THE VITAL CORPORATION

How American Businesses—Large and
Small—Double Profits in Two Years or Less

Garry Jacobs and Robert Macfarlane

PRENTICE HALL
Englewood Cliffs, New Jersey 07632

Prentice-Hall International (UK) Limited, *London*
Prentice-Hall of Australia Pty. Limited, *Sydney*
Prentice-Hall Canada, Inc., *Toronto*
Prentice-Hall Hispanoamericana, S.A., *Mexico*
Prentice-Hall of India Private Limited, *New Delhi*
Prentice-Hall of Japan, Inc., *Tokyo*
Simon & Schuster Asia Pte. Ltd., *Singapore*
Editor Prentice-Hall do Brasil, Ltda., *Rio de Janeiro*

© 1990 *by*

PRENTICE-HALL Inc.
Englewood Cliffs, NJ

10 9 8 7 6 5 4 3 2 1

Library of Congress Cataloging-in-Publication Data

Jacobs, Garry
   The vital corporation : how American Businesses—large and small-
-double profits in two years or less / by Garry Jacobs and Robert
Macfarlane.
     p.   cm.

   Includes bibliographical references.
   ISBN 0-13-946450-6
   1. Corporate profits.   2. Corporate profits—United States.
I. Macfarlane, Robert. II. Title.
HG4028.P7J33   1990
658.15'5—dc20   89-28975
                                            CIP

ISBN 0-13-946450-6

PRENTICE HALL
BUSINESS & PROFESSIONAL DIVISION
A division of Simon & Schuster
Englewood Cliffs, New Jersey 07632

Printed in the United States of America

"You are what you believe in. You become what you believe you can become."

Bhagavad Gita

Acknowledgments

Many individuals and organizations have made significant contributions to this book. We would especially like to thank more than 200 managers from the following companies for time, energy, interest, and frankness with which they shared their experiences, insights, achievements, difficulties, and unfulfilled aspirations. Wherever possible, we have tried to acknowledge individual contributors in the text of the book.

AMRE	**Mesa Airlines**
Ben & Jerry's Homemade, Inc.	**Nedlloyd Lines**
C & J Industries	**P.A.M. Transport**
Expeditors International	**Patten Corporation**
Federal Express	**Ross Incineration Services**
Gartner Group	**Trimedyne**
Linear Technology	**Vipont Pharmaceutical**
Listen Up, Inc.	**Waltz Brothers**

We would also like to acknowledge the pioneering work of The Mother's Service Society of Pondicherry, India, in conceptualizing the process of corporate growth and socioeconomic development that is the inspiration for the ideas presented in this book.

At our office, Jan Feldberg and Salli Smith spent literally hundreds of hours arranging appointments, transcribing interviews, and preparing manuscript. We convey our deep appreciation to them for their patient, dedicated work.

Companies Referred to in This Book

American Express
AMRE
Apple Computers
Audio Associates
Audio Centre
Audiocraft
Bajaj Auto, Ltd
Bang & Olufsen
Ben & Jerry's Homemade, Inc.
Bryn Mawr Stores
C & J Industries
Chargeurs
Chrysler Corporation
Delta Airlines
East Asiatic Company
Elizabeth Carbide
Expeditors International
Federal Express
Ford Motors
Gartner Group
General Electric

IBM
J & M Incorporated
Kennedy & Bowden Machine Co.
Linear Technology
Listen Up, Inc.
London Life Insurance
Marriott Corporation
Merck & Co.
Mesa Airlines
Minit International
Northwestern Mutual Life Insurance
P.A.M. Transport
Patten Corporation
Pflanz Electronics
Precision Grinding, Inc.
Ross Incineration Services
Scandinavian Airlines
Sound Advice
Trimedyne
Vipont Pharmaceutical
Waltz Brothers

Industries Referred to in This Book

Airfreight
Airlines
Appliances
Audiovideo Manufacturing
Automotive
Computer
Consumer Services
Electronics Retailing
Financial Services
Food
Freight Forwarding
Hazardous Waste Disposal
Home Improvements
Hotels and Restaurants
Information Services
Insurance
Pharmaceuticals
Semiconductors
Shipping
Tool and Die Machining
Trading
Trucking

The Challenge

To speak of doubling revenues or profits in one or two years sounds like hype and cheap propaganda. But this is no pipe dream. Almost every company has doubled or tripled its revenues or profits once or many times in the past. Only then, the process occurred more or less by itself or in response to a fortunate external circumstance. When doubling happens in this way, we rarely reflect on the real how or why that made it possible. Rapid growth in revenues and profits is the result of a process which every company can consciously utilize to accelerate its growth and dramatically improve its bottom line.

Energy is the driving force for growth. Every company possesses five unlimited sources of energy that can be converted into dynamic engines for rapid growth and high profitability. These engines propelled the growth of a Silicon Valley chipmaker from $7 million to $60 million in five years. They enabled a struggling $5 million Chicago precision machining company to escape bankruptcy and convert $350,000 of losses into $350,000 of profits in one year. They drove the growth of a Brussels shoe repair service into a global service company with over 4,000 retail outlets around the world. By tapping just a little of the power of these engines, an ailing airline went from losses of $20 million to profits of $80 million in one year. Ford Motors rode these engines from losses of $3 billion to become the most profitable car maker in the world. And one impetuous, entrepreneurial firm harnessed its powers to build a high-flying $4.6 billion company from scratch in 15 years with the aim of becoming the largest transportation company in the world by the end of the century.

These engines are available to every company, because you already possess them. All that is needed is consciously to turn the keys that unlock their potential and release their powers for rapid growth and high profitability. Then doubling the company or the country will look like a modest proposal.

Garry Jacobs
Robert Macfarlane
Pondicherry, India

Introduction

This is a book about the *process* of corporate growth, what makes it happen, what makes it stop, and how it can be accelerated in any company to dramatically increase revenues and profits within a very short time. The emphasis in the preceding sentence is on the word "*process*." Growth is a natural process that is occurring all the time, all around us. People grow, companies grow, nations grow too. This growth usually occurs in response to some fortuitous opportunity in the environment, or it is compelled by the pressure of external conditions. But these are only stimuli that initiate the process, not the process itself. The process of growth is an internal mechanism in all living organisms and is propelled by its own energies. In companies, that process is initiated and directed by management.

Companies are growing all the time without ever fully understanding how or why that growth takes place. In other words, the process of growth is usually unconscious or at best semiconscious. But occasionally there are individuals, such as Tom Watson at IBM or Fred Smith at Federal Express, who have acquired a deeper understanding of the process and have utilized it to accelerate the growth vastly and multiply the profits of their companies. This knowledge and productive power are available for all who seek to acquire it. It is a knowledge that individuals can discover for themselves by observing and understanding the process as it expresses in their own lives and their own companies. Those who acquire knowledge of the process have the capacity to achieve extraordinary results in business.

We live in a country that has grown phenomenally over the last two centuries to become the most prosperous nation in the world. Our growth has been swift, spontaneous, and exponential—so much so that we have not had the time or inclination to stop and reflect on the process by which we achieved it. Today this nation is beset with problems—a burgeoning national debt, an enormous trade deficit, a simultaneous mixture of unemployment among low-income groups and lack of skilled people for higher paying jobs, and the ever-present specter of inflation. As a nation, we lack the same knowledge that most companies lack, the knowledge of the process of growth that made the nation great and the power to make it far greater still, if only we fully utilize the country's and our own potentials.

In a real sense, individuals who discover the process of growth and accelerate the growth of their own businesses do a real service to the nation. They are the pioneers who show us what is possible and blaze a trail for others to follow. This book is intended for the trail blazers, who in growing their own companies, serve the nation and help it grow.

The book can be read on three levels: theory, example, and practice. It presents the basic principles of the process of corporate growth. These principles are illustrated by inspiring examples of companies of all sizes and descriptions drawn from a wide range of industries, which have utilized the process to grow very rapidly and double or triple their profits in a short time. For those who are practicing managers, the book also contains a number of specific strategies for applying the principles in your own company or department and a series of detailed exercises to assist in making the ideas and their application as real and relevant to your company as possible. These strategies and exercises have been tested and proven extremely effective in our work with a wide range of companies.

Table of Contents

"I set the limits on my growth."

Terry Crabbe, Sound Hounds

Chapter One

THE CHALLENGE

Adobe Systems
Alaska Air Group
ALCOA
Allegheny Ludlum
Altos Computer
AMAX
American Express
AMR
Applied Materials
Aristech Chemicals
Avery International
Bank of Boston
Bank of New England
Bank of New York
Bethlehem Steel
Boole & Babbage
Bowater
Blockbuster Entertainment
Businessland

Carpenter Technology
Carroon and Black
CBS
Centel Cable Television
Chambers Development
Chapparal Steel
ChrisCraft
Colgate-Palmolive
Commodore International
Contel
Cyprus Minerals
Danaher
John Deere
Diamond Shamrock R&M
Dresser Industries
Dreyer's Grand Ice Cream
DSC Communications
Federal Paper Board
First Financial Management

M. A. Hanna
Intel Corp.
Int'l Minerals & Chemicals
Intertan
Linear Technology
Louisiana Pacific
LSI Logic
Magma Power
Manufacturers National Bank
MCI Communications
Merchant National Bank
Micro Mask
J. P. Morgan
Multimedia
Navistar International
New York State Gas & Electric
Niagra Mohawk Power
Nike
Norfolk Southern
Nucor
Oracle Systems
Pacific Resources
Pacific Western Bancshares
Penn Central
Pennwalt
Pennzoil
Phelps Dodge
Phillips Petroleum

Precision Grinding, Inc.
Procter & Gamble
Provident Life & Accident
Puget Sound Bancorp
Pyramid Technology
Quantum Chemical
Republic New York
Reynolds Metals
Riggs National Bank
Seeq Technology
Signet Banking
Southeast Banking
Southwest Airlines
Stanford Telecommunications
Sterling Chemicals
Stone Container
Storage Technology
Texas Industries
Timken
Transcisco Industries
Union Carbide
United Artists Communications
United Illuminating
UNOCAL
USX
Vista Chemical
Wells Fargo & Co.
Wendy's International

What do all the companies in this list have in common? Each of these companies reported profits last year at least twice as large as their profits the year before—in some cases as much as five or ten times larger. A few of them also doubled their revenues last year.

What distinguishes these companies from one another? Just about everything else. They come from all parts of the United States, a complete mix of manufacturing and service businesses, high tech and low tech, old and young, very large ($20 billion) to very small ($1.1 million).

We could probably fill a book with the names of companies that doubled their profits or revenues last year. Would the name of your company be on our list? If not, why not? If yes, will it be on next year's list too? That is the subject of this book.

Howard K. Cooper, president and CEO of Trimedyne, a Los Angeles-based high-tech medical equipment manufacturer, is obsessed with these questions. His company more than doubled its sales and profits in 1988. Revenues grew from $12 million in 1987 to $31 million, while pretax profits increased from $500,000 to $6.5 million. For Cooper, the challenge has been: "How to introduce my people to the concept of 2X, meaning twice again next year. Some guys would be happy to do $12 million again. But we (top management) won't be and neither will the shareholders." What about you?

The whole thing is not really about numbers. Doubling is only a figure of speech. The real issue is about being the very best possible, achieving the maximum possible for your business. For some, doing the maximum possible may be tripling revenues in one year like Palma Tool & Die in Buffalo, which went from $400,000 to $1.2 million in 1987, or tripling profits in one year like Eastman Kodak, whose earnings soared from $374 million to $1.2 billion in 1987. Or more.

Over the last few years we have observed young companies emerging from obscurity to take old established industries by storm, like P.A.M. Transport, a trucking company started in 1980 with 5 trucks and 15 trailers and now one of the ten largest irregular truckers in the country with over 700 trucks and 1,500 trailers. We have also seen established companies suddenly awaken from slumber and soar into prominence like Patten Corporation, a real estate company founded in 1965, whose revenues grew to $4.3 million over its first 15 years and then rocketed between 1984 and 1988 to $116 million with profits of $15 million. Along with everyone else we have watched megacorporations amble along for years with flat sales or slow steady growth and then surge forward dramatically like Ford Motors, which lost billions of dollars in the early 1980s and then bounced back to raise revenues by 80% and more than double net income between 1985 and 1988.

Numbers do not tell the whole story. They are only an indicator, an expression of something going on deeper within these companies. Doubling is as much a question of quality as of quantity. This book is about raising the quality of corporate performance from that of an average or above-average performer to become the very best. The question, as Trimedyne's Cooper put it, is "Even in the professional ranks, what makes the difference between just an ordinary player, a professional player, and the champion?"

We may measure that difference quantitatively in terms of seconds clocked, yards run, points scored, or games won. But being a champion is essentially a question of quality.

THE MYSTIQUE OF RAPID GROWTH

Over the last few years we have studied and surveyed more than 1,000 companies around the world from North America to South India and back—companies ranging in size from a few hundred thousand dollars to tens of billions, companies in a wide spectrum of businesses from basic manufacturing—the tools, dies, and molds used to make just about everything else—to ice cream, toothpaste, stereos and integrated circuits; from down-to-earth, traditional services like selling land, remodeling homes, transporting cargo and repairing shoes; to sophisticated, high-tech businesses in the finance and information industries.

These companies differ widely in age, size, origin, geography and culture. They also share a lot in common with each other and with other companies in terms of the way they were founded, the types of experiences they have had, and the challenges and problems they have confronted. But the most significant common denominator that links them all together is that they have grown rapidly and profitably, and even more important, they have managed to maintain high rates of profitable growth over a considerable period of time.

Growth is a refreshing and invigorating experience, and there is something particularly exciting and exhilarating about rapid corporate growth. Growth is both a natural and universal phenomenon common to all living things. Therefore, it is doubly strange that corporate growth should be the subject of so many superstitions and misconceptions. Few issues are so frequently discussed these days and yet so steeped in mystery as the phenomenon of rapid corporate growth.

When we talk of rapid growth, companies like Apple Computers, Federal Express, The Limited, and Circuit City may come to mind. But there are many others—thousands of companies of all sizes and descriptions and in every conceivable type of business—that are experiencing rapid growth at this very moment. In fact there is nothing very uncommon about rapid growth at all, except perhaps that we think there is. And that is a very important "perhaps," because it often prevents companies from growing as fast and as far as they can. The myths and superstitions surrounding corporate growth would not be so important if they did not have such a profound impact on the performance of most companies.

How would you react if someone walked into your company and said that you can double your revenues or profits within 24 months? Skeptical? Suspicious? Amused? Probably not unlike Ray Kennedy, CEO of Kennedy & Bowden Machine Co. in Nashville, Tennessee, who commented: "The first time I heard the idea, I thought it was pure hype!" But in the last one year, Kennedy's profits have increased by more than 50%. His initial reaction only illustrates how unusual rapid growth seems, despite the fact that it is happening all the time, all around us and, not uncommonly, to us as well—for virtually every company has grown rapidly at one time or another.

Then why all the mystery? The mystique of rapid growth is reinforced by a host of myths and superstitions that prompt us to admire rather than imitate the accomplishments of other companies and to dream of greater success rather than striving to achieve it. This corporate lore is supported by a vast array of common sense, conventional wisdom, and objective fact. But that does not make it inevitably true or compelling. The real issue is not whether it is ever true, but whether it need be true for your company.

To quantify the potentials which we believe exist for every company, we speak in terms of doubling revenues or profits within a year or two. Such a goal may seem unrealistic to some and modest to others. But in either case, the real challenge we propose is to go beyond the ordinary and unexceptional to attain the highest possible and achievable. Our experience has convinced us that the highest possible is almost always far more than what even the most dynamic and ambitious companies attempt to achieve.

This is so because, while a great many companies experience rapid growth, very few really understand how to tap consciously and utilize systematically the sources of energy that drive and propel it. But before coming to that, the first necessity is to dispel the myths that conceal the underlying process.

THE FIVE MYTHS

Myth 1: There are inherent limits to how fast companies can grow. Of course there are limits. The question is: How fast is fast? When "reasonable" companies plan for rapid growth, they think in terms of 15%, 20% or at best 30%. But much higher rates of growth are being achieved by many companies. According to *INC.* Magazine, the 100 fastest growing public U.S. companies in 1987 grew at a compound annual rate ranging from 93% to 579% between 1982 and 1986. The 612 companies which have appeared on the *INC.* 100 since 1979 have grown at an average compound rate of 90%, doubling in size on average every 56 weeks.

Such high rates of growth are certainly impressive, but they immediately raise other dominant myths about rapid growth: growth of this magnitude can only be achieved from a very small base and in newly emerging industries.

Myth 2: Opportunities for rapid growth exist only in new, nontraditional or high-tech industries, which are not yet dominated by giants. If Fred Smith had believed this generalization, he never would have started Federal Express and entered the parcel delivery business, which had been dominated by the Postal Service and UPS for nearly a century.

It is true that many fast-growing companies come from high-tech industries. But this generalization conceals the fact that a great many others do not—companies like Century 21 (real estate), Kinder Care (day care), Liz Claiborne (garments), and Nike (shoes). In fact the top three companies on *INC.*'s 1988 list are specialty discounters—Entertainment Marketing, Home Shopping Network, and Warehouse Club. *INC.*'s top ten for 1988 also included Care Plus (home health-care services), Sahlen & Associates (security services), and Vipont Pharmaceuticals (oral hygiene products).

There is nothing very high-tech or nontraditional about vinyl siding. AMRE, Inc. began doing custom home installation of external siding in 1980. In 1983 the company had revenues of $4.4 million. By 1986 it had grown ninefold to $40 million. Sales doubled in 1987 to $78 million and nearly doubled again to $140 million in 1989.

The Biggest Firm in Town: Other very fast-growing companies can be found in unlikely industries and unusual places too. Tontitown, Arkansas, is not exactly a thriving metropolis, but being the largest company in this small town is nonetheless a considerable distinction—even if the town has a population of less than 700. In 1980, with $3,000 of capital, Paul Maestri founded P.A.M. Transport under in his home town a large oak tree. The company has doubled in size every year since it was established. By 1989, P.A.M. had become a $75.8 million company.

Myth 3: The bigger you are, the slower you grow. True enough, most of the companies on the *INC.* list were under $10 million in size when they went public. But a number have already crossed the $100 million or the $500 million mark and are still going places—companies like Liz Claiborne, whose sales rose from $117 million to $1 billion between 1982 and 1987 (a five-year growth rate of 47% compared to the industry's 8%) while profits increased from $10 million to $114 million.

Still one could argue that a few hundred million dollars is relatively small. What about the big guys? In 1970 IBM had revenues of $7.2 billion. Over the past 17 years, it has grown another eightfold to $60 billion in 1988. The revenues of Federal Express nearly doubled between 1984 and 1986, growing from $1.4 billion to $2.6 billion. In the last two years revenues have risen another 80% to over $4 billion. Of course, Federal Express knows that it cannot keep growing at that rate indefinitely. That is why it has set only a modest growth target for the rest of the century—to become the largest transportation company in the world! Companies like Federal Express and IBM are exceptional, but hardly unique. Other major corporations like Apple, Coca-Cola, and Marriott also have targets to at least double in size over the next few years. What about your company?

But after all, anyone can increase revenues simply by lowering prices and cutting profits—which brings us to the fourth myth.

Myth 4: The larger you grow, the smaller your margin of profit. Let us concede from the beginning that this is certainly most often the case. The question is whether the fact is the result of the myth or vice versa? Bajaj Auto Ltd. has dominated the Indian motor scooter industry for nearly 30 years. The company grew from $1 million in 1961 to $36 million in 1976. Over the next decade sales grew another tenfold and pretax profits rose ninefold. In 1986 sales rose 60% to $420 million and operating profit increased a staggering 72% to $100 million. But by this time the Indian market had begun to really heat up with the entry of more than 30 new competitors including the world's largest players—Honda (world 1), Suzuki, and Piaggio (Vespa). In 1987 Bajaj's revenues crossed $500 million, after-tax profits doubled, and the company now ranks second in the world in its industry with plans to double production again by 1992.

Sterling Chemicals of Houston is a company that shatters all the myths. This fledgling three year old created from Monsanto's petrochemical manufacturing facilities recorded sales of $699 million in 1988 with profits of $213 million and a return on equity of 235%!

Myth 5: Rapid growth cannot last. We come finally to the most devastating of the myths about rapid growth, most devastating because it is most often true. Almost every company grows rapidly at some points in its existence, but in most cases spurts of rapid growth tend to be just that, short-lived bursts followed by leveling off and in some cases decline or extinction. Rapid growth is not only very common; it is usually very fleeting too. Rapid growth is not only exhilarating; it is also extremely demanding and sometimes fatal. Some companies actually grow themselves right out of existence.

We can, of course, quote exceptions to this rule like Apple Computer, whose sales climbed from $1 million in 1977 to $335 million in 1982, then rose to $2.67 billion in 1987, while profits multiplied 5.5 times to $218 million. In 1988 sales grew another 54% to $4.1 billion and profits nearly doubled again to $400 million. But the fact remains that rapid growth is for the most part a transient phenomena. Nearly 40% of the companies that appeared on *INC.*'s 1987 list did not return in 1988. In a survey of 770 U.S. corporations, which we conducted in collaboration with American Management Association, periods of rapid growth lasted an average of 29 months.[1]

Yet still we refer to this frequently documented occurrence as a myth, not only because it is not always true, but also because it need not be true for any company that fully understands the process of growth and anticipates its demands.

The Greatest Myth of All: These five generalizations obviously cannot serve as guidelines for a company that wants to grow and keep growing rapidly and profitably. Shattering their hold on us is the first step toward rapid growth. Even when we give up one myth, we frequently adopt another in its place. Very often even when we say and genuinely believe we are free from them, they guide our every action—the plans we make, the type and number of people we recruit, the size of the computer we buy.

How much do you plan to increase sales or profits next month? Next quarter? Next year? Are you hiring people who can help take the company to a far higher level and continue to grow with it? Are you equipping them with all the skills they will need to manage that growth? Are you putting in systems capable of handling a much greater volume of work in future? Or do you say: "Let the growth happen and then I will do all these things."

What we should part with is The Myth of Limits. *The only really binding limitations on our growth are the constraints placed on us by our limited perception of what is possible and our limited aspiration to achieve it.* Terry Crabbe, founder of Sound Hounds in Victoria,

B.C., put it succinctly: "I set the limits on my growth!" Or as Lee Southard, president of Vipont Research, expressed it, "You can be whatever you resolve to be. Everything is possible!"

THREE CONCLUSIONS

Our study of rapidly growing companies has led us to three fundamental conclusions:

> *Our first conclusion is that rapid, sustained and profitable growth is possible for any company that really wants it and is willing to make the effort. The emphasis is on* **wants** *and* **willing.**

But doesn't everyone want to grow rapidly and profitably and keep on growing? Not by a long shot! Sure, almost all companies will welcome growth if it comes their way. But that is not enough. Few companies really, genuinely believe that rapid and continuous growth is possible for them, and even fewer are willing to expend the energy needed to achieve and sustain it.

So everything comes down to the questions: Do I really believe that rapid growth is possible? and Do I really want it? This book is intended to help the reader answer the first of these questions in the affirmative.

But the second question—Do I really want it?—we each must answer for ourselves. Actually the two questions are much more closely interlinked than may at first seem evident. For very often our lack of understanding or appreciation of a possibility is actually an expression of a lack of aspiration or an unwillingness to take the effort needed to achieve it. To put it plainly, when we say we do not understand or do not believe, we really mean we do not care or are not willing to try.

Many companies today cannot really afford the luxury of choosing between rapid and more moderate rates of growth. Our society is changing so rapidly that companies which do not seek to perform at their maximum may not even survive—as Chrysler almost did not survive. Dave Norman, cofounder of Businessland, put it bluntly: "If you don't grow, you'll die."

> *Our second conclusion is that rapid growth in revenues and profits is the result of a process, a process that can be learned. Many entrepreneurs may be born with innate talents for enterprise, but the knowledge and skills needed to make a company grow and keep growing can be acquired by anyone.*

In the remaining chapters of this book, we attempt to describe that process and to illustrate how it works in companies of all sizes drawn from a wide range of industries. This process is not something we have invented. It is the natural process by which all companies grow, but usually that process is unconscious. How many companies really understand what has propelled their growth up to the present? How many ever ask the question? In our experience very few, even among the most successful.

Usually growth occurs unconsciously in response to the pressure of external forces or as the result of favorable circumstances, such as an expansive market or a new technology. Companies respond to these conditions by releasing their energies and tapping inner potentials which have been there all the time unutilized or underutilized beneath the surface, just as psychologists say that the average person utilizes less than 10% of his or her mental capacities during normal life. This need not be true either for the individual or the company. If we become fully conscious of the process by which we have grown up to the present, we acquire the ability to stimulate and accelerate that process in the future.

Every company has already doubled in quality and quantity many times. What most of us understand as the result of luck or hard work is an expression of a process we do not perceive. Normally we think doubling is possible only if luck is on our side—if the market suddenly takes off or if we discover a great new product or if someone offers to double the investment in our company. Doubling is possible without waiting for such fortuitous circumstances to occur by fully utilizing the potentials which lie within every company.

> *Our third conclusion is that the process of growth is fundamentally the same for the individual, the company, and the nation. In fact the three are inextricably intertwined, that is, personal growth, corporate growth and national growth go together.*

Companies that strive for the maximum personal growth of their people tend to grow the fastest and the farthest. So, too, individuals who strive to release fully their personal energies and utilize fully their capacities for the growth of the companies they work for tend to grow the most as well, both in terms of career advancement and development of personality.

DOUBLE AMERICA

The same is true of the nation. *The New York Times* recently published an editorial entitled "Two Trillion Dollars Is Missing," in which it mourned the declining rate of growth in industrial productivity and concluded:

> By world standards, the American economy remains a continuing success. By the standards of what America might achieve *if its creative energies were fully utilized*, it is only stumbling along. *No one knows how to excite and harness those energies.* But the stakes, from maintaining national security to rescuing poor children, are immense. The rejuvenation of the incredible productivity machine stands as the highest priority of America's new political era.[2]

Obviously we must first understand how to release and harness fully our own creative energies and those of the people we work with and the companies that constitute this great national economy. In the last 200 years the quantity and the quality of American life have doubled many times—in terms of productivity, national wealth, educational attainments, scientific knowledge, technological development, and so on. How far have we as a nation really understood the secrets of our own success, the source of the enormous creative energies that have propelled our growth, and the process by which we have released and harnessed those energies to double our achievements time and again?

In the world of today, the time required for doubling is shorter than ever before—as the rapid emergence to power of countries on the Pacific Rim makes abundantly clear. Yet as the *Times* article reminds us, our own rate of growth is declining, while that of others around us continues to accelerate. Between 1948 and 1965, output per hour in the United States rose 3% per year. Had it continued to grow at the 1965 rate, our gross national product today would be $2 trillion higher than it actually is and per capita income would be 40% higher than it is now. That additional national income would generate enough tax revenues to eradicate completely the federal budget deficit.

Is that decline inevitable? Certainly not. Like today's developing countries, our rapid growth in the past was fueled by tremendous gains in productivity based on the spread of education and the application of advanced technologies. Have we exhausted or even begun to exhaust the potentials of these two engines of growth? All recent studies of our educational system state emphatically that a doubling of the quality and quantity of our educational attainments is not only possible but essential for the future strength of the nation.

The same is true of technology. The American farmer is regarded as among the most advanced in the world. Yet according to agriculture scientists, only 50% of the proven technological discoveries made in our nation's laboratories are utilized to enhance commercial production on our farms. How much more potential lies unutilized for applying advanced industrial technology in the hundreds of thousands of factories across the country?

Nor are education and technology our only underutilized resources. There is a technology of organization, what is commonly called management, that we are only just beginning to understand and have hardly begun to utilize, a resource that can contribute as much to national productivity in the century that is soon to begin as scientific technology has in the one that is coming to a close.

The challenge to double sales and profits is not intended just for companies. It is addressed to every individual reader and to the nation as well—to raise performance and productivity to the maximum level we are capable of—to double the prosperity and quality of life in America. If a continuation of past growth rates in productivity would be sufficient to eradicate the federal deficit, one of our most pressing national problems, how much more prosperous could our nation be if we try to improve upon our past performance rather than merely trying to match it?

The idea of doubling America is not mere speculation. It is already happening. In 1988 alone American exports rose by 26%, the trade deficit declined by 21%, and the profits of the nation's 500 largest industrial corporations rose by $115 billion or 27%—at which rate they would double in three years! What then can we not achieve by a concerted effort to utilize fully all our resources and fully tap all our potentials?

PROFIT PLANNING
FOR PRACTICING MANAGERS

This book has been designed to assist practicing managers to apply the ideas it contains directly to their companies/divisions/departments to accelerate the growth of their businesses and dramatically increase profitability. If you complete all the exercises suggested in the book, you will have created a detailed blueprint to achieve maximum growth and profits for your company.

As you read through the concepts and examples in this book, practical, useful ideas may occur to you for application in your company. We encourage you to pause in your reading to note ideas and decisions you take for the improvement of your business. Appendix A contains a model for an Action Plan form and instructions on how to use it to record your decisions. The use of the action plans will help you to translate directly the concepts and examples into practice.

The key for applying the ideas in this book to your business is the Profit Plan. A model form for the Profit Plan is given in Appendix B. The profit plan will help you assess the actual impact on your company's revenues and profits of the decisions you take and the action plans you develop. Subsequent chapters of the book contain specific exercises to aid you in evaluating the relative strengths and weaknesses of your company and in identifying practical strategies appropriate to improve its performance. At the end of most chapters, you are asked to write action plans to apply the ideas in the chapter and to assess the impact of your plans on revenues and profits.

Chapter Fifteen contains detailed instructions for reviewing the decisions and Action Plans you have developed and for completing the Profit Plan.

STEP ONE

The first and most important thing you should do to apply the ideas in this book for the improvement of your business is to *choose a goal*. The effectiveness of the strategies described in the book depends on the clarity of your goal and the intensity of your commitment to it.

Define your goal in terms of the dollar growth in revenues and profits you want to achieve in the next 12, 24, and 36 months.

The goal you choose should be challenging and realistic. It should be one you can enthusiastically pursue. It should not be either so easy that it is not inspiring or so difficult that it seems impossible to realize.

First, choose the goal for growth in revenues over the next three years. Then project the growth in profits which will result from that revenue growth based on current operating margins. Beyond this, what additional growth in profits do you want to achieve through improved productivity and efficiency. Add these two together to generate a profit goal for each year.

Formulate your proposed goals now and write them down in line 1 of your Profit Plan form. In the last chapter of the book, you will be asked to review these goals in the light of all you have read and thought and to revise it if appropriate. You can always change your goals later, but it is important that you choose now before proceeding to the next chapter.

SUMMARY

- The challenge to every company is to at least double revenues and/or profits within 24 months.

- Doubling means to accelerate growth of revenues and profits to the maximum level possible for your company.

- Doubling is happening to companies all the time. Most likely it has happened to your company one or more times in the past.

- Rapid growth in revenues and profits is possible for any company that really wants it and is willing to try. It is the result of a natural *process*. That process usually occurs unconsciously. By discovering the process and making it fully conscious, any company can achieve high rates of growth.

- We must release our energies from the common myths and superstitions that limit our awareness and aspiration for growth.

- The first step is to set a clear goal and make a firm commitment to achieve it.

Chapter Two

MOBILIZING THE FIVE ENGINES OF GROWTH

In the first chapter, we issued a challenge—double your performance. We also tried to raise and dispel some of the myths that block or slow growth. In spite of this, many of you might be thinking right now: "Doubling may be possible for other companies, but . . . our's is a mature market . . . We have intense competition from Japan . . . Without a huge investment, we cannot grow . . . We cannot get the people we need. . . ." The reasons may vary, but the conclusion is the same: "We are different."

If that is what you are thinking, then at least in this respect you have a lot in common with others. For most companies believe that their circumstances are somehow different than others—especially from companies that are more successful than they are.

How can we be so confident that doubling is possible for your company? For two reasons. The first is that we have seen companies in much more difficult circumstances than these—companies in the deepest trouble and on the verge of extinction—not only survive their ordeal but launch themselves on a fresh round of rapid and profitable growth. And so have you. Chrysler Corporation did it in the early 1980s at the very peak of the Japanese onslaught—hardly the right time or the right place for a comeback—after drawing down to its last $1 million in cash to meet daily expenses of $50 million. Chrysler not only survived, but has achieved record profits, doubled in size, and increased its market share since then. Hundreds of midsize and thousands of smaller companies have done it too.

The second reason we are so confident about doubling is that, considering the unfathomed potentials that lie dormant within every company, doubling is a modest goal. Whatever your business, you possess five unlimited resources upon which to draw for growth, five engines, any one of which is powerful enough to double your revenues or—at the very least—your profits within a year or two.

These engines are nothing new. You do not have to buy them or install them. You already possess them. If you did not, your company could not exist, could not survive, could never grow. Think for a moment. What are the essential components needed for any business to exist, survive, and grow, regardless of the industry?

The words we use to answer this question may vary as does the relative importance we place on one or another of the components. But whatever our method of classification, to be complete it must include five fundamental components.

There must be a need in society that the company serves, what is commonly called a *market*. There must also be a *technology*, a know-how for producing a product or providing a service that the company offers to meet that market need. There must, of course, be *people*—managers and workers who contribute their energies and ideas, talents, and skills to deliver the products or services to meet the market need. There must also be *capital* in one form or another from one source or another to support and finance the activity. And, finally, there must be something that often seems vague and nebulous but that is absolutely indispensable to give life to the other four—there must be an *organization*.

Organization provides the structure and systems that direct the people and utilize the capital and technology to provide the products and services to meet the needs of the market.

The ancient philosophers spoke of the five cosmic elements from which all things in the universe are born and constituted—earth, water, air, fire and ether. The five engines are the creative forces from which all businesses are born and which give life to them. These five—market, technology, people, capital and organization—are all essential for the existence of any company. And they are more than that. They are not only the five basic elements out of which businesses are created. They are also powerful engines that can drive the growth of revenues and profits in every company. Each of these five is a vast reservoir of potential energy that can be released and utilized for higher sales and higher productivity. Drawing on the power of any one of them is enough to catapult a company into rapid growth. Drawing on the powers of all of them, even to a very limited extent, is enough to convert a near-fatal crisis into an opportunity for expansion.

Everyone knows that an expansive market can be a powerful driving force for growth, that technology can propel a company upward, that capital is essential for increasing productive capacity, that good people and good organization are keys to success. Everyone knows that some companies are market driven, some are product driven and still others are people driven. So what?

No matter how well we understand the importance of these five engines, no matter how seriously a company strives to exploit their powers, no matter how effectively you harness their potentials for growth, you can never exhaust their latent capacities. And if every reader, every company, knew and believed that and acted on that basis, they would already be doubling every year or two and our nation's $2 trillion shortfall in GNP would be a $2 trillion or perhaps a $10 trillion surplus. It is not as if the existence of these five engines is a secret from anyone. But the real depth and extent of their powers is as much a secret today as the energy pent up within the atom was to our ancestors in earlier centuries—unimagined and unutilized.

Think for a moment about your company or about a company you know well. Which of these five have been the engines that propelled its growth? How has the company harnessed their powers? How far has it really utilized their productive potentials? What more can be done to tap their capacities?

In later chapters we will explore many of the latent powers of each of these five and see how they can be applied in any business. For the moment let us contemplate a few of the miraculous feats they perform.

A CHIP OFF AN OLD BLOCK

Although most of the headlines are grabbed by the digital chips used as micro-processors and memory storage devices in computers, analog chips represent about 25% of the total market for integrated circuits. Analog chips convert signals electronically from real world parameters such as temperature and pressure into digital language.

In 1981 three executives left the giant chip producer National Semiconductor to found a new company in Silicon Valley named Linear Technology, specializing in the manufacture of proprietary analog chips used in computers, defense and a wide variety of other electronic equipment. Since 1984 Linear's sales have soared nine-fold from $7 million to a current annual rate of $63 million with net profit margins in excess of 17%.

Linear's phenomenal growth has been generated by tapping a few of the latent potentials of the engine market. Linear has energized its market by carefully attuning all its activities to meet the needs of its market and to deliver exactly what the customer wants. That is no short order in a business which involves 20 different manufacturing processes, which produces thousands of different products specifically designed to customer requirements, and in which the key to product development is the individual circuit designer.

One of the challenges for any company is to bridge the gap between what they make or offer to customers and what the customers really want. This may not be a serious problem for the owner of a small corner grocery store who is at once checkout clerk, purchasing agent, and stock boy. But as soon as a company gets much larger or more complex than the corner store, a chasm begins to grow between what we think our customers want and what they actually want. We have seen many $1 million businesses in which the chasm had already widened into an unfathomable and sometimes fatal abyss. How does your company prevent a fissure from forming between it and the changing needs of its customers?

The dangers of producing what we know or like rather than what the customer really wants are especially great for technology-intensive companies like Linear, which are founded and managed by engineers and scientists. Yet Linear has discovered a way to bridge this gap and energize its market by means of a unique product development system. Each circuit designer goes out into the marketplace with the salespeople to talk with customers and find out what they want. Then the same person comes back to the laboratory and designs a product to meet that need. The designer then moves with the product through the production phase and goes back into the field to meet customers again and ensure that the product works as it was intended. When customers call in with questions or complaints, they can speak to the expert who actually designed the product, not to a customer service representative. With a base of 4,000 customers, that says a lot about the company's commitment to its customers. "I look at it as a triangle," says design director Tom Redfern. "There is a customer, the manufacturing and a designer. It is very important for the design guy to be plugged into the customer."

Linear's CEO, Robert Swanson, commented, "We go to great lengths to distill the information coming in from the field so what we design fills the real need." The result is a phenomenally high percentage of Linear's products are successful in the marketplace. Almost no product is a failure and some are very big success stories. For a technology-intensive business, Linear has shown that tapping even a single cylinder of the engine market can be a powerful lever for very rapid and very profitable growth.

A FRESH PERSPECTIVE

The energy that has fueled Linear's growth issues from an attitude, the attitude of looking at work from the customer's point of view. It may sound simple, but it is not—at least judging by how uncommon that attitude is. *Therein lies a key to energizing any company—changing the way we look at people, events, and things around us.*

A change of perspective is also a key to unleashing the power of the engine technology. We use the word technology in its broadest sense as the "know-how" for running a business, the know-how for producing products and providing services as well as the products and services themselves.

Information can be a product, and providing it to others is a service that requires sophisticated know-how. Gartner Group is the recognized leader in a very fast-moving service industry—providing information about developments in the computer industry to manufacturers, financial analysts, and end users. The company's growth has been energized by its fresh way of looking at the technology of the services that it provides.

Just before he founded the company in 1979, Gideon Gartner recognized the growing need in the marketplace for up-to-date, reliable, expert information on new developments in the computer industry. At the time, Gartner was a partner at Oppenheimer, catering to needs of institutional investors on Wall Street for information that would impact on their investments in the computer industry. But no one was using the fast moving Wall Street style to provide information on developments in the industry to other key decision makers, such as vendors in the computer industry who needed to understand the marketing and product strategies of their competitors and large computer users who needed to know developments that might influence their decisions to purchase new systems.

So Gartner redefined the product to meet these needs and create a new market by providing information of a practically useful nature to decision makers and presenting it in a simple and concise form for easy reference. *Adding just one new dimension to the way we look at a product or service reveals new applications and provides greater value added to customers.* This is only one of the ways in which the greater potentials of technology can be tapped.

During his prior employment at IBM and Oppenheimer, Gartner had learned a variety of methods for collecting, interpreting, and utilizing this type of information. But the challenge in starting his own company was to institutionalize the research process, so that every Gartner researcher would produce practically useful, accurate, timely information consistent in content with the information supplied by other researchers in the company and in an easy-to-read brief format. "The better quality has to do with our approach to research, to research concept," says Gartner.

The company has achieved a high standard by methods more commonly associated with manufacturing firms—standardized procedures, quality control and evaluation systems, and continuous training programs. The essence of this technology is set forth in the company's "bible," the research notebook written by Gideon Gartner. This research technology has enabled the company to expand its research staff rapidly and still maintain a reputation for innovation and high quality standards. *Technology is also energized by implementing high corporate values like quality, systematic functioning, innovation, and freedom.*

These strategies have enabled Gartner to convert technology into a powerful engine for growth and a lucrative source of revenues. From 1979 to the time it was acquired by Saatchi & Saatchi in mid-1988, the company's revenues grew from $500,000 to $36 million, averaging an increase of about 52% each year over the last three years. Current revenues are at $62 million.

CAPITALIZING ON A DREAM

When we speak of engines of growth, the one that first comes to mind is often capital. At Patten Corporation, capital was not the first engine, but it has certainly been one of the most important. In the mid-1960s, when Harry Patten founded the company in Stamford, Vermont, there was a surging demand among the urban population to fulfill their dream of owning a home in the countryside. Harry had developed a talent for recognizing good potential homesite property and a simple mechanism for marketing it to city dwellers through classified ads in major metropolitan newspapers. For the next 20 years, Patten Corporation remained a small land company buying 50- to 100-acre rural plots and dividing them into 5- to 20-acre homesites for resale.

Then in 1984 Harry met a young Boston financial consultant who saw the enormous potential of his business and offered to raise capital for its growth. That year the company raised $20 million and the company's sales jumped from $4.3 million to $11.2 million. New offices were opened in Maine and New Hampshire. The following year, Patten Corporation went public and raised another $7.2 million in equity. Sales soared to $33.2 million. By 1988 the company was operating 38 branch offices, primarily in the Northeast and midatlantic areas of the country, with revenues of $116 million, profits of $17.5 million and a strategic plan for doubling again by 1993.

Capital was the engine that enabled Patten to utilize the latent potentials of his long years of experience in the acquisition and marketing of rural land to expand his business 26-fold in four years. But the power of this engine goes way beyond mere investment value. Apart from its role as a factor of production, there is a whole other way of looking at finance as a means to energize the other components of a business. Again it comes back to attitude, to perspective. When finance is looked at as a measure and an index rather than an end in itself, it acquires new creative power. We pursue that idea further in a later chapter.

A PERSONAL APPROACH

Expeditors International, based in Seattle with offices in 40 cities around the world, is the largest forwarder of airfreight cargo from the Far East to North America. Over the last five years its revenues have risen from $3.5 million to $147 million, and profits have crossed $7 million. What has been the engine that has generated such phenomenal growth? "The people," says John Kaiser, Expeditors' founder. "In a service business, you don't have anything that anybody else couldn't get. It requires minimal capital to get in. We have a relatively good organization. The engine or drive has been the people. We've been able to motivate the people."

Kaiser's comment is based on an understanding that goes back to the time when the company was founded. In 1979 when Kaiser and ten associates with many years of experience working for another forwarding company established Expeditors, they agreed that each of the founding partners should make a sizable personal investment in the company and share in a percentage of the profits. As new offices were opened overseas, a similar arrangement was made so that branch managers also became owners and shared in the profits.

Expeditors has combined good compensation with another powerful energizer—freedom. "Our philosophy at that time was to spread the wealth amongst the people and make sure they all have a vested interest in the organization," Kaiser explained. "One of the things that made this business grow is that the people that came on board were very confident. We make a conscious effort to make our managers at the branch level as independent as possible. If you create an atmosphere where people can operate independently and you have the right people, that's the real key in our business."

Expeditors illustrates a few of the many ways in which people can be made an engine of growth—recruiting very experienced managers from the same industry, making them investors and profit sharers, and giving them a wide latitude of freedom.

GIVING NEW LIFE TO A DYING INDUSTRY

Of the five engines, organization contains the greatest creative power for growth, yet it is the least understood and the least utilized. In 1957 two Harvard MBAs travelling in Europe discovered and demonstrated this power to people around the world—literally!

Applying the market research techniques they had learned in business school, they discovered that shoe repairing was a dying industry in Europe, where becoming a cobbler did not attract young people entering the work force. For instance, while the population of the Netherlands had increased by 50% during the previous 20 years, the number of cobblers had declined to half the previous level. The demographics were similar in other European countries. As a result, it took an average of six days to get a pair of heels repaired in Paris or Zurich. Seeing opportunity where others saw none, the two entrepreneurs opened up a fast shoe-repair service right in the midst of the prestigious Bon Marche department store in downtown Brussels. The shop, known as Mister Minit, offered fast (two minutes for a heel repair), quality, convenient, clean service for a premium price. These were the heydays of the spike-heeled shoe, and the cobblestone streets of Brussels played havoc with the new fashion. The new business was an instant success. Within a year, Mister Minit shops had been opened all over Belgium.

The ability to recognize an unmet social need was the initial power behind the development of the business. But the real growth of this company had not yet begun. For that, the entrepreneurs had to find a means to reproduce their local success in hundreds of locations throughout Europe, and they did. The means they discovered was the engine of organization.

The company decided to reduce all its operations to a set of codified and standardized systems, so that virtually every step in the process of establishing new service centers, recruiting and training personnel, procuring materials, relating to customers and accounting for the results was explained and documented as a standard operating procedure (SOP). As we sat in Geneva talking with the company's chairman and co-founder, Hillsdon Ryan, he waved his hand at a row of at least 15 four-inch thick manuals on the board room bookcase, which set forth the organizational technology that enabled the company to grow so rapidly.

Along with these systems, the company introduced a supervisory structure that was designed to make each of the service center managers an entrepreneur in his own right, while also ensuring uniform performance standards throughout the company. "The supervisory structure is absolutely one of the keys to our success, an important key," says Ryan. "We've kept a lot of the spirit of freedom. We've kept a flat organization. It is all based on very good codification of our experience in systems, because in a service business of our kind where the units are reproducible, they lend themselves to systems."

The power of that engine was made clearly evident by the remarkable expansion of the company over the next few years. First it spread horizontally by opening centers in other European capitals. Then it expanded its range of services from shoe repair to key cutting, engraving, rubber stamps and knife sharpening. Later the range was broadened further to include instant printing of cards and letterhead, watch repair, sewing, and one-hour photo film development. Finally, it focused on backward integration of the retail service outlets with distribution centers and manufacturing plants for the equipment, fixtures and raw materials such as key blanks and rubber stamps, incidentally becoming the world's largest producer of rubber stamps.

The standard operating procedures were expanded to include detailed guidelines for establishing new foreign subsidiaries. For a period in the early 1960s, the company was opening up new subsidiaries at the rate of one every two months as it expanded within Europe, then to Australia, Japan, Korea, Taiwan and Singapore. "These are detailed SOPs on how to operate the unit," Ryan explained. "You'll find this in every country in its own language. Here we have four volumes of standards for the photo business. As far as I know, no one else in the business has this. What we did was search the whole business and write our own procedures for everything by subject. We did this early in the game, so we can now reproduce our units anywhere." And the company has done just that. By 1989 Minit International was operating 4,600 service centers in 2,500 cities and towns in 25 countries globally and employing 11,000 people. Organization was the driving force for this phenomenal growth.

DRIVERS, TEST YOUR ENGINES

The word *driver* is important. For if you perceive that any of the five engines we have described are somehow beyond your reach or control, then we have failed to convey the point. *You* have the power to drive each of the five engines and harness its energy for growth.

When we speak of market, we do not mean that big, impersonal and unpredictable world out there that is beyond any and everybody's control. Rather, we refer to *your* perception of that market and the relationship you forge with it, both of which are directly and totally subject to your control.

When we speak of technology, we do not refer to the vast movement of scientific and technological evolution which is continuously changing the way we interact with each other and the world around us. Rather we mean the way you perceive the products and services you provide and the methods you employ to generate them.

When we speak of capital or finance, we do not confine ourselves to the quantity of money invested in your company or the sources and means of finance you draw upon to obtain it. Finance is also a way of looking at things—not just passively in order to track performance, but actively in order to manage it.

When we speak of people, we are not thinking in demographic terms of numbers, age, sex, or qualifications, but in terms of people's energies, knowledge, skills, and capacities; their understanding and their attitudes; and how these can be fully mobilized for their personal growth and the growth of the company.

When we speak of organization, we do not refer to the organizational chart that describes the division of responsibilities and levels of authority within a company. This is only an abstract, two-dimensional, structural representation of a complex, living organism with manifold and immense productive capabilities. An organizational chart has never doubled anything, except perhaps payrolls and bureaucracy, while organization in the true sense has virtually unlimited creative power.

Words are a great limitation, because we must use common nouns to describe uncommon powers. Once again, think about your own company. What is the source of its energies? What has propelled its growth?

We have included a business self-evaluation form at the end of this chapter to assist you in assessing the relative development of each of the five components of your company as they exist today. Knowing where we are is the first step for accelerating growth. Our understanding of where we are is usually based to a great extent on impressions. An exercise like this enables us to formalize and objectify our assessment and to compare it with the perception of other people. Take a few minutes to evaluate your business.

SUMMARY

- Five essential components are necessary for the existence, survival, and growth of a business—market, technology, people, capital, and organization.

- Each of these five contains vast untapped potentials that are within the reach of every company.

- Any one of them can be converted into an engine for doubling a company's performance.

- Development of all five releases opportunities for endless expansion.

BUSINESS SELF-EVALUATION QUESTIONNAIRE

Instructions

This questionnaire contains five sections, one for each of the five engines. Each section consists of 20 statements.

Evaluate how true each of these statements is for your company on a scale from 0 (low) to 10 (high) as shown. You may score the statements with any whole or decimal number—for example, 2, 3.5, 6.7, 9.

Never true at all	A little true	Partially true	Mostly true	Always fully true
L_I__I__I__I_I_I__I__I_I__I__I_I_I__I__I_I__I__I__I_I__I				
0	2.5	5	7.5	10

After answering all the questions, add up the subtotal for each of the five components.

To assess the absolute and relative strength of each of the five components, calculate a percentage score for each section by dividing each subtotal in half (e.g., if the subtotal score on market is 140 out of 200, the percentage score is 70%).

Market

1. We know exactly who our customers are.
2. We are in contact with all potential customers for our products/services.
3. We understand the needs and preferences of our customers.
4. We are able to anticipate the changing needs of the market.
5. We are able to meet these changing needs.
6. We know our present market share and what we have to do to increase it.
7. We closely observe the marketing strategies of other companies in our market.
8. Our customers are pleased with the service they receive from our company.
9. We always deliver our products/services promptly.
10. We go out of our way to satisfy even the unreasonable demands of our customers.
11. Someone is available 24 hours a day, 7 days a week to answer questions or solve the problems of our customers.
12. We give timely and accurate information to our customers.
13. All our people have a friendly attitude in their interactions with our customers.
14. Every member of our sales staff knows how to listen to customers, win their confidence, and make them feel happy about the products/services we offer.
15. Our showrooms, offices, and all other facilities open to the public are immaculately clean, orderly, and pleasing to the eye.
16. Our company employs highly innovative marketing strategies.
17. Our company's advertising campaigns are effective and imaginative.
18. All salespeople undergo continuous sales training to improve their sales skills and product knowledge.
19. There is a smooth flow of information from the sales force back to the customer service department and vice versa.
20. We conduct regular sales meetings to discuss performance, set targets and develop new sales programs.

Technology

21. We offer the best value (quality for the price) available in the market.
22. Experts in the industry would characterize our product/service as "first with the latest."
23. We incorporate all new technological developments in our industry.
24. We operate at high levels of efficiency with the minimum of wastage.
25. We utilize the most advanced systems for quality control.
26. The productivity of our people is among the highest in the industry.
27. The productivity of our equipment/facilities is among the highest in the industry.
28. We are constantly trying to upgrade and improve our products/services.
29. Top management is fully aware of the importance of technology.
30. We are highly creative and innovative in developing new products/services.
31. We offer the widest range of products/services to our customers.
32. Our company fully guarantees the products/services we sell and backs them with a quick and fair claims service.
33. Every member of our customer service department possesses a high level of technical knowledge and competence.
34. Every member of our sales staff possesses complete technical knowledge about the products/services we offer.
35. Every member of our production/operations staff possesses a high level and broad range of technical knowledge.
36. We allocate sufficient funds for the development of new products/services.
37. Production/operations is well coordinated with sales and marketing.
38. We continuously train our employees to improve safety and eliminate all types of accidents.
39. We are constantly trying to reduce the production cost of our products/services.
40. Those involved in product development are well trained for their work.

Organization

41. All activities of the company are carefully planned in advance and closely monitored during implementation.
42. Routine operations, projects and paperwork are completed on schedule.

43. Our organization is flexible and responsive to the changing demands made on it.

44. Our organizational structure is clear to everyone in the company and there are clear job descriptions for each position.

45. Higher levels of management respect the authority and freedom given to people at lower levels of the organization.

46. Decisions are taken and executed promptly.

47. We consciously build new systems large enough to support future expansion.

48. We order products/materials on time to ensure sufficient supplies.

49. The company is structured so as to minimize duplication of work and maximize efficiency.

50. Recurring problems are dealt with by introducing new systems or by improving existing ones.

51. When something goes wrong, it is easy to determine who is responsible and accountable.

52. Decision making is decentralized throughout the organization so that decisions are taken by the lowest-level employee competent to do so.

53. All departments/offices/divisions are well coordinated so that information and work flows smoothly back and forth between them.

54. Decisions taken by top management are quickly and smoothly transmitted down to the lowest level of the company.

55. Information and ideas generated at lower levels of the organization are transmitted quickly and accurately to top management.

56. All file cabinets, offices, storage facilities, and warehouses are maintained in a clean and orderly fashion.

57. The forms and systems employed by all departments and offices conform to a common standard.

58. The files maintained by each employee are organized so that other employees can easily access them and find materials in their absence.

59. Meetings are carried out in an effective and productive manner.

60. All systems are documented by written standard operating procedures to facilitate training of new persons and ensure uniformity of operations.

People

61. We consciously recruit people with high energy levels and the right type of personality.

62. In recruiting new employees, we give high priority to selecting people with the highest level of education available.
63. Our company has a refined system for evaluating job applicants.
64. All new employees go through a comprehensive orientation program and job-related training before beginning work.
65. We strive to develop all the capacities and potentials of our people.
66. All employees receive regular job performance appraisals to help them improve their performance and plan for their career development.
67. Our employees feel a high level of enthusiasm and job satisfaction.
68. Our employees feel a minimum of stress on the job.
69. Our employees work together harmoniously as a team without conflict.
70. We give our people a great deal of freedom for individual initiative and creativity.
71. Our employees believe they are compensated fairly for the work they do.
72. Our compensation system links material benefits with individual or group performance.
73. Our company offers excellent long term benefits as part of its policy to provide job security to its employees.
74. We give social recognition and personal attention to employees that do a good job.
75. The company encourages and supports the ongoing education of all its employees.
76. Our managers possess a high level of organizational and managerial skills.
77. We systematically train and develop the managerial skills of young managers and potential managers.
78. All supervisory and managerial personnel in our company are continuously being trained to improve their interpersonal skills.
79. People within the company are self-disciplined in their work.
80. We continuously evaluate the training needs of each position and employee and provide appropriate training to ensure that individual skills meet job requirements.

Capital

81. We utilize all possible sources of capital from banks, suppliers, credit, financial markets, and so on.

82. Our cost accounting systems enable us to measure accurately the cost of each activity and operation involved in producing products and services.

83. We closely and regularly monitor our costs on each category of expenditure and compare it to past levels or established standards.

84. We pay our bills on time.

85. We collect receivables on time.

86. We have detailed budgets for planning and projecting expenditures and cash flow.

87. Our accounting systems are updated daily and maintained up to date.

88. Our accounting systems measure the productivity of people in every activity and are used as an effective instrument to encourage high individual performance.

89. We carefully control expenditures to keep them within budget.

90. We maintain active and close relations with our shareholders, investors, bankers, and other financial institutions.

91. We carefully invest surplus cash to achieve maximum returns.

92. All people consciously strive to minimize costs and eliminate waste of any description.

93. We control inventory levels to achieve the maximum number of turns.

94. All purchases of goods/services are routed through a central purchasing department to ensure we buy at the best prices.

95. Our company is highly successful in evaluating credit risks and minimizing bad debts.

96. Our company's return on investment is above average for the industry.

97. We regularly monitor an array of financial indicators to forecast future activity and respond appropriately to new trends as they develop.

98. Our managers carry out tasks appropriate for their level of compensation and delegate all tasks which can be done more cost effectively at lower levels of the organization.

99. Our financial people possess all the knowledge and skills required to carry out their responsibilities effectively.

100. Our facilities and equipment (physical assets) are carefully maintained to minimize wear and tear and ensure long life.

"Growth is our double-edged sword."

David Barasch
Ben & Jerry's

Chapter Three

===

A SURE-WIN DIET FOR DOUBLING YOUR SALES AND PROFITS

THE MOST IMPORTANT ENGINE

Refer back to the business self-evaluation questionnaire at the end of the last chapter. Which of the five components has been the most important engine for the growth of revenues and profits in your company up to now? Which should be the engine for its future growth? Which of the five has the greatest inherent power to propel growth?

The relative importance of these five has always been a lively issue for debate. Dedicated salespeople will emphatically insist that the market—the customer—is the real key to any business. With equal vigor, design and production engineers will stress the dominant role of technology in the success of a business. Of course, every human resource manager knows that people are the real key. As one put it: "Without people you've got nothing!" Financial analysts often laugh at the other three and quietly remind them that, after all, capital is the foundation, the means, and the end of every business, without which the others are powerless. And occasionally—very occasionally—you run across an experienced executive who will present a view similar to that of Andrew Carnegie, who once said: "Take away everything else, but leave me my organization and in ten years I'll be back on top."

And as with people, so with companies. In board rooms across the country there are intense debates as to whether the company should be market driven or product driven, people oriented or systems oriented, dedicated to profits or to quality, and so on. Ask most managers, and they will immediately tell you one or another of the five is most important. And within the same company, you can hear many different views.

Who's right? Which is the most important engine for growth? Steve Bedowitz, CEO of AMRE, insists quite emphatically: "All of them. Every single one of them makes up the engine. It is not any one alone. I know a brilliant man who has great ideas, but every time he starts, he goes bankrupt because he doesn't have all the pieces of the engine. No one piece can stand alone. There are a lot of pieces. One reason we will keep on growing is because we found all the pieces to put together."

Bedowitz has hit on the secret. A closer look at any business will reveal that not one but several engines have played important roles in its growth and that all five have been developed at least to the minimum level required to support that growth.

People was certainly a driving force for the growth of Expeditors, but the highly decentralized entrepreneurial structure the company has developed relies to a great extent for its success on the standardized operating procedures employed by all the branches and the strong control systems top management employs to monitor their activities.

Technology has been a major driving force behind the growth of Gartner Group, but the company's ability to attune its research products very carefully to meet the information needs of its customers (market) and its ability to attract and motivate bright, high-energy salespeople, who are nearly twice as productive as the competition (people), have also been critical success factors.

Linear Technology's growth is the result of a fine balance and coordination between research (technology) and the market supported by an environment that provides great freedom and high levels of compensation to its people.

The rapid influx of new capital enabled Patten Corporation to increase its inventories and expand its operations 26-fold, but it has been the company's ability to recruit and motivate managers properly for its new branches (people) and its expertise in identification and acquisition of the right properties for investment (technology) that has ensured that proper utilization of those funds to return consistently high profits.

The global expansion of Minit International was made possible by the organizational structure and systems it put into place. But recruiting the right type of people who possess qualities of both craftsmen and entrepreneurs, training them in a wide variety of technical skills, and motivating them to high levels of productivity and customer service was made possible by the emphasis the company placed on the engine people.

The real issue is not whether a company should be market driven, product driven, people driven, systems driven or profit driven. *If any company wants to grow and keep growing profitably, it needs to develop all five, because each of these five is an engine that contains within itself virtually unlimited potentials for expansion, and to tap the potentials of any one more fully, the others must be developed proportionately as well.*

That is what Waltz Brothers discovered in 1986.

A BANKER'S ERROR

Waltz Brothers is a precision machining company founded in Chicago 50 years ago by three brothers, who all retired in 1976 leaving the business to their four sons to manage. The company specializes in machining parts to incredibly close dimensional tolerances of three-ten thousandths of an inch. The four cousins worked hard to build on the good reputation established by their fathers and their work soon began paying rich dividends. In the early 1980s, the company became a major supplier of computer disk drive shafts to IBM and to companies in the aerospace industry.

In 1985 sales soared and revenues rocketed from $3 million to $5 million in one year. Excited by the great potential for continued growth, the company purchased new equipment, moved into a new modern building in a suburb of Chicago, hired lots of new people and took every new job it could get its hands on.

For a while rapid growth was exhilarating. Then problems began to surface. In a business where quality and on-time delivery are paramount, quality declined and deliveries fell behind schedule. Only 40% of jobs were completed on time. Dissatisfied customers started sending back rejected parts. Then they stopped sending in new orders. Orders by one major customer dropped from $500,000 to $10,000. As suddenly as the surge of new business had appeared, it suddenly disappeared and with it the partner's profits and their dreams.

One day their banker called them in to point out that the company was losing money at the rate of $350,000 a year. It came as a big shock to the partners, because profit was something they had always taken for granted. The banker asked them how they planned to repay the plant and equipment loans. Then he said, "Your days are numbered. By our estimate you can survive for only one or two more months." The cousins were stunned by the imminent demise of a business which their fathers had nurtured and developed over five decades and which had recently seemed on the verge of taking off.

In that brief meeting with their bankers, the Waltzes discovered what thousands of companies have learned in the past. Rapid growth is not only one of the most exhilarating experiences that a company can have, it is also one of the most challenging and potentially dangerous. It is not very difficult to grow rapidly, but it is difficult to grow rapidly and profitably and to keep growing profitably over a prolonged period of time. That explains why 23% of the fast-growing companies on *INC.*'s 1988 list were losing money.

All these fast-growing companies have discovered the explosive power of at least one of the five engines. But why when they are so buoyant and expansive do they so often run into trouble? Because they have not learned the second basic truth about the five engines, a truth that we all were taught at the dinner table when we were children—the importance of balance.

The Waltzes discovered that truth after their meeting with the banker. When the Waltzes returned to their office, their sole objective was to prove that the banker's prophecy was wrong. They realized that in expanding rapidly they had focused almost all their attention on two of the five components—market and technology, the customer and the machine—and in the process had neglected other essential components of profitable growth—people, organization, and capital. Sales had grown faster than their operating systems could handle and their people could manage. Expenditure rose faster than their financial systems could control. In other words, in growing rapidly the five components had grown out of balance.

So the Waltzes formulated a comprehensive strategy for saving their company by eliminating weaknesses in each of the five components and restoring the balance between them at the same time. First, they took a serious look at their market and decided they had to change their approach. They redefined their mission as a company, evolved a new marketing strategy, and made a serious effort to improve the service they provided to customers. They set as a goal to raise on-time deliveries from 40% to 90%. Rejection rates were brought down from 8% to less than 1%. On-time deliveries rose above the 90% standard.

They energized their people by introducing a series of training programs. They hired an outside agency to teach eight-week courses on statistical quality control and gave their supervisors a five-week advanced course in supervisory skills. They also introduced a profit-sharing program to enable their employees to participate in their success. As a result, productivity soared and costs fell.

They also tapped the potentials of the component capital. They introduced some stringent cost cutting, eliminating every unnecessary expense—including free coffee in the office. They found they could achieve a 25% cost savings on raw materials by negotiating long-term contracts with vendors just as their customers negotiated with them. Expendable tools was another area that improved. Machining bits were being thrown away prematurely. By purchasing one with a better coating, they found productivity could be raised. Then they introduced a sophisticated budgeting system to help them control costs and closely monitor key performance indicators which enabled them to project workforce requirements accurately in advance of actual need. They carefully analyzed new machinery purchases to determine whether the investments were actually justified.

They also tapped some of the potentials of technology. They purchased a computer-controlled grinder, which met a small need, and then marketed their new capabilities and filled the expanded capacity.

And finally, they restructured and streamlined their organization by redefining the responsibilities of the four partners and improving the systems for inventory control, budgeting, monitoring performance, scheduling, and quality control.

As a result of these efforts, net income went from a negative $350,000 in 1985 to a positive $30,000 in 1986 and to $500,000 in 1987—a net increase equivalent to 17% of revenues in two years. The company also received a prestigious quality award from IBM.

Waltz Brothers recovered from the brink of bankruptcy by tapping some of the latent potentials of the five engines and by restoring the balance between them. What the Waltz Brothers have done in a time of crisis, every company can do at any time to grow rapidly and profitably.

A DELICATE BLEND

The real key to nonstop growth is a harmonious and balanced development of all five components, either successively or simultaneously. Each of the five is a powerful engine for growth, but each also depends on the other four in order to flower fully and express its potentials. When the development of any one of the five exceeds the present requirements of the company, the surplus energies from that component overflow and begin to stimulate the development of the others. When people are energized, customers are attracted to the company, systems work faster and better, money is utilized more efficiently and technological innovation increases. When the market is energized, employees are more enthusiastic, development of new technologies is stimulated, and systems are constantly being improved. When the organization is tuned to perform at peak levels of efficiency, people feel more relaxed and happy, service to customers is superior, costs are reduced, and coordination among research, production and the market improves.

The reverse is also true. The lack of development of any one of the five components retards the development of the other four. The market for our product may be strong. But if we lack the technology needed to maintain quality, we cannot fully tap that market. We may have the most talented and highly motivated people, but without the right type of structure to direct them and the right type of systems to carry out routine operations effortlessly, anarchy and burnout will be the main result. We may have the best technology, but if we lack people with enough energy and the right skills, the market may not respond to what we offer.

UNIVAC learned from IBM the cost of ignoring one of the five components back in the 1950s when it became the first company to bring computers to the marketplace. Despite the fact that the UNIVAC machine was considered far superior, IBM took away

75% of the computer market within the first five years. IBM knew that a highly educated, trained, and motivated sales force (people) was as important for success as a good product (technology).

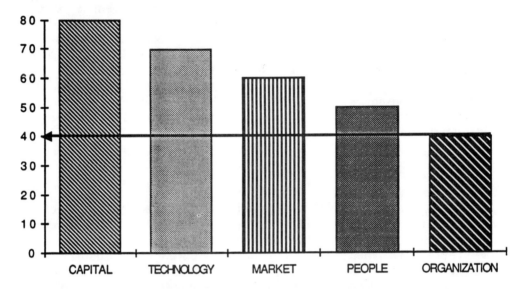

Figure 1. A Typical Profile of the Five Engines of Business.

Figure 1 is a typical profile of the five engines of a business. It shows that the components market and technology are relatively well developed. Like Mister Minit and Linear Technology, it is in close touch with the needs of its market. Like Gartner Group and Patten, it has developed technology to a high level. But the components people and organization are relatively weaker, as they are in a majority of fast-growing companies. The horizontal line shows the level of full utilization of potentials based on the development of the weakest component, organization. The areas of market and technology above the line represent capacities that cannot be fully utilized for lack of appropriate supporting strength in people and organization.

A THREE-ENGINE PLANE

As the Waltzes found out, an unbalanced development of the five components can slow or stop growth in its tracks, and that is precisely what happens to most fast growing companies. Like many other small commuter airlines, the birth of Mesa

Airlines in Farmington, New Mexico, in 1982 was spawned by deregulation of the commercial airline industry. However, unlike many other young commuter services, Mesa has been able to remain profitable.

One of the keys to Mesa's survival and growth in a highly competitive market, where even the majors have taken some beatings, has been its ability to identify markets with latent demand for commuter services in which it could effectively compete against other carriers. When competition on the Farmington-Albuquerque route heated up, Mesa dropped its fare from $48 to $25 to match the competition. When competitors later raised their prices again, Mesa kept its low because it had discovered a significant increase in demand for seats at the lower rate, which enabled it to achieve 20% higher load factors than their competitors.

But apart from just competing cost-effectively, Mesa has been able to actually create new markets between cities where air travel had not existed earlier. Founder-President Larry Risley explained: "We want to get the price down as low as we can and get the volume up as high as we can. . . . That way we get people traveling. We make less profit per seat, but because we fill more seats, the flight is making a profit . . . We've stimulated the market with fares. We get people talking about how easy it is to travel from point A to point B. That's how we built the market from Farmington to Albuquerque, which was nonexistent. . . . The engines that have propelled our growth have been the ability to recognize the potential markets and fit the right size equipment to them, so that we could operate profitably." Mesa has become adept at entering new markets, testing out new fares and quickly withdrawing from those that are not profitable.

Market, technology (the right equipment) and capital (cost management) have been the engines that propelled the growth of Mesa from $2.1 million in 1984 to $14.4 million in 1987. During this same period, profits also rose from $185,000 to $790,000. Then quite suddenly, everything stopped. Even with three engines driving it forward, the airline lost its momentum.

When we visited Mesa in mid-1988, Larry Risley explained why Mesa had stopped growing last year.

> We've hit a point of stabilization. Our growth is down to 4–5% annually. What caused us to stop growing was our inability to staff it properly. I'm not saying that we quit growing purposely. I'm saying it went beyond my capacities at the time. I didn't learn quick enough. My management staff didn't learn quick enough. It put us on the back side of the power curve. Our reliability was going down. Our customer confidence was starting to fall. The employee loyalties began to drop—morale and all. You couldn't go out and put your finger on the cause exactly.

Mesa stopped growing because it lost its balance. While Risley was focusing on market, technology, and capital, the people and organization components got left behind. The company was so busy developing its markets that it forgot to develop its people and its organization. As market expansion continued, it quite literally overran the runway. Mesa was slow to build up the management team, structure and systems needed for nonstop growth. Risley continued to manage the company as he had when it was much smaller, keeping information "close to the chest," and refusing to delegate.

THE DOUBLE-EDGED SWORD

Mesa has been fortunate. Even though growth has slowed, the company has remained profitable. It may be able to restore the balance and take off again in the near future. Many other companies are not so fortunate. In the early 1970s a dynamic young entrepreneur with a real talent for marketing and a real appreciation for high-technology products opened up an electronics store in Chicago. The store's sales grew rapidly, and it was quite profitable. Soon the entrepreneur opened a second store, then a third. Within a few years the company was operating eight stores in Illinois, which the CEO visited regularly by private plane. Revenues soared to $8 million, but profits remained at about the level they had been when the company operated only two stores. By 1978 the company was in trouble. To the surprise of top management, an analysis of the business revealed that only the first two stores were making money, and, in fact, the other six had never been profitable. Although the company had expanded its number of outlets, it had never built up an organization to manage its growing empire, and it had never put in the financial systems to control inventory and costs in multiple locations. The owners did not even recognize they had a problem until it was too late. Here too, an unbalanced development of the five components halted growth.

The experience of this company is in striking contrast to that of another firm in the same industry, Audio Craft in Cleveland. The company is a leader in its field with one of the best profit records year after year. An analysis of the company shows that all five components are well developed and in balance. The company shares the traditional strengths of other companies in the industry—a very strong commitment to customer service and a high level of technological expertise. But Audio Craft is also strong in three areas where many of its competitors are relatively weak—finance, organization and people. CEO Wayne Puntel is famous among his peers in the industry for the sophisticated systems he has installed to help him manage and control his six stores efficiently and effortlessly. He also has developed very effective training programs to improve continuously the skills of his sales force and strong incentive and recognition programs to motivate and reward them. In spite of this high performance, Puntel is continuously striving to generate more power from the five engines by developing them further in a balanced manner. Last year that effort generated an additional 40% increase in profitability.

When things get out of balance, some companies take a conscious decision to slow down or stop the growth before it leads to trouble. At the time we visited Ben & Jerry's Homemade Ice Cream in Burlington, Vermont, the founder and president, Ben Cohen, had just put out a directive—"No more growth." Ben and cofounder Jerry Greenfield started the company in an abandoned gas station in 1978. Between 1981 and 1988, sales multiplied 75-fold to top $45 million. Now there is heated debate concerning an issue quite familiar to ice cream lovers—is it possible to have too much of a good thing?

The growth of this company has been propelled by the engines market (great ads and promotions), technology (a wonderful product) and highly motivated people. Its one weak point has been organization. "Growth is our double-edged sword," says David Barasch. "The number one issue here is whether we should keep growing. Do we have the internal organizational tenacity and structure to be able to do it? Do we have the right people? The right checks and balances? It all boils down to communication . . . things happening out of coordination . . . the feeling that we are swimming upstream."

Ben described the issue from his perspective: "Growth has been a heated topic in our company for the last eight years. The word growth is interesting. You have inner and outer growth, qualitative and quantitative growth. Right now I want to stop the quantitative growth, so that we can concentrate on the quality." To which Jerry retorted, "We talk about slower quantitative growth, but we continually make decisions that will fuel greater growth!"

The issue that Ben and Jerry are coping with is far from academic. Companies that refuse to pay attention to these symptoms are forced to compensate by driving their people harder or spending more and more money or compromising further and further on quality or lowering prices to maintain growing volumes. The result is steadily rising costs and complications, steadily deteriorating customer and employee satisfaction—until finally the floor or the roof caves in and they are forced to stop and pick up the pieces, if it is not already too late. Two of the 100 companies listed by *INC.* in 1986 were already out of business one year later.

Any company that focuses on one or two components to the exclusion of the others runs the risk of becoming a leaning tower—a company like Chrysler Corporation in the 1960s and 1970s that focused on technology at the expense of the other four (particularly market), until the company was brought to the brink of disaster.

CORPORATE ANATOMY

There are many similarities between the functioning of the human body and the functioning of a company. But they differ in one major respect. As a biological life form, the body naturally grows and develops in an organic manner. The growth of each part of the body occurs simultaneously and in correct proportion to all the others. The right arm and the left lengthen proportionately. The nerves, muscles, and blood vessels extend in proportion to the growth of the bones. As they grow, the links between them—the cartilage, ligaments and tendons—automatically extend to ensure proper connection between the bones and muscles.

In a company, however, balanced and proportionate growth cannot be taken for granted and is, in fact, rather unusual. Like the body, organizations do expand in many directions simultaneously. Structures, systems, positions, policies, and rules grow along with the number of people and offices and the volume of production. But they often grow at different rates and in different directions. Frequently they grow without proper systems and procedures to link them together. Therefore, in examining the anatomy of a company, the human body is a good image of how a company should but usually does not grow.

The body and the organization differ in one other important respect. The growth of the body is not only organic, it is also subconscious, which means that it is not under our conscious control. Organizations grow subconsciously too. They expand naturally without anyone really thinking about all the parts and their interrelationships. But they do have a choice. Companies can exert conscious control over their own development and achieve through effort and alertness what the body accomplishes through subconscious processes. The ability of management to understand the subconscious process of human physical development and replicate it in the company is a key to nonstop, rapid corporate growth.

The five engines constitute the anatomy of a business. They are like the essential organs of the body—the brain, heart, lungs, stomach and liver. Their role in corporate growth can be understood from three distinct perspectives. First, each is important and crucial in its own right. The heart, like the market, must be strong and healthy. The brain, like the people, should be alert and energetic, and so on.

Second, each must also be developed in proper proportion to the others. As the lungs must be sufficiently developed to provide all the oxygen needed by the brain and heart, technology must provide new products and services to serve a growing market. As the liver must be capable of purifying all the blood which the heart pumps, capital must be capable of providing sufficient support for innovations in technology.

Third, in addition to their absolute importance and the need for balanced development, there is also a need for harmonious interaction and close coordination between them. When the heart beats faster, the lungs must pump more oxygen and the liver must filter more blood. When the market expands, people in all parts of the company must be able to respond with energy and skill. Capital must circulate more quickly. Production and research (technology) must accelerate their activity. If for even a short interval the synergy is lost between the organs of the body, the body collapses into coma. The same is true of companies.

This harmonious coordination is not only essential for life. It is also the key to health and vitality—both for the body and the company. Companies that are able to establish and maintain very high levels of synergy between the five engines are able continuously to grow rapidly and profitably.

THE VIEW AT THE TOP

What determines the relative strength, balance, and coordination of the five engines in a company? It starts with the people at the top—their understanding, their attitudes, and their preferences. If the CEO or the top management team believes that this is a technology-driven company, it will be. If they believe that people are the driving force, people will be. The real balancing act takes place in the minds of the leaders.

There are many ways to spoil a healthy diet. We have been in companies where top management believes only in the market and never builds up an organization or people to support the market. We have been in companies where the CEO was so committed to organization that he has systematized the life out of the company. We have even met senior executives who put so much emphasis on training that salespeople, who are subjected to the same "motivational" video-taped training programs year after year, secretly speed up the tapes whenever the training supervisor is not looking.

The role of the CEO is to ensure that all five powers are seen in proper perspective, that their capacities are fully recognized, and that their interrelationships are fully appreciated. Fred Smith, founder and CEO of Federal Express, has understood that maintaining a dynamic balance between the five engines is an important part of his job.

> I purposely populate the ranks of the senior officers with champions of disparate points of view. I don't want a chief financial officer who is an existentialist. I want a chief financial officer who is very dollars and cents oriented, almost to a fault. Then over on the marketing side, I'd like somebody who is very dissatisfied unless we're prepared to give away the product and pay the customer. In this way you create a contention in the organization where there are alternative points of view. That keeps me intellectually honest. . . . As you grow you have to be careful that you don't get the components out of balance. Companies that survive have this sort of intuitive knowledge.

A BALANCING ACT

The view from the top is not the only view or necessarily the most objective. CEOs who ask other managers of the company to evaluate the relative strengths and weaknesses of the five components are often surprised to learn how differently the company is perceived from other vantage points. One CEO who had performed the exercise three or four times over two years commented jocularly, "Every time I rate the company, my scores go up. Every time the rest of the management team rates it, their scores go down!"

Chuck Kittleson of Century Stereo in Palo Alto administered the questionnaire to his employees and then undertook a systematic effort to strengthen the company on all the areas they had identified as relatively weak, even those that appeared relatively minor. Apart from the changes he implemented, the effort itself had a profound impact on morale and performance. Over the next one year, the company's profits doubled.

Henry Triesler, president of Precision Grinding, Inc., in Phoenix, gave the questionnaire to all his managers. He then held weekly staff meetings for the next six months discussing their answers to each question and eliciting suggestions on how to raise the company's performance in each area. This exercise helped his company go from heavy losses to strong profits in a little more than a year.

The very act of giving serious attention to all five engines has a power to release some of their latent energies. That was enough to double the performance of these two companies. Then what will be the result if these powers are fully tapped and systematically utilized? An endless expansion of revenues and profits.

Examine the relative strength of the five engines of your company and sketch them on a bar chart. Which are the strongest? In an absolute sense according to your own ratings, how much further scope is there to strengthen these strong components? Which are the weakest and how much scope is there to strengthen them? Now compare the relative levels of their development. How evenly are they balanced? How much developed capacity in the stronger components remains unutilized because one or more of the other components is not sufficiently developed to support it?

Where should a company be concentrating its efforts for further growth? Should it focus on the stronger components or the weaker ones? About 50% of companies have excess unutilized capacity already developed (a strength which is not able to express itself fully) in at least one component. If fully utilized, this capacity is often enough to double the company's performance. But utilizing that excess capacity requires the proportionate strengthening of the other components. Companies that focus on fully exploiting their strengths invariably end up reinforcing the weaker areas to restore a balance between the components. The balancing occurs naturally, even if the strategy is not conceived in this manner. If you review the growth of your own company, you should be able to identify this process at work.

An understanding of where we are is the first essential step. But recognizing the power of the five engines and the importance of balanced development is not enough to generate and sustain high rates of rapid, profitable growth. For that, we must know how to tap the potentials of each of these five, to release their energies, to channel them effectively and convert them into practical results in terms of high performance, high profits and increasing revenues. For that there is a process, the process we referred to in Chapter One, a process that anyone can learn and apply in their own business. This leads us from the subject of corporate anatomy to the realm of corporate physiology.

SUMMARY

- Companies grow by developing the potentials of the five components and converting them into engines for growth.

- Each component can be developed in itself and each can drive the growth of the other four. But each depends on the development of the other four for bringing out its maximum potentials.

- As the strongest of the five components drives growth, the weakest component prevents the developed potentials of the stronger ones from fully expressing themselves and sets an overall limit on the growth of the company.

- The key to nonstop growth is to maintain a dynamic balance and equilibrium between the five engines as they develop and the company grow.

Chapter Four

ACCELERATING THE ENERGY CONVERSION PROCESS

Harold Corner is a powerhouse of energy. When he speaks, people listen. When he says that American business can beat the foreign competition—including the Japanese—he speaks with authority and experience. Corner is one of the old breed—or is it the new breed?—of entrepreneurs that believes anything is possible and means to prove it.

But Corner did not always feel and talk this way. Back about six years ago, Corner was in trouble. The early 1980s were a tough time for companies in the tool and die industry. Intense competition from Asian manufacturers had already driven many major U.S. manufacturers overseas, reducing the demand for tools and dies at home. Then the industry was hit by a second wave of attack from foreign tool and die makers entering the previously inviolate domestic market, which conventional wisdom said would never happen since close communication between tool maker and manufacturer makes proximity very important. But it did happen to the industry and to Corner.

Corner is founder of C & J Industries in Meadville,·Pennsylvania, and a former president of the National Tooling and Machining Association. He awoke one morning to find many of his long-established customers buying molds from his Japanese competition. And the reasons were not difficult to understand. The Japanese were offering their custom-made molds delivered in the United States at lower prices and with faster delivery dates averaging 16 weeks compared with C & J Industries' 32 weeks.

Unlike many in his industry who resigned themselves to apparently inevitable decline, Corner decided to take up the challenge and fight back. He set as his goals to cut his production costs to less than, and his delivery dates to sooner than, those of his foreign competitors and announced his intentions to every employee in the company. He then set about reviewing and revamping virtually every system, operation, and activity in the company to raise performance to the highest possible level. He introduced a massive training program for upgrading the skills of people at all levels of the company, including special training on how to use systems more effectively. He also launched a quality program to get all his people involved in improving the molds they made.

Over the next 30 months, Corner brought down his production time from 32 weeks to 16 weeks and cut operating costs by $540,000. Business poured in, and the company began to grow rapidly. During this period sales increased by 40% to exceed $10 million in 1987, then rose another 30% in 1988 and are projected to reach $17.5 million in 1989—a near tripling of the company's revenues. Corner's remarkable turnaround illustrates the latent potential available to any company for tremendous improvements in performance within a short period of time. It also illustrates key elements of the process by which companies energize themselves for growth. It all starts with energy.

ENERGY

Over the last few years we have asked more than 1,000 U.S. and foreign companies to describe to us their most recent experience of rapid growth. Their responses reveal that during periods of rapid growth, companies share several common characteristics: a high level of energy and enthusiasm, a clear sense of direction, smooth running systems, good coordination and teamwork, good morale, pride, nonstop recruitment of new people, and continuous learning of new skills. These characteristics reduce to four essential elements: high energy, clear direction, streamlined organization, skilled and motivated people. The relationships and interactions among these four are the keys to the process of converting corporate potentials into practical results in terms of high performance, high profitability, and rapid growth.

In our study of major U.S. corporations with long histories of sustained growth, described in *The Vital Difference: Unleashing the Powers of Sustained Corporate Success*, coauthored by Garry Jacobs and Frederick Harmon,[1] we described the tangibly intense atmosphere of energy we experienced in high-performance companies like Apple Computers, Intel, Merck Pharmaceuticals, Marriott, Coca-Cola, General Mills, Delta Airlines and Northwestern Mutual Life Insurance. High energy is the fuel and driving force for high achievement. It excites and enthuses people to great efforts and accomplishments. It spurs the organization to perfect its operations and raise the quality of its performance. It attracts customers, motivates employees, and stimulates creativity and innovation. The generation and unleashing of that energy and its effective utilization by the company are the keys to an endless expansion.

The single most common characteristic reported by fast-growing companies is a high level of energy. The task of accelerating the growth of a business requires an enormous amount of energy and hard work. Most companies feel comfortable growing leisurely at rates of 5%, 10%, or 15% a year and find that demanding enough on their energies. To grow at higher rates—30%, 40%, 50%, or more—is considerably more demanding.

Regardless of the rate of growth, energy is the fuel for that expansion, and accelerated growth, like high-speed driving and flying, demands a proportionately or disproportionately greater amount of fuel. Without that energy you cannot even think of doubling. You cannot plan for it or build for it.

That energy starts with the people at the top—the founder, the CEO, and the management team. They must generate energy, embody it, radiate it, communicate it to everyone else in the company, and express it in everything they do. That energy is needed to maintain and develop every component and every activity of the company: to formulate and implement plans, to give and carry out instructions, to maintain regular production, to meet delivery schedules, even to maintain facilities in a clean and orderly fashion.

Energy is needed to inspire people, to excite customers, to attract investors, to negotiate with vendors, and to carry conviction with the board and the management team and every employee in the company.

Think about the energy level in your company. Before planning to double or triple the company, you should be sure there is sufficient energy to achieve that goal. Are you generating and releasing sufficient energy to carry on routine operations effectively and to propel the growth of the business? Unlike the fuel capacity of a car or plane, the energy of a company is not fixed or subject to any finite limits. Our own energy level and the energy level of our people is under our control and it can always be increased. In later chapters we will be examining many ways to release further energy in yourself, in your customers, in those who report to you, and even in your boss, if you have one.

Energy is the starting point, but energy alone is not enough. By itself it is aimless, uncontrolled, and unproductive. It will not produce anything. It may even become destructive like the raw energy of a cyclonic wind or a raging river. For a company to utilize that energy effectively, it must possess the other three characteristics we referred to earlier—a clear direction, a streamlined and efficient organization, and skilled and well-motivated people. Direction, organization, and people focus and channel the energy and convert it into higher sales and profits.

DIRECTION

Companies give direction to their energy by formulating goals to define their purpose and intentions. These goals are both quantitative and qualitative. Quantitative goals define how large the company wants to become—large in terms of revenues or profits or production volumes or offices in the city, the state, the country, or the world. Companies also direct their energies by establishing shorter term quantitative objectives—for example, to double revenues in two years, to triple profits in three, and so on.

Quantitative goals describe what or how much a company wants to achieve. Qualitative goals define the manner in which it wants to achieve them. Disney wants its theme parks to be spotlessly clean and its employees to be cheerful and friendly. Federal Express wants every parcel to be delivered on time. Marriott focuses on carrying out every routine activity in a systematic manner. DuPont gives a near fanatical importance to safety. Merck is obsessed with product quality. Northwestern Mutual places a tremendous importance on communication and teamwork. Delta wants all its employees to feel happy and secure as part of the corporate family. IBM is deeply committed to the growth and development of its people.

Qualitative goals like cleanliness, orderliness, punctuality, safety, systematic functions, communication, coordination, service to customers, teamwork, and development of our people are what we mean by corporate values. These values help us to communicate to everyone in the company and to our customers and vendors precisely what type of performance we are trying to achieve. They direct the energies of our people, not only at the level of senior management, but all the way down through the organization by clearly stating how each activity should be performed.

Values focus and concentrate energy. Think of how much energy it takes for Disney to maintain a commitment to the value of cleanliness when 100,000 visitors—including children of all ages—go through the park in a single day. Or how much energy is required for Federal Express to achieve 96% performance on their value of on-time delivery, when a single plane delayed by bad weather could result in 30,000 disappointed customers.

According to the laws of physics, when energy is given a specific direction it becomes capable of accomplishing work. By giving direction to the energies in a company, corporate values and objectives convert those energies into a force. They not only focus the available energy—they also magnify it.

We all have seen the power of a goal to release people's energies for an extraordinary effort. In the last two minutes of the 1989 Superbowl game, the San Francisco 49ers drove 95 yards to score a touchdown and come from behind to beat the Cincinnati Bengals for the national championship. During that drive Joe Montana and his team moved down the field with a power and effectivity they had not displayed during the previous 58 minutes of the game. That is the power of a goal to release and direct energies for accomplishment.

How effectively does your company give direction to the energies of its people? How clear and inspiring are its values and objectives? How fully are they understood and endorsed by people at different levels? In later chapters we will be looking at ways to increase commitment to corporate goals and enhance their power to release and focus people's energies.

A SUPERTANKER CHANGING COURSE

Nedlloyd Lines is a 100-year-old Dutch shipping company, a $1 billion company with the largest worldwide network of routes, the largest fleet under the Dutch flag, and a very strong financial position. Those who know this somewhat traditional and conservative company well refer to it as "a sleeping giant in the process of awakening." As a first step toward achieving that goal, the top management of the organization has been actively trying to raise the level of energy and enthusiasm within the company by opening up the channels of communication, getting people involved, and giving them an opportunity to participate in discussions about the company's future. The second step has been to provide a clear direction for the channeling of those energies. Senior management has formulated a strategic plan to double revenues over the next 5 years, that is, to achieve in the next 5 years growth equal to that which the company achieved over the last 100. Announcement of the company's plans to purchase $750 million in new container vessels over the next 5 years has sent shock waves throughout the company and the rest of the industry.

Having successfully initiated this process and stirred the energies of this vast company, the chief executive, Theo M. Oostinjen, has a major concern. Will Nedlloyd's organization be able to channel properly and utilize effectively the energy that is being released? "How can we ensure that all the energy which is released will be properly harnessed for productive purposes, that it does not generate unrealistic expectations and impatience that end in frustration?"

Oostinjen's concern should be shared by every executive who tries to accelerate corporate growth—because releasing energy and giving it a direction are not sufficient to achieve results. That energy needs to be controlled and properly channeled into productive activities. It needs to be converted from raw force into organizational power. That is the role of an organization.

ORGANIZATION

When a company's energies are given a clear direction, they are ready for purposeful action. But that still is not enough to ensure that the company will grow rapidly and profitably and keep on growing. A mob possesses a high level of excited energy and a passionate direction, but mobs are only effective for destructive purposes, and even then they are not very efficient. Even in physics, a force must act on or through some instrument in order to accomplish work. Heat cannot do work in a vacuum. Electricity cannot do work unless it is converted into mechanical power by a machine.

For the directed energy in a company to become a productive power, it has to be channeled through an organization and harnessed to carry out specific tasks. Organization defines levels of responsibility and authority: who will make which decisions, who will give what instructions, who will execute each type of work, who will monitor and evaluate the work. Organization defines systems and procedures: how each operation is to be performed, how it will be communicated, and how different operations will be coordinated. Organization utilizes the energy of countless people—workers, supervisors, technicians, engineers, scientists, administrators, sales and marketing personnel, accountants, managers, and so on—to carry out a multitude of specialized activities according to specific plans to implement the company's values and achieve its objectives.

Imagine Joe Montana trying to drive his team downfield without assigning each player to a specific position (job) and without a portfolio of carefully orchestrated plays to run (operating systems). He might find ten receivers going deep for a pass on a play he intended to run. Even if his team consisted entirely of highly motivated superstars, their enthusiastic energy and physical power would be no match for any well-organized team of professional players running well-practiced plays.

Think of your organization as a power plant which harnesses the raw energy of a river and converts it into productive power. How much of the available energy is the organization able to mobilize? How effectively does it control and channel that energy for productive work and expansion? How efficiently does it utilize the energy in its routine operations to maximize profitability? In subsequent chapters we will be examining strategies to convert a good organization into a championship team.

SWITCHING PEOPLE ON

Organization focuses and distributes the energy precisely to the points at which it is needed and guides its expression through policies, rules, and systems. This gives organization a tremendous power to accomplish work. But the quality and effectiveness of that work finally depends on one more crucial element—people. The skills and attitudes of our people are the last vital link in the process of converting that raw energy into practical results—high performance, high profitability, and rapid growth. A company may have the best laid plans and the most sophisticated systems, but if the skills and attitudes of its people are not appropriate, it cannot achieve the maximum results.

How many companies seem to forget this self-evident fact? You pay $3,000 for a round-trip airline ticket to the Orient and when you ask the flight attendant for a blanket so you can sleep through the long flight, she tells you matter-of-factly that there are none left—without so much as a smile or an apology—a $3,000 ticket with no blanket, no apology, and no smile!—either because she has not been properly trained or she is not properly motivated. Here you are flying on a $50 million plane belonging to a billion-dollar airline with tens of thousands of employees and a worldwide network of routes, but what you remember about the flight is the blanket, the smile and the apology that the company forgot. It is a matter of skill and attitude.

You check into a luxury resort hotel at 3:00 in the afternoon with confirmed reservations made weeks in advance and the check-in clerk informs you that your room is not ready and asks you to check back in an hour or two. When you ask him to call you in the restaurant as soon as the room is ready, he informs you that there is no procedure for doing so. Is there a procedure for the room not being ready on time? It is a matter of skill and attitude.

There are literally hundreds of skills and attitudes that impact on the performance of our people. Each is like the hair-thin filament in a light bulb. There may be plenty of power flowing through the electrical wires, but if that tiny little filament is broken—no light. If even a single skill or positive attitude is missing, the circuit is not complete.

The reverse is also true. In every company there are hundreds of small connections that are not being made right now, because a small filament is missing. Provide that missing link and astonishing results may follow. One CEO saw his business literally triple in a year, growing from $400,000 to $1.2 million, after he took a course to improve his interpersonal skills and he learned how to be more friendly in dealing with his customers. One course—one skill—tripled his business.

Do your people have all the skills they need to get the maximum results from their efforts and maximum profits for the company? What more can you do to switch on your people for peak performance?

SAS TAKES OFF

When Jan Carlzon took over as CEO of Scandanavian Airlines in 1981, the company was losing altitude. It had lost $20 million the previous year. The market was stagnant. Energy and morale were low. Performance was sagging. In a business dedicated to getting you there fast, SAS had acquired a reputation for late departures and late arrivals. Punctuality had deteriorated so much that customers sometimes joked that the company's customer service was so good that if you were late arriving at the airport for your flight, chances were the plane would still be there waiting for you.

Much has been written about the story of SAS's turnaround, including a book by Carlzon himself. The steps that he took to revitalize the company are an excellent example of the power of the process we have been describing. His first task was to raise the energy level. He did that by pouring his own energies into the company, meeting with his management team and addressing groups of employees to stir them out of complacency.

Next, he gave a new direction to the company by formulating a new mission, values, and objectives. The mission was "to become the world's best airline for the business traveller." The values he focused on were punctuality (on-time departures), pleasing the customer, and employee involvement. He set a standard to raise on-time departures to 100%. The objectives were explicit too: increase profits by $25 million in one year and by $50 million in three years. To ensure that the message was communicated down to every employee in the company, he distributed copies of a small booklet to all 20,000 employees describing the new mission and goals. These goals evoked an enthusiastic response from the people, a new energy, and focused that energy for a dramatic comeback. Carlzon writes: "Once they understood the vision, our employees accepted responsibility enthusiastically, which sparked numerous simultaneous and energetic developments in the company. . . . The new energy at SAS was the result of 20,000 employees all striving toward a single goal every day."[2]

For these new energies to be converted into improved service and financial results, Carlzon realized that major changes would have to be made in the company's organization, which at the time was slow, unresponsive to customers and employees, authoritarian, and bureaucratic. So he conceived of the now famous idea of turning the organizational pyramid on its head, viewing the people on the front lines in touch with the customer as the real top of the pyramid and the other levels of management as essentially supporting staff to assist the front lines in carrying our their jobs more effectively to fulfill the mission, values, and objectives of the company.

Whether the pyramid was ever actually turned upside down is open to question, but there is no doubt that Carlzon did institute very tangible changes which flattened the SAS organization and had a very real impact on its ability to channel corporate energies. The major change was to shift the focus of the entire company from managing a business to serving customers better. Responsibility for achieving corporate goals was clearly assigned. Many more decisions were delegated to people on the front lines, empowering them with authority to act to improve customer service. The jobs of middle managers and even executives were redefined to focus on the values of service and punctuality.

The new organization was also streamlined by improving systems and reducing paperwork to a minimum. New systems were introduced to make delegation more effective. Everyone was involved in achieving the corporate goals. Procedures were modified to reduce the time required to service planes between flights. A computerized monitoring system was introduced to measure performance on cargo delivery times and flight departure times.

Beyond all these changes, Carlzon focused on one more critically important element in the equation for energizing the company—the skills and attitudes of the people. Unless each individual in the company possessed the skills needed for high performance and an enthusiastic commitment to the corporate goals, there was no way to ensure that the company would achieve those goals. To provide those skills, the company conducted customer service training programs for 12,000 employees. They also introduced cross-training, so that employees could perform more than one job.

Changes in the organization had a positive impact on employee attitudes. Delegation got people more involved. It created an atmosphere in which new ideas could sprout at any level of the company and have a chance to be heard. It "unleashed our employees' creativity through decentralization."[3] The company instituted awards, celebrations and other forms of social recognition to acknowledge peoples' efforts and contributions to improved performance.

The results of these efforts: On-time departures improved dramatically. In the first year alone, profits increased by $80 million, against a goal of only $25 million. In a stagnant market, passenger volume increased by 30% in three years. In 1983 *Air Transport World* named SAS Airline of the Year, fulfilling Carlzon's aspiration to make SAS the best.

ENERGY CONVERSION AND DISPERSION

The process which Carlzon initiated at SAS closely parallels what Harold Corner did in his company and what we have seen companies of every size and description do to energize themselves to increase profits dramatically and grow rapidly. This process can be thought of as a series of lenses that focus and magnify corporate energies and convert them into material results. The first lens consists of the ideas that give direction to the energies. This lens focuses and converts the energy into force. The second lens consists of the organization that harnesses and controls that force and converts it into a productive power. The third lens is made up of the skills and attitudes of our people, who express that power in millions of tiny acts every day—what Carlzon called "moments of truth." Figure 2 depicts this process of converting energy into material results.

Think about how your company generates, releases, directs, and channels the energies of its people. How effective is the company in converting these energies into productivity, profitability, and growth?

The questionnaire at the end of this chapter is intended to assist you in evaluating the company to identify ways to increase the flow and conversion of energy into revenues and profits.

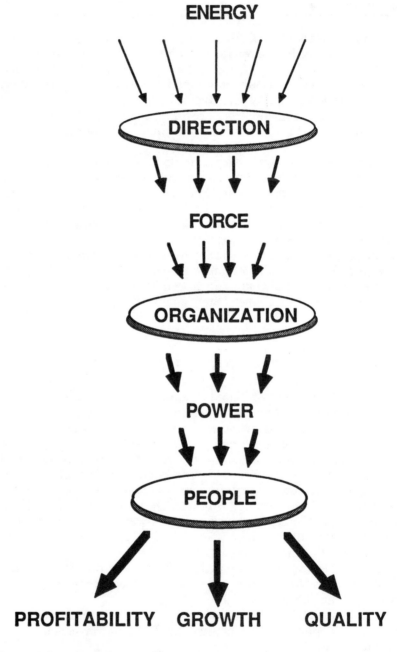

Figure 2 Corporate Energy Conversion

52

SUMMARY

- Energy is the source of productivity and profits and the driving force for all growth.

- Companies develop the five components and convert them into engines by generating, releasing, directing, and harnessing energy for productive work, revenues, and profits.

- Companies focus and magnify their energies by means of three lenses—direction, organization, and people.

- They give direction to their energies by their commitment to quantitative and qualitative goals, that is, objectives and values.

- They convert these energies into productive power by channeling them through the structure and systems of an organization.

- People finally determine the quality and magnitude of the results through the skills and attitudes with which they express the energies in work.

ENERGY CONVERSION QUESTIONNAIRE

Instructions

This questionnaire contains five sections: energy, direction, structure and systems, communication and coordination, and attitude and skills. Each section consists of 20 statements.

Evaluate how true each of these statements is for your company on a scale from 0 (low) to 10 (high) as shown below. You may score the statements with any whole or decimal number—for example, 2, 3.5, 6.7, 9.

Never true at all	A little true	Partially true	Mostly true	Always fully true
0	2.5	5	7.5	10

After answering all the questions, add up the subtotal for each of the five sections to determine which areas need improvement to increase the generation and conversion of energy in your company.

Energy

1. This is a high-energy company.
2. This energy is expressed as an intensity noticeable to everyone.
3. The CEO has a missionary zeal.
4. Senior management shares that zeal.
5. Managers exhibit high levels of energy and enthusiasm.
6. Customers feel attracted to this company.
7. People love to work at this company.
8. People are hard working.
9. Our employees are cheerful and enthusiastic.
10. Physical activities in the company are brisk and quick.
11. Our employees feel a minimum of fatigue and burnout on the job.
12. Fresh ideas are continuously being generated and encouraged.
13. People are always willing to make a new effort.
14. The company is highly innovative and creative.
15. People are focused on their work (not distracted by nonwork-related activities).
16. All facilities are maintained at the highest level of cleanliness.
17. All areas are maintained at the highest level of orderliness.
18. Regularly scheduled activities (weekly, monthly, quarterly) are carried out at the appointed time without fail.
19. Decisions are taken and implemented promptly.
20. The company is able to perform at peak levels without feeling strained.

Direction

21. The company has a clear perception of its mission and central purpose.
22. The CEO understands and embodies the mission and central purpose of the company.
23. Senior management understands and endorses the mission and central purpose of the company.
24. People at all other levels of the company understand and endorse the mission and central purpose of the company.
25. The CEO knows what is required to develop and balance the five components of the company to achieve its mission and central purpose.

26. Senior management knows what is required to develop and balance the five components of the company to achieve its mission and central purpose.
27. The company prepares strategic plans including long-term financial projections and pro formas.
28. The company prepares short-term operational plans.
29. Each department prepares detailed budgets.
30. The company plans for future organizational needs.
31. The company plans for its future human resource needs.
32. The company prepares detailed sales and marketing plans.
33. The company plans for future products and services.
34. Employees enthusiastically endorse and pursue the company's goals and plans.
35. The company strives to achieve high corporate values.
36. The CEO embodies these values and strives to make them real in every activity in the company.
37. Senior management follows the lead of the CEO and strives to achieve high corporate values.
38. People at all other levels accept and endorse these values.
39. Clear standards of performance have been established for expressing these values in daily activities.
40. The company has clear policies and rules which support efficient operations and motivate people.

Structure and Systems

41. The company's organizational structure and functioning is clear to all employees.
42. The CEO and the top management team have clearly defined responsibilities and authority for achieving corporate objectives.
43. The CEO and the top management have clearly defined responsibilities and authority for implementing corporate values.
44. The responsibility and authority of each manager for achieving corporate objectives is clearly defined and understood.
45. The responsibility and authority of each manager for achieving corporate values is clearly defined and understood.
46. The structure of the company is flexible and adaptable to new organizational requirements.

47. People are held responsible for their performance.
48. There is a high level of discipline.
49. People are given a good deal of freedom for constructive individual initiative.
50. The organizational structure facilitates open and effective communication.
51. Operational systems function smoothly, efficiently and automatically.
52. The company has systems to monitor and measure performance on corporate goals.
53. The company has systems to monitor and measure performance on corporate values.
54. Managers spend an appropriate amount of time planning for growth and development of the organization rather than on operational tasks.
55. Systems are regularly reviewed to determine their effectiveness and efficiency.
56. Every department has developed standard operating procedures for all their routine activities.
57. The meetings held at all levels of the company are well organized, effective and completed on time.
58. There are systems in place to support the implementation of corporate values.
59. When customers enquire about the status of their orders, our systems enable us to respond immediately.
60. Systems are designed to minimize duplication and nonproductive reporting.

Communication and Coordination

61. There is good communication between the CEO and senior management about the company's goals and values.
62. There is an open-door policy at all levels of the company.
63. There is good communication between senior management and all department managers about the company's plans, goals, and values.
64. There is good communication between departmental managers and their staff about the specific activities and projects required to achieve the plans and to implement the values.
65. There is good open communication among the top management team.

66. There is good communication/coordination between sales and marketing and production/operations.
67. There is good communication/coordination between the finance and accounting departments and other departments in the company regarding plans, budgets and other financial matters.
68. There is good communication/coordination between R&D and production/operations.
69. There is good communication/coordination between sales and marketing and R&D.
70. There is adequate written communication to support the decisions that are taken in meetings or other informal discussions.
71. There is a minimum of rumor and gossip within the company.
72. The company strives to share all relevant information with its employees in a quick and open manner.
73. Each individual/department receives feedback on their contribution to the achievement of corporate goals.
74. There are formal channels for communicating information of general interest to all employees, such as a company newsletter, company meetings, etc.
75. Employees have a high level of confidence in the information they receive from top management.
76. There is open and good communication between the company and its customers.
77. There is good coordination between field staff/offices and corporate headquarters.
78. There is good communication between top management and the board of directors/shareholders.
79. There is open and good communication between the company and its suppliers.
80. There is a channel by which the lowest level employee can effectively communicate with top management when the situation warrants.

Attitude and Skills

81. Our people take pride in doing the best job possible.
82. Our people feel closely identified with the interests of the company and are eager for its growth.
83. People within the company actively appreciate each other's point of view.

84. Our people express a cooperative attitude in all activities.

85. There is a culture of positive thinking and a "can do" attitude throughout the company.

86. People in the company are never satisfied and always want to improve our performance in every activity.

87. Everyone feels that they should constantly be learning new things.

88. There is an attitude throughout the company of wanting to please our customers, both external and internal customers.

89. There is a strong feeling of belonging to a team throughout the company.

90. Everyone feels they should put the company's interests ahead of their personal preferences and ambitions.

91. Our managers possess all the necessary skills to be effective in their jobs.

92. Our sales staff is very knowledgeable and skilled.

93. Our managers and customer service representatives have very good interpersonal skills.

94. All of our employees possess the skills needed to effectively organize their time and work.

95. Employees engaged in bookkeeping and accounting possess all the knowledge and skills needed for their work.

96. Our technical staff are highly skilled in their specialized areas.

97. Our managers are highly skilled in motivating their people.

98. All our people have good communication skills.

99. All executives and managers possess effective decision-making skills.

100. All executives and managers are skilled in organizing and conducting effective meetings.

Chapter Five

HOW TO REENERGIZE YOUR COMPANY FOR RAPID GROWTH

Probably most readers can recall a time, however brief, when everything worked as we have described in the last chapter, a time when the quality of your products or services neared perfection, schedules were met on time, people and activities interacted smoothly and harmoniously—almost without effort—customers were blissfully happy and employees were filled with enthusiasm. Chances are this was also a time when the company was very profitable and growing rapidly as well. If everything was going so well, why didn't it last? Why is it that most companies find it so difficult to sustain high performance and rapid growth for more than a few years? Why is rapid growth usually such a short-lived phenomenon?

The answers to these questions are relevant to every company that wants to grow rapidly—regardless of whether it has or has not ever grown rapidly in the past and regardless of whether it is or is not growing rapidly at the present moment. For in any case the issue boils down to two questions: What makes rapid growth happen? What makes rapid growth stop?

We have already addressed the first of these questions in the last chapter, where we described the process that generates rapid growth. But that process does not occur in every company, and it is not easy to sustain for long periods in any company. Therefore it is not enough that we know what generates growth. We must also understand what impedes and stops it.

In our study of fast-growing companies, we stumbled on a paradoxical fact that sheds light on these questions. Apart from the list of positive characteristics reported in the last chapter, these companies also reported a set of negative characteristics which almost all of them shared in common. The paradox is that these negative characteristics are exactly opposite and in direct contradiction to the positive ones reported by the very same companies during the same period! Along side high energy, a clear sense of direction, good morale, pride, enthusiasm, teamwork, good systems, good co-ordination, and continuous training, these same companies reported high levels of stress, fatigue, burnout, chaos and confusion, breakdown of systems, conflict within the organization, poor coordination and communication, continuous shortage of skilled people, and no time for training.

How is it possible for the same companies to report that both enjoyment and stress are very high, that both teamwork and internal conflict are widespread, that systems are at once smooth running and inadequate, that training is nonstop and nonexistent? How is it that such high-performing companies should resemble all too closely in some important respects the thousands of ordinary, average companies that are unable to generate rapid and profitable growth? This apparent contradiction contains an important key to why most companies are unable to maintain high rates of growth and why others are unable to grow rapidly in the first place.

The contradictory descriptions reflect the fact that rapid growth is experienced differently in different stages of its progress. Rapid growth usually occurs as a steeply ascending curve followed by a steeply descending curve. The positive characteristics associated with growth—the energy, clear direction, enthusiasm, teamwork, and smooth systems—are commonly associated with the ascending curve when growth is taking off and profits are soaring. As growth gains momentum, enthusiasm rises. People feel excited and eager to meet the challenge. Differences of opinion and preference get pushed into the background as everyone focuses on common goals. There is no time for quarrels or disputes. The organization comes alive and functions at peak performance.

NOT ANOTHER ORDER!

As growth accelerates, the demands of work on each individual, department, system, and operation become proportionately or even geometrically greater. Space becomes scarce, phone lines are constantly busy, computer systems are overloaded. These conditions place more and more demands on individuals to adjust to or compensate for the shortages by greater personal effort and longer working hours. Stress, fatigue, burnout and internal conflicts increase. Employee turnover rises. Even routine operations—relaying messages, returning phone calls, filing letters, paying bills and salaries(!)—no longer function automatically and require individual attention, because the systems are no longer adequate and there are not enough trained and experienced people. Often the hiring of new people at this stage compounds the difficulty because the new people need attention, and their work needs to be closely supervised to ensure that quality is maintained. As stress, pressure, and haste increase, so do errors, confusion, and frustration. Quality declines. Service degenerates. Profits fall. The descending curve has begun.

At times like this you can hear people say—sometimes in apparent jest, sometimes in deadly seriousness—"Oh, not another new order!" Or depending on the context, a variation on this theme is repeated, such as "Not another new office to open!" "Not another new customer to serve!" or "Not another new product to develop and produce!" Not surprisingly, life gradually responds to this voiced attitude or silent prayer in one way or another. Customers get frustrated by poor or slow service and go elsewhere with their orders. New products get buried in R&D and never leave the drawing boards. Management cancels plans for expanding into new territories. Growth slows or stops altogether. This explains why out of the 100 companies on *INC.*'s 1986 list, 37% were growing too slowly to remain on the list in 1987 and 20% reported lower absolute revenues. That is why Mesa Airlines saw its growth rate drop to under 10% last year. That is what prompted Ben Cohen to issue the edict at Ben & Jerry's: "No more growth."

ENERGY DISPERSION

The process we have been describing is exactly opposite to the one we described in the last chapter. There we saw how companies release and garner all available corporate energies, and then focus, direct, magnify, and multiply them to achieve extraordinary results as Harold Corner did at C & J Industries under intense pressure from Japanese competitors and as Jan Carlzon did at SAS to transform a substandard airline into one of the best in the world.

In this chapter we see how even highly successful companies dissipate, scatter, disperse and waste the energies that they have released, the way a poorly tuned engine burns excess fuel and dissipates the energy through friction as waste heat. The reverse of the process by which companies convert energy into results is the process by which they disperse those energies in wasteful and unproductive activity. In fact, these are but two expressions, positive and negative, of the same phenomenon. Regardless of whether your company is growing rapidly, leveled off, in a period of decline or near the bottom of the curve, the process of energy conversion and dispersion is the same.

Figure 3 depicts a company that is well past the peak of rapid growth and on the descending curve. Revenues are flat, profits are falling. The company possesses considerable energy but dissipates most of that energy and reaps minimum results for

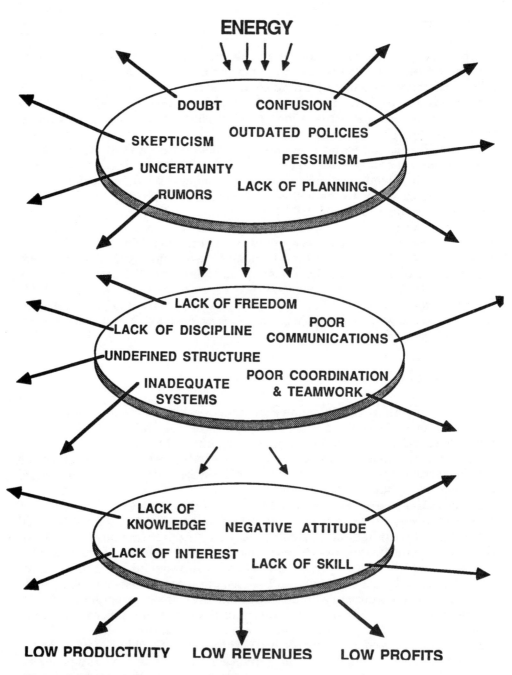

ENERGY

DOUBT   CONFUSION

OUTDATED POLICIES

SKEPTICISM   PESSIMISM

UNCERTAINTY

RUMORS   LACK OF PLANNING

LACK OF FREEDOM

LACK OF DISCIPLINE   POOR COMMUNICATIONS

UNDEFINED STRUCTURE

INADEQUATE SYSTEMS   POOR COORDINATION & TEAMWORK

LACK OF KNOWLEDGE   NEGATIVE ATTITUDE

LACK OF INTEREST   LACK OF SKILL

LOW PRODUCTIVITY   LOW REVENUES   LOW PROFITS

Figure 3 Corporate Energy Dispersion

maximum effort. As in Figure 2, there are three lenses. But in this case the lenses are dispersing the energy rather than focusing and magnifying it. The first lens is direction. Instead of being concentrated on pursuit of corporate values and objectives, the energy is diffracted and scattered. The company does not have clearly defined goals. Its values are vague. There is no formal planning. Various departments pursue conflicting priorities, leading to doubts and confusion. The company is rife with rumors. People are skeptical and pessimistic.

The second lens is organization. Instead of harnessing and channeling the energy, the energy is being obstructed by lack of clear lines of authority, absence of discipline and constraints on individual initiative. It is being consumed by outmoded, cumbersome, inefficient systems and wasted by duplication of work due to inadequate communication and poor coordination.

The third lens is people. Here the energy is expended inefficiently due to inadequate knowledge and skill and diminished by negative attitudes among employees about the company and its activities.

All three of these diffractive lenses are found in most companies. They account for the very poor conversion of energy into results, which retards growth and minimizes profits. The efficiency of energy conversion in the average company is not unlike that of the early steam engines of the last century—lots of sound and lots of heat to do a little work.

THE OTHER END OF THE RAINBOW

Like all other living things, companies exist and oscillate between two extremes or poles of existence. At one pole they are exploding with a boundless youthful creative energy, expansive, exuberant, lightning quick and responsive, aware of boundless opportunity, performing at peak levels, and growing by leaps and bounds. At the other end they are dull, heavy, and slow, overcome by inertia and resistant to change; old in their thoughts and actions, aware only of limitations and obstructions; stagnant and gradually degenerating. In between these two extremes are the companies that have leveled off. They have not yet started up the ascending curve to rapid growth nor have they started down the descending curve to losses and possible extinction.

Whether a company is at one extreme or the other or somewhere in between has relatively little to do with age or size. We have seen very young, small companies behaving like aged invalids and very ancient, large ones behaving like exuberant children. But a company's position on the spiral of ascent and descent has everything to do with its attitude and the way in which it utilizes the energies at its disposal.

When an unsuspecting Englishman, Ben Thompson-McCausland, took over as CEO of London Life in 1980, he encountered a company headed straight for the bottom of the barrel. His charge was clear: "London Life is a first class company. Wake it up, but let there be no blood baths." In his struggle to find an antidote for corporate degeneration, he discovered a formula for eternal corporate youth.

Imagine a company wearing wire-rimmed bifocals and you get the picture. London Life was founded in 1806, making it one of the oldest mutual life insurance companies in the world. It was a company with some notable strengths—good quality and a good range of products, a record of sound investment performance, loyal employees who took pride in the company's heritage and past achievements, a tradition of service, and the goodwill of its policyholders.

But as the new CEO soon discovered, the company was really living in the past and on its past, while slowly but surely heading for the precipice. When Thompson-McCausland assumed charge, he found the company in a serious state of deterioration and drift. "All energy had gone out of the company." There was an atmosphere of complacency and inertia—no deadlines and no sense of urgency. "The company was suffused with a feeling of sleepy security."[1]

There was no sense of direction either. Values like service, which the company had prided itself on in the past, had lost all meaning. The quality of service had been declining for years. Responses to inquiries were slow. Employees reacted to customer complaints with excuses and defensiveness, or did not bother answering them at all! There was no planning and no budgeting. New ideas were discouraged; good ideas were shot down.

The organization was fragmented and highly bureaucratic. It was divided into several autonomous empires. There were no clear lines of authority. Status and security were given greater importance than productivity. In one department there were five employees, four of them supervisors! Systems were sloppy and outdated. Coordination was poor. Each branch office functioned according to its own standards and procedures.

People felt secure in their jobs and were well paid, so there was very little staff turnover. There were no targets set for individuals or departments. No one was evaluated or held accountable for achieving results. Therefore, talents were ignored. "The idea of standards of performance was completely alien." Morale was low. People felt defensive and afraid. Gossip and quarrels were rife. There was an antitraining attitude in the company. Training for managers was nonexistent. Selling was considered a dirty word.

For the previous 20 years, the company had been gradually losing market share to the competition. In 1976 alone the company lost a major government account and 44% of its most profitable premium income. A 1980 industry survey showed London Life's expense ratios were the highest of the nine companies examined and dangerously out of line with the rest of the industry. In other words, London Life was a company whose lenses were cloudy, full of cataracts, and all out of shape.

What would you do if you were in Thompson-McCausland's position—assuming, of course, that it was too late to back out of the assignment?

RESTORING LIFE TO LONDON

Thompson-McCausland had an intuitive understanding that energy was the key, that without energy he could not accomplish anything. So the very first thing he did was to start moving around briskly through the company, meeting everybody, taking interest in every operation, speaking enthusiastically, asking thousands of questions—even running up and down the stairs. He made himself a living example and embodiment of energy, dynamism, and speed, and set a demanding pace for every activity in which he got involved. "Energy was the one thing I concentrated on. It was a charismatic approach, energy, and example."

Then he set a new direction for the company. He started talking about change and growth, about improving performance and rejuvenating the company, about restoring London Life to the heights it had occupied in the past. He opened up communications, encouraged suggestions from all quarters, and challenged pessimistic attitudes. He asked senior managers to identify the company's values and define clear standards for how those values should be expressed in action. He then extended the process to middle managers and to groups of employees at all levels of the company to build awareness and acceptance of those values. He got everyone involved in thinking and talking about how to improve the company, in developing performance standards and contributing their ideas on how to achieve them. A consensus gradually emerged. A previously unknown energy, enthusiasm, and excitement began to surface in this once placid and lethargic company.

Top management formulated a new mission: "To be the best-run life office in the land." It set quantitative targets for growth—40% a year, compared to an industry average of 15%. The plan was "received with horror."[2] Time deadlines were set for every routine activity. Meeting schedules were rigorously enforced to ensure that too much time and energy were not spent in talking rather than doing.

Then he and his staff turned to look at the organization. It was immediately clear that the existing structure was inadequate for the task. Already managers were having problems directing and utilizing the new energy for productive purposes. People now became easily frustrated by conditions they had quietly endured for years.

So they set about creating a new simplified structure, abolishing the dotted lines and devious routes by which people reported, got their work done and exercised control over others. Many supervisory positions were redefined and assigned clear operational responsibilities. Branches were given a much higher level of decision-making authority and greater freedom for initiative. Frequent meetings were instituted to foster coordination and teamwork, especially between the head office and the branches. Thompson-McCausland found that "the new structure gave rise to a sense of renaissance."

The initial response to these efforts was extraordinary. Against a target of 40% growth, new business increased by 87% in 1982. Morale improved dramatically. People worked hard and happily. The company began to grow again. It was on the upward spiral.

But it soon became evident that much more needed to be done in order to sustain that growth. The organization was still a constraint and a stumbling block. Systems were quickly overloaded and rendered useless by the increased volumes. Management instituted a complete review of the company's systems and an effort to upgrade them to handle the growing volume of business quickly and smoothly. Quality circles were instituted to get everyone involved in making improvements. There was even a circle for messengers and file clerks, which came up with some good suggestions to stream-line the process of file retrieval.

The greater the efforts they took, the greater the improvement in performance. Yet they always seemed to be chasing an elusive target. For the more they improved, the more business grew and the more needed to be done to keep up with the increasing volume of work. For this reason, it took a full three years to bring down customer response times to the desired level.

Yet for all their efforts, it was clear to Thompson-McCausland and his team that something more was needed. The higher quality standards, sales goals and volumes of work not only strained the company's systems to the limit, it put enormous demands on the skills of the people as well. So management introduced a comprehensive training program to impart new and higher skills to people at all levels of the company, from senior management to secretaries and receptionists. At the top, the company instituted a two-year corporate development program to improve managerial and interpersonal skills with an emphasis on participation and teamwork. The program released tremen-dous energy, revealed hidden talents, and generated a sense of fulfillment. At lower levels, the program covered a broad array of skills ranging from time management, decision making, and assertiveness training for subordinates to creative thinking, report writing, and managing one's in-basket. Improving people's skills was highly motiva-ting. Thompson-McCausland found that "training released much more energy."

Thompson-McCausland removed the bifocals and restored clear vision to this once aging company. Gradually this somber and formal corporate personality was trans-formed into a youthful, dynamic, and exciting company again—as it had been in its prime many decades earlier—and a rapidly growing one too. From 1980 to 1984, London Life's new premium business increased 4.5 times, its total income and invest-ment fund both doubled, and its expense ratio declined by 41%.

REFOCUSING THE LENSES

The conditions Thompson-McCausland found at London Life are not as uncommon as we may like to believe. They are quite similar to the conditions that Lee Iacocca encountered when he took over at Chrysler in the late 1970s, of which he later remarked: "If I had the slightest idea of what lay ahead for me when I joined up with Chrysler, I wouldn't have gone over there for all the money in the world."[3] The situation he encountered was so de-energizing that instead of thinking how to double the company he was literally seeing double! Yet Iacocca was able to reverse the lenses and convert $3.3 billion in losses which Chrysler accumulated from 1978 to 1981 into $3.3 billion in profit over the next three years and to double the revenues of what was already a $12 billion company in the process.

In actual fact, these conditions exist to some extent in every company. Like the lenses in our eyes, the lenses of a company have to be continuously refocused on a constantly changing and moving world both outside and within the company. This task can never be complete, so long as a company wants to keep growing and surpassing its previous performance. And regardless of its age, as soon as it stops wanting growth, it embarks on the descending curve which London Life had ridden nearly to the bottom, before refocusing its lenses and reversing the direction of its energy flow.

GROWTH IS AN ENDLESS CHALLENGE

Even after the dramatic turnaround of SAS, Jan Carlzon found that the job was not over. In winning international recognition, 1983 was a year of attainment for SAS and for Carlzon. But for Carlzon, it was followed in 1984 by "a year of agony."[4]

The problem was that SAS had achieved all that it had set out to achieve . . . and more. Carlzon explains how by fulfilling and exceeding its goals, SAS had inadvertently rendered itself directionless once again. The first lens got out of focus.

> I was quickly learning yet another lesson about running a business organization: when you reach your goal, you become a prisoner of success. . . . Between 1981 and 1984 all our forces were aligned, and each and every person was striving to surpass his previous best efforts. But now we had arrived at our objective—before we had given much thought to what we wanted to accomplish next. The absence of new goals was producing some negative effects at SAS. The atmosphere of togetherness was eroding. The purpose of our work began to be questioned frequently. And *our employees' newfound energy began to be redirected* toward narrower and more personal objectives. . . . By establishing our original goal, we had placed a demand on our employees. But now that there was no goal, *a kind of reversal had set in.* We had unleashed new energy, new motivation; with the goal achieved and the motivation still there, people began setting their own individual goals, scattering in all directions and making different demands of the company. *It was a graphic illustration of the need for top management to direct all forces toward a common goal."* [5]

And so Carlzon set about refocusing the lenses again by launching what he calls "the second wave." He established a more challenging direction for the corporate energies—to make SAS the most efficient airline in Europe by 1990 in preparation for deregulation of the commercial airlines there. Then he introduced further changes in the organization to further flatten and decentralize it, redefining the roles of middle and top management and further empowering people on the front lines.

The SAS experience dramatically illustrates the power of the process of energy conversion. It also points to the inadequacy of a limited goal like doubling. So if you have not yet chosen to triple or quadruple your business, set your sights higher!

ACTION PLAN FOR CORPORATE ENERGY FLOW

What about the three lenses in your company? What is their energy coefficient? To what extent do they focus and magnify corporate energies? To what extent do they diffract and disperse them? Refer back to the questionnaire at the end of the last chapter. Are you fully releasing the potential energies of your people? Are you giving clear direction to those energies through commitment to values and objectives? Does the organization effectively harness and channel those energies for productive work? Do your people have the right attitudes and skills to effectively express the energy and achieve maximum results?

Develop an Action Plan using the form in Appendix A. List on the form the actions you propose to take to improve the generation, direction, organization, and expression of energies in your company and to eliminate the dispersion and loss of energies due to lack of direction, organization, skills, and attitudes. If possible, try to estimate roughly the impact which these actions will have on the revenues and profits of your business over the next few years.

SUMMARY

* In most companies high profitability and rapid growth are rare and short-lived, because their three lenses are out of focus and their energies are scattered.

* When companies lack clear goals and priorities, their energies are dispersed and they lose direction.

* When the organization is inadequate to sustain growth or when its structure and systems are outmoded and cumbersome, energies are dissipated through stress or are smothered through inefficiency.

* When people lack the right skills and right attitudes, energy is short-circuited, growth stops, and profitability is poor.

* The key to constant growth is to release continuously, focus, and magnify corporate energies through a constant refinement and realignment of these lenses.

"What we need in this country is more people that can capitalize on opportunities, not more opportunities."

Lee Southard
Vipont Research

Chapter Six

IDENTIFYING UNLIMITED GROWTH OPPORTUNITIES

Planning strategically for growth involves asking and answering three fundamental questions about your business: Where are we? Where do we want to go? and How are we going to get there? Thus far we have been primarily concerned with the first of these questions—where are we. We have looked at the five components of your business and raised questions to help you evaluate the relative strengths and weaknesses of these powerful engines. We have also examined the process of energy conversion and raised questions to help you determine how effectively your company generates, directs and utilizes the energies at its disposal to achieve maximum results in terms of productivity, profitability, and revenue growth.

Now we come to the second basic planning question: Where do we want to go? The answer to this question sets the direction for channeling corporate energies. It also plays a crucial role in determining how much energy is available for direction. The higher our goals, the greater the energy they release. Energy is released when we become aware of a greater unrealized possibility and make a firm decision to convert that possibility into a reality. Awareness of the opportunities available for growth is the first step toward achieving them.

In this chapter we will be focusing on opportunities that exist in the external environment for the growth of your company. In subsequent chapters, we will examine some of the potentials buried within your company that also represent untold opportunities for its growth.

According to common conception the true entrepreneur is one who has a vision of an opportunity that others do not see. It is that vision that inspires his thinking, excites his imagination, releases his energies, and propels him into action. A vision of opportunity is the basis for all high achievement.

AMRE

Steve Bedowitz and Robert Levin of AMRE had such a vision of the home improvements industry. Levin explained: "Steve and I saw that nobody had grown big in this industry. Most of the guys were salesmen or carpenters." Like Art Bartlett, founder of Century 21, in the real estate industry and Harry Patten in the land business, Bedowitz and Levin saw an opportunity in a fragmented industry composed of thousands of small mom-and-pop operators. In 1981 AMRE got its first license to sell siding under the Sears name in Austin, Texas. Steve then realized that "here is a vehicle that is easily expandable. The name Sears gave us the little extra that made it easier for us to expand across the country, so that's when the idea came to us to specialize in just a few products but take it national." The company quickly established operations throughout Texas and neighboring states and then expanded across the country.

Awareness of an opportunity is essential, but awareness alone is not enough. There must also be a compelling urge for achievement. That urge or determination to achieve releases our energies for effective action. As we said in the first chapter, you must really want it. Says Levin:

> The real difference, the reason why we made it was our goals. The typical business person's goal is to make enough money for themselves. Our goal on a continuing basis was not how much money could we make, but how big could we grow the company. There is a big difference. We both always wanted to build a big company and we set out to do it. From the beginning we have always set goals. Short term, long term. We've amazed ourselves at how close we've come to hitting them. Setting the long term goals and living with those is the real secret of any good organization. We still have aspirations, things we want to accomplish."

Nor are their goals limited to being the dominant force in the $5 billion siding industry. Siding is only a small part of the $100 billion home improvements industry. And home improvements is really just one of the many fields in which they can express their organizational capabilities. As Bedowitz explained, "In essence, we are not a siding company. We are a direct consumer-marketing company with many other potential fields for our growth. My goal is to be a Fortune 500 company by 1992."

THE TWIN KEYS

Back in the 1960s Fred Smith had a vision that legend says he first described in a college essay. His vision was

> to build a transportation company that would be to the automated, computerized, technologically based industries of today what the railroads were to the industries of the late nineteenth century, what the truck lines were to the traditional manufacturers of the 30s and the 50s; that is, to be the primary artery of today's high value-added industries, the clipper ships of the computer age. My goal when I started the company was to create a totally unique transportation system that I felt was the total underpinning of the computer age. I mean it was a huge vision and it still is. It hasn't changed one iota.

In an industry dominated by giant UPS since 1907, Smith was able to see tremendous opportunity where others saw none, because he understood the significance of changes in life style. He saw that the pace of modern life was accelerating rapidly and that people were no longer satisfied with one-week or even three-day parcel delivery. By simply abridging that time to overnight, he founded a new multibillion-dollar industry.

For 16 years Smith's vision has guided the growth of Federal Express. That vision consists of two parts—a perception and an aspiration. He *saw* a possibility and he *wanted* to achieve it.

> I believe Federal Express will be far and away the largest transportation company in the world. Now we're probably number 8 or 9, but I don't have any question about the fact that we're going to be bigger than all of them. My unfulfilled aspirations are twofold: first, to do all over the world basically what we have done for the United States; and second, to make Federal Express a flawless organization in terms of the quality it produces.

Smith's perception has set the direction for the growth of Federal Express over the last 16 years and will continue to do so well into the next century. His determination to realize what he perceived as possible has been the catalyst which released and set in motion his energies and the energies of his people. That commitment continues to propel the company forward.

Smith's awareness and aspiration fixed the boundaries or limits on what the company could accomplish, but its actual achievements have depended on his ability to inspire others in the company to believe in and seek to fulfill his vision.

> I think that the most important thing that we have done here at Federal Express is to make sure that everybody in the company shares in the vision of this institution.

The vast majority of people want to do something that they feel is important in their lives. One of their primary motivations is to be on a quest, to be on a mission.

The leader's vision determines what is possible, but his or her ability to generate acceptance of the vision in people at all levels of the company—to create a consensus of thought and enthusiastic support for action culminating in the wholesale release of collective energies—determines to what extent that vision will actually be realized.

The leader must have an awareness of opportunity and an aspiration to realize it. These two result in a commitment to pursue the opportunity. When that commitment is complete, it is expressed as an infectious and overflowing enthusiasm. That enthusiasm releases the energy of the leader and sparks the imagination of key people in the company. When the leader succeeds in communicating the vision and in creating a commitment and consensus among others in favor of pursuing the opportunity, their enthusiasm and energies are also released, and the whole company is propelled into action.

A perception of opportunity and a will to achieve it are the twin keys that unlock the powers of rapid growth. If the perception is narrow and circumscribed—if we fail to see that there are infinite opportunities within and around us—or if the aspiration is limited, if the goal we set is not high enough to keep us stretching, so will be our achievement.

HUNTING FOR TREASURE

In Alexander Dumas's *The Count of Monte Cristo*, a poor innocent sailor is thrown into prison where he is befriended by a learned priest who gives him the map to a fabulous treasure buried on a deserted island. After the priest's death, the sailor escapes from the prison, recovers the treasure and becomes one of the wealthiest men in the world.

We write with conviction about the opportunity for every company to grow rapidly and profitably, because every company has not one, but five treasures within its reach and available for exploitation—not on some far-off island—but right in its own backyard. We referred to these treasures earlier as the five engines of a business. We have also cited examples of companies in crisis that have successfully tapped these opportunities for growth, like Chrysler Corporation and C & J Industries did in the face of intense competition from Japan and SAS did in a stagnant commercial airline market.

What are these opportunities? Where do they come from? How can we identify them?

Life is continuously throwing up new opportunities in every industry for those who have the eyes to perceive them. It does not require a visionary's genius, just an open mind and a will to see. New opportunities are constantly emerging because society is continuously evolving, and the rate of social development is greater today than at any prior time in recorded history. Every change that occurs as part of this process has direct or indirect impact on virtually every aspect of social life and, therefore, on virtually every business as well.

Earlier we described the five engines as the essential components of a business, but they can also be viewed as the five basic social resources upon which each business draws in order to constitute itself and to grow—capital, technology, market, people, and organization. Each significant change in society influences one or more of these five components, adding some new dimension to it or altering the way it functions. The effort to become aware of these changes and identify their significance generates a perception of new business opportunities. This perception is worth more than all the capital invested in a business, ten times more. For that perception creates capital and the fruits of capital—profits.

During the nineteenth century, capital was considered synonymous with business. The barons of industry in those days were known as capitalists. Countries with established capital markets and companies that could amass capital flourished. As the last century came to a close, a second engine—technology—became increasingly important. Rapid advances and revolutions in technology have been the most important engine of industrial development during the last eight decades. Even today they continue to be a powerful force for change, a prodigious generator of new opportunities.

But now more than any time in the past, there are many other social changes taking place that influence these five engines and generate new opportunities faster than we can perceive or respond to them. All the five engines are very actively producing fabulous treasures for those who see and seek them.

Ordinarily we view the changes taking place around us from the perspective of our present needs and activities. We take note of those with immediate and direct impact on what and where we are today. We ignore many important but apparently unrelated trends because we do not see how they will or could impact on the five social resources that constitute our business. If we really want to understand the full significance and potential of these changes, we must step out of our present context for a moment, cast off our mental set, and look freshly at what is really going on. Every development in society completely redraws the whole map of the future and creates new opportunities all around us.

It is worth the time and effort to try to understand the forces that create new opportunities—worth its weight in gold. Stop for a while and think about it. What social changes in the past have created new opportunities for companies in your industry? What further changes are taking place today that may generate new opportunities for your industry in the future?

TECHNOLOGY

Technological change was not always as warmly welcomed as it is today. When the windmill was first introduced in Holland centuries ago, the church considered it a sacrilege for anyone but God to direct the wind. The priests actually instructed their parishes not to use wind-milled grain. When the first British clock manufacturer tried marketing wall clocks in India 150 years ago, the company found it difficult to convince customers that the clocks really served a useful function. As a last resort, the company installed clocks free of charge in customers' homes for a one month trial. By the time they came back the next month to remove the clocks, most consumers were sold on the new device. In the late 1940s, a brilliant but unknown inventor named Chester Carlson developed an ingenious black box capable of reproducing the image of a printed page on plain paper—a process he called xerography. Carlson took his marvelous invention to more than 20 of the leading manufacturers in the United States, companies like IBM, General Electric, and RCA, and offered it for sale. Everywhere he was turned down because the companies did not see a market for the product. Finally a company named Haloid, forerunner of Xerox Corporation, decided to stake its future on a "chance."

Today the customer is far more ready and willing to accept new products and technologies, even if they are unorthodox and unusual, provided that they have some intrinsic value and utility. The number of new products and processes being developed is increasing exponentially. The time from invention in the laboratory to acceptance in the marketplace has shrunk from decades to months. These trends signify that more and better opportunities are being thrown up for grabs every year, every month, almost every day.

Listen Up, a high-end, audio-video retailer based in Denver, was one of the first in the country to recognize the potential of a new technology for home entertainment, the compact audio disc (CD). At a time back in 1983 when CDs were not even available for sale in the U.S. market, the founders of Listen Up, Walt Stinson and Steve Weiner, flew to Japan to see the technology and carried back suitcases full of CDs to sell in their store. The new technology spurred the explosive growth of their business. Stinson can vividly recall the time between 1983 and 1986, when revenues rose from $6 million to $12 million. He suddenly found that "we had a tiger by the tail. We doubled our revenues in three years. We didn't mean for that to happen. That's too fast, I believe. It was too fast for us. But we got into something that we couldn't control. We grabbed the tiger by the tail and hung on." Stinson and Weiner saw an opportunity around the corner, which the large record and hi-fi chains failed to see. Then they actively sought out that opportunity and converted it into growth—and gold.

In virtually every industry, the rapid development of new technologies generates opportunities for new and improved services as well as new products. Computers are enabling companies to network directly with their customers and provide them with new services. Federal Express is installing terminals in its customers' facilities that enable customers to order and track parcel deliveries and even handle freight billing. Gartner Group is developing a system that will enable customers to get up-to-the-minute information on important changes in the computer industry by online time sharing and electronic mail. Expeditors International is providing customs clearance services for its customers via computer, and so on.

Think about your industry and your business? What are the technological developments that have created opportunities for new or improved products or services in your industry over the past decade? What technological developments are now emerging that represent new opportunities in the immediate future? What other developments are on the horizon that hold promise down the line?

STAYING IN STYLE

Technological development is still a very important engine of new opportunities, but it is not the sole source. Today both business and the consumer have been trained to understand and recognize the significance of technological changes and to welcome them with anticipation. But our society is not nearly as astute in grasping the significance of changes in other spheres of life.

One of the most sweeping social changes of the past quarter century is the increasing demand for speed, which Fred Smith capitalized on to build Federal Express. Companies in virtually every industry—from fast food and shoe repairing to containerized shipping and mold making—are discovering new implications and new opportunities arising from the increasing importance of speed.

"Healthy, wealthy, and wise" goes the saying. Many companies have been wise enough to see an opportunity for great wealth in the American public's growing preoccupation with health and exercise. Reebok multiplied its revenues nearly 100-fold in four years, growing from $13 million in 1983 to $1.4 billion in 1987, by recognizing the significance of a life-style change in its industry. Co-founder Paul Fireman explains:

> There was a social change going on which nobody had noticed. We realized that the aerobics craze was for real and that there was a huge untapped market of women seeking both comfort and style. The industry was only focusing on jogging shoes. It wasn't growing with the customer."[1]

Reebok's stylish recreational shoes have attracted some 20 million new customers, many of whom have purchased four or more pairs in different colors.

The phenomenon of the working woman is a social change with far-reaching implications for businesses in such varied fields as processed food, day care and garment manufacturing. Liz Claiborne, Inc., recognized an opportunity resulting from the increasing number of working women and decided to specialize in designing stylish clothes for them. "We knew we wanted to clothe women in the work force," says cofounder and vice chairman Jerry Chazen. "We saw a niche where no pure player existed. What we didn't know was how many customers were out there."[2] Over the last eight years Liz Claiborne's sales have grown at an average compounded annual rate of more than 40%, while earnings have soared tenfold.

Charles Lazarus saw a different opportunity arising out of the same social change. He realized that the busy working woman would like a place to shop for her children that was quick, easy, and relatively inexpensive. So he founded the Toys "R" Us chain of warehouse-style stores, which offer a much wider range of playthings than traditional department stores. By 1988 the company was operating 350 stores with sales of over $3.1 billion.

What recent social or life-style changes have generated new opportunities in your industry? What social trends could represent opportunities for you in the future?

ORGANIZATION

Society is continuously generating new, more complex and efficient types of organization. The explosive growth of the fast-food industry initiated by McDonald's in the mid-1950s was fueled by a new type of organization—the franchise restaurant chain. Since then franchising has stimulated the growth of an incredible variety of industries, ranging from health clubs to home security.

Earlier, we described how AMRE became a dominant force nationally in the long-established home improvements industry, which previously had consisted primarily of local, mom-and-pop operations. When the company first proposed to extend its collaboration with Sears outside of Texas, Sears rejected the proposal on the grounds that a larger operation could not be effectively managed, as several past failures had proven. Yet AMRE persisted, and given the chance showed that it could succeed where others had failed.

AMRE accomplished its coup in just eight years by creating a highly centralized and efficiently run marketing operation to direct and coordinate the activity of local sales offices and warehouses throughout the country. Homeowners responding to AMRE's advertisements call into a central office, which qualifies each potential customer and then assigns them to a particular sales office. Every morning the manager of each branch office receives an electronic message listing the details of potential customers. The branch office then schedules two appointments that day for each salesperson in the office.

Expeditors International and Patten Corporation saw similar opportunities in two other primarily mom-and-pop industries, freight forwarding and selling rural land.

They tapped these opportunities by developing organizations that could operate efficiently on a larger scale. Minit International successfully took on an established shoe repair industry worldwide and rose to a globally dominant position in 20 years by introducing a new type of organization into the industry based on thousands of decentralized service units run by entrepreneurial managers and supported by central manufacturing, distribution, training and marketing facilities in each country.

The *just-in-time* concept is an organizational development that is creating opportunities in a wide range of industries. Federal Express operates a Parts Bank in Memphis to stock products and replacement parts for large manufacturers and mail-order catalog retailers. Many companies have reduced or eliminated their warehouses, utilizing the Federal Express system to store and deliver their products from point to point for sale or use precisely when needed. Parts Bank customers can send replacement parts or products via Federal Express for delivery by 10:30 the next morning practically anywhere in the country.

A central part of Nedlloyd Line's strategic plan for the 1990s is a similar organizational strategy for providing just-in-time logistical services for large-volume shippers. When American manufacturers ship their products to Europe, Nedlloyd will assume complete responsibility for bulk transport of products by ship, rail, and truck on both sides of the Atlantic. They will then stock products for the shipper in Nedlloyd-operated warehouses and ship individual consignments to European customers as directed.

Organizational developments are also affecting the relationship between manufacturers and their vendors. There is a shakedown going on in American industry today. To stay competitive, many American manufacturers are reducing the number of vendors they work with quite drastically, but are increasing the scope and extent of their dependence on those that pass muster. Companies such as GE, McDonnell-Douglas, and Kodak are working with vendors of parts, components, and tools to develop closer, more synergistic and long-term relations. Critical suppliers are being included as part of the product development team and given input into product design at an early stage. Some major manufacturers are directly linking up their computer systems with those of vendors so that communication of information and design specifications is greatly facilitated. Others are demanding guarantees from their vendors of on-time delivery and quality in return for guaranteed orders. Many vendors see these organizational developments as threats. Others, like C & J Industries, welcome the changes and view them as opportunities.

CHANGES IN LAW AND POLITICS

Deregulation has been a mother of many business opportunities during the past decade. The survival and phenomenal growth of Federal Express was made possible by deregulation of the air cargo industry, which Smith campaigned for vigorously in the late 1970s. The proliferation of commuter airlines like Mesa, regional airlines like America Air West, and the doubling of airline passenger volume in five years were also a direct result of airline deregulation, which has been so successful that it is slated for introduction in Europe by the earlier 1990s. Deregulation of interstate trucking created the occasion for P.A.M. to enter a highly competitive business dominated by established giants and grow to $70 million in seven years. Deregulation in telecommunications gave birth to a litter of thriving Baby Bell companies.

Increased regulation can also stimulate new opportunities. The hazardous waste industry has expanded very rapidly in the 1980s due to the plethora of new legislation regulating the disposal of hazardous industrial wastes.

Political and economic events outside our country have a far greater impact than ever before. Most of us are conscious of external changes that threaten to force changes in the way we do business. But how many are equally aware of the external changes that could generate lucrative opportunities, if we take the effort to change our way of doing business before we are forced to by circumstances? How many companies have seriously considered what business opportunities could be generated for them out of *perestroika* in the Soviet Union; the liberalization of the Eastern bloc; the cessation of hostilities between Iran and Iraq; the economic unification of the European Economic Community in 1992; the transfer of power in Hong Kong in 1997; the rapid development of future industrial giants like Brazil, China, and India; and so on?

Traditionally, the American tool and die industry has catered almost exclusively to domestic manufacturers and always assumed its foreign competitors would do likewise. Now all the rules of international competition have changed and the devaluation of the dollar has opened up worldwide opportunities for U.S. toolmakers. Yet in a survey we conducted, very few said that they saw exports as an important opportunity for them. But a few companies in the industry are aggressively exploring foreign markets and meeting with considerable success. Last year Enpro Systems of Houston, a $9 million manufacturing and fabrication business, appointed its first international sales representative and committed $100,000 for marketing overseas. In fewer than 12 months, the company has established world-wide agents for its industrial valves and booked several million dollars in foreign orders.

Twenty years ago, even ten years ago, how many really foresaw the positive impact which the Pacific Rim would have on their own businesses today—on the quality, cost, and delivery time for manufactured products; on the demand for tools and components; on the price of consumer products; on foreign exchange rates and exports; on financial markets and investment opportunities; on foreign investments in U.S. companies, manufacturing facilities, and real estate; and so on? The founders of Expeditors International did. They recognized that the growth of imports from the Pacific Rim countries meant more incoming airfreight. In their eyes that translated into a lucrative opportunity for freight forwarders and consolidators. Starting from scratch in 1979, Expeditors has grown to become the largest airfreight forwarder from the Pacific Rim with revenues of over $147 million.

Think about the impact of changing legal and political conditions on the world around you and the potential for converting them into opportunities for the growth of your business.

VISION PAYS

Awareness is capital. Perception is profit. Newly emerging opportunities are like waves emerging out of the ocean. Companies that perceive and exploit an opportunity are like surfers taking the wave for a ride. It is all a question of timing and positioning. Figure 4 depicts a wave of opportunity and three companies in the industry. The company at the top perceived the wave just as it was rising out of the ocean, positioned itself properly, and was carried forward and upward by the momentum of the wave to 1,000 times its original position, as did Apple Computers, Federal Express, Liz Claiborne, and Reebok, which saw before others the newly emerging opportunities in their industries and rode the wave on its crest to a thousand times their original size.

The company positioned in the middle was not the first to perceive the emerging opportunity, but was quick to follow the lead of the pioneer. This company has been carried upward to ten times its original size, like Ben & Jerry's in the gourmet ice cream market, Mesa Airlines, and hundreds of other companies which appear on the *INC.* list for a year or two.

The company at the bottom missed the boat and was left behind. Either it was too slow to perceive the opportunity or it failed to heed the advice of its customers or the example of its competitors, or it perceived the opportunity as a threat and chose to ignore it, hoping it would go away.

What are the opportunities now emerging in your industry as the result of developments in technology, life style, social attitude, organization, law or politics, devaluation of the dollar, and so on? Where is your company positioned on the wave of opportunities that have emerged in your industry? Is it a visionary and a pioneer? If not, does it at least respond quickly and adeptly to the example of the industry leaders? What national or international events may create new opportunities for your company in the future?

Some companies may think that they are too small to be affected by or benefit from national or international developments. Then what about state and local developments? Some small companies may feel that they are fully dependent on their large industrial customers and have no destiny of their own. Then think about how these factors could generate opportunities for your customers and ask how you can also take advantage of the opportunities available to them.

There is no shortage of opportunity. As Lee Southard, president of Vipont Research put it, "There have always been more opportunities out there than there are people who can actually go after them and master them and make them work. What we need in this country is more people that can capitalize on opportunities, not more opportunities."

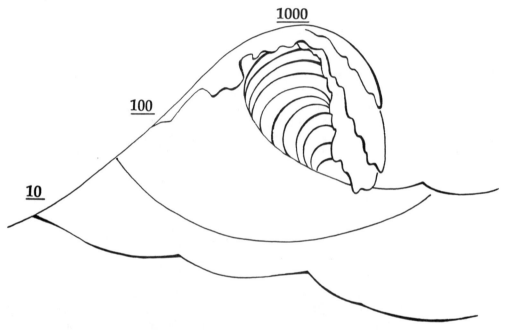

Figure 4. Wave of Opportunity.

ARE YOU READY?

There are a number of things your company can and should do to foster the awareness and develop the perception of newly emerging opportunities.

1. Encourage your customers to speak out, and *listen* to what they say. What do they like? What would they like better? What are their problems? Every problem is a potential opportunity.
2. Keep abreast of the latest developments in your industry through conferences, seminars, and trade journals.

3. Do not restrict your exposure to your own industry. Keep informed and observe trends and developments in closely and distantly related industries that could conceivably have an impact on your business.
4. Read the newspaper for social trends and changes in life style, not just for hard news. Imagine what the future could be if these trends continue.
5. Closely monitor the new initiatives of competitors.

ACTION PLAN FOR OPPORTUNITIES

1. Review the basic factors that create opportunities and identify the opportunities in your industry which your company can and should take advantage of to achieve your revenue and profit goals.
2. Write an Action Plan for developing each of these opportunities.
3. Estimate the impact of these Action Plans on the revenues and profits of your company over the next three years.

SUMMARY

- The external environment is filled with unlimited opportunities for the growth of every company.

- Society is continuously evolving. Every change in society creates new opportunities.

- New opportunities are generated by technological, life-style, organizational, legal, economic, and political developments.

- Opportunities are like waves. Companies that recognize them early and respond quickly are carried forward by the momentum of the wave and propelled to great heights. Timing is crucial.

- Awareness of these opportunities releases corporate energies.

- Commitment to tap them mobilizes the company for growth.

Chapter Seven

RECOGNIZING THE POWER OF VALUES

In the last chapter we looked at some of the opportunities for rapid growth which are constantly being generated by changes in the external environment. These changes create enough potentials for any company to double. But the opportunities created by these external treasures pale into insignificance when compared with the vast riches which every company can unearth within itself. The key to those riches is values.

The word values is often used to describe something rather vague and nebulous, a grandiose idea or ideal, a corporate ethic or philosophy. But when we use the word, we mean something very different—something very real, very concrete, and very powerful. Values possess power, a phenomenal power—the power to energize a company for rapid growth in revenues and profits—and this is a power which is fully available and accessible to every company. Like opportunities in the external environment, the only essential conditions are: (1) you must be aware of their enormous potentials, and (2) you must really want to tap them.

Earlier we said that companies direct their energies by focusing on the achievement of corporate goals. The goal may be to achieve a quantitative target for units produced and sold or dollars of revenue and profit. The goal may also be to improve the quality of performance—to do work better, faster, more efficiently, more safely, more systematically, with improved communication or coordination, in a manner more pleasing to customers or more satisfying to employees, and so on. These qualitative goals are what we mean by corporate values.

BANG & OLUFSEN

Robert Cavalco discovered the power of values a few years ago after he took over as CEO of Bang & Olufsen of America. BOA is the U.S. subsidiary of a $300 million Danish electronics manufacturer, known throughout the world for its technically sophisticated and superbly designed audio and video home entertainment systems. Bang & Olufsen is the Mercedes-Benz and BMW of hi-fi.

When Cavalco joined BOA, he found the company facing fierce competition from Japanese electronics manufacturers. As a result, sales had remained flat at around $22 million for the past three years. Cavalco started looking for some chemistry to turn a difficult situation into an opportunity for growth and he found one, not outside in the marketplace, but within the company itself.

The opportunity he hit upon was a value—customer service. He decided that it was not enough that his company offered the most elegant products on the market or offered acoustical quality equal to the world's best. BOA would offer the most elegant and best quality service to its customers as well.

Having identified an opportunity, he took the idea to his four senior executives and shared his thoughts and enthusiasm with them. Customer service was something that they could share and get excited about. Then he carried it to his employees at BOA's Chicago headquarters and spoke with missionary zeal about the company's new direction. He talked with the company's sales representatives and customer service representatives, but he did not stop there. He got virtually everyone in the company involved, even the shipping and warehouse crews, the accounts receivable and credit personnel. He brought in a consultant to work with groups of employees to define what customer service should mean to the company and elicit their ideas on how to improve it. The idea seemed to appeal to everyone and it caught on.

Cavalco and his management team spent the next few months traveling hectically around the United States meeting their customers and asking them, "What can we do to help and serve you better?" He and his team listened carefully and responded immediately wherever possible. They took action to liberalize the company's merchandise return policy, offer more flexible credit terms where appropriate, increase the speed of order processing, and improve the quality of packing. They sent out a traveling sales training program and trained 1,500 dealer salespeople. Cavalco took many other steps to improve communication with his dealers. He even sent his chief financial officer to give free consulting services to electronics retailers who needed advice on how to manage their own companies better.

The immediate results of these initial efforts were visible to everyone who knew and dealt with the company. Although few tangible changes had yet been made in the company's policies or practices, these efforts generated tremendous energy and excitement. Employees became more active and enthusiastic. Customers began to look on the company differently, as a friend and a partner. By the end of the year, Bang & Olufsen was rated the best customer service company by specialty home entertainment retailers. And after three years of no growth, the company's sales grew by 35%. That is the power of a value.

POWER OF VALUES

There are seven important reasons why values have power.

Values Release Energy

Values release energy because they motivate people. "People get far more excited about doing something as well as it can be done than about doing something adequately," says Steve Jobs.[1] They motivate people to work together collectively to improve overall corporate performance. Everyone likes to be part of a company that is known for its quality or its service, its integrity or its fairness, its friendliness, or its contribution to the community. People feel pride and satisfaction in being with an organization that has quality and class.

People at London Life Insurance had gradually lost that sense of pride and satisfaction over the years as the quality of performance slowly deteriorated, so slowly that they still perceived the company as high quality long after that quality had begun to fade. After Ben Thompson-McCausland arrived, people became conscious of what the company had been in the past and could be again in the future. They took up the challenge to reestablish the company's great traditions. Once-divided departments and groups started working together as a team to establish and achieve higher standards for speed, quality of work, customer satisfaction, and communication. "We took a deliberate decision to commit ourselves to the values," Thompson-McCausland says. The focus on values released tremendous energy.

Values also motivate people to improve individual performance on their own jobs. Profit and revenue growth may be powerful motivating goals for the owners of a company, the CEO, and senior management. But what does the accountant, the receptionist, or the warehouse clerk have to do with profit? Even if the company has a profit-sharing plan, many employees cannot easily see a direct relationship between their activities and corporate profits. But everyone can relate to values, because values apply to every job, every activity, every operation in a company. Achieving a high level of performance on any value is self-gratifying, self-rewarding, even when it is not linked to compensation.

At London Life everyone got involved and felt the personal impact of the focus on values, even the file clerks and secretaries. Employees worked together in groups to identify which values needed to be strengthened and the best way to do it. This gave each individual a sense of participation and ownership in the values. Once a consensus had been established, each person had a responsibility for increasing the quality of performance on his or her own job. The values became a personal challenge to every employee to improve execution of work.

Values Promote Nonstop Expansion

Every sales manager knows the power of setting targets for a sales force. The mere fact of establishing a quantifiable objective propels people to achieve it, on condition that they perceive it as a realistic target. But as Jan Carlzon found out, quantifiable objectives motivate only until you reach them. Once you achieve or exceed them, as SAS achieved and exceeded its three-year profit target the very first year, they no longer possess the power to raise performance further. That is why SAS leveled off after its initial explosive surge.

Values, on the other hand, are not subject to this limitation, for they can never be fully and finally achieved. The achievement of better quality and improved teamwork today is no assurance that they will still be better tomorrow, any more than cleaning a room today ensures that it will remain clean tomorrow. Values are like ever-receding or never-ending goals. The higher the values, the more the energy and effort required to achieve and sustain them. The more you pursue them, the greater the energy they release and put into action.

Values Are Precise Measures of Performance

Goals are measures by which we evaluate our performance and strive to improve it. The effectivity of any measure is directly related to the quality of the measuring instrument. The finer and more perfect the result we seek to achieve, the more precise must be the instrument we use to evaluate our performance. We can use a yardstick to measure the length of a room or a bolt of cloth without much difficulty, but the same instrument is unsuitable for measuring the precision of a small ball bearing or the dimensional accuracy of a hair-thin filament. For that we need a micrometer.

High corporate performance requires perfect precision in decision making, product quality, timeliness of action, personal behavior, clarity of communication, and in countless other respects. Although revenues, profits, production volume, and other quantitative goals are good measures for overall corporate performance, they are too broad and crude to serve as effective and motivating measures of individual and group performance on many jobs and activities. But the quality of performance on every job, every activity, and every act can be accurately assessed in terms of values.

American Express is a company dedicated to the value of customer service. The company has discovered how effective values can be for measuring and improving performance. It has set clear standards for what type of service it wants to deliver: replace lost or stolen charge cards within 24 hours, process new card applications within 15 days, ensure that bills are completely error free, and so on. It has a very sophisticated system for measuring the quality of service by monitoring performance on over 100 different activities. Every month the top management of the company reviews performance on these activities and takes action where necessary to bring it up to standard. The company also has over 100 recognition and reward programs in place to motivate its people to deliver the very best service possible to American Express customers. Cash awards of up to $1,000 are given for outstanding individual service. These and other programs help to explain the conclusion of one expert on the credit card industry: "There's no getting around the fact that American Express's service is far and away the best in the industry."[2]

Values Generate Profits

Take a close look at any company with a sustained record of high profits over a considerable period of time. Almost invariably you find that it is one that produces high-quality products, delivers excellent service to its customers, insists on cleanliness and orderliness of its facilities, avoids waste of money and materials, functions systematically with good coordination and teamwork, shows respect for its people and provides continuous opportunities for them to grow, and so on. In surveys of over 1,000 American and European companies, we found that companies that rated their implementation of key corporate values the highest also reported the highest levels of revenue growth and profitability in their respective industries.

Robert van Harten, a Dutch researcher, suggests there is a relationship between implementation of high corporate values and the long-term share value of public companies. It is common knowledge that share value does not always directly reflect short-term financial performance. Nonfinancial factors such as the perceived quality of management undoubtedly influence investors. The quality of management is a nebulous entity which has not been adequately defined up until now. The implementation of values is a very direct and appropriate measure of the quality of management.

Studies of performance on specific values indicate a direct link between financial performance and implementation of values. The value quality has become the buzzword and cure-all of the 1980s, and rightfully so. Quality is powerful stuff. An analysis of 2,600 companies over 15 years by the Strategic Planning Institute of Cambridge, Massachusetts, revealed that "financial performance is tied directly to the perceived quality of a company's goods and services." Companies that offer the highest quality of products and services achieved the best long-term financial results in terms of market share, return on investment, and asset turnover.

Punctuality or speed is another crucial value for high performance, one whose importance is greater than ever before. *Fortune* recently ran a feature article entitled "How Managers Can Succeed through Speed." The article cites a study by McKinsey & Co. of manufacturers of high-tech products, which shows a direct linkage between punctuality and profits. Companies that are able to bring out new products according to schedule earn 33% more profits on them over five years than do companies that come to market six months late.[3]

Values Apply to Every Activity

As Cavalco found out at Bang & Olufsen, improving corporate performance on a single value can virtually transform the way a company functions. Take punctuality or speed of response for example. Punctuality applies to virtually everything a company does—from the speed with which it answers the phone, replies to letters, processes orders, pays and collects money, to the speed with which it adopts new technologies, develops new products, introduces new systems, responds to new market opportunities, recruits and trains people, plans and evaluates work, and so on. Actually it is not possible to raise performance on any one value very high without improving performance on other values as well. Punctuality is improved through more systematic functioning, better coordination and teamwork, enhanced communication, and so on.

When C & J Industries decided to improve delivery time on its molds, it had to raise performance on a host of other values. First it increased communication and coordination among sales, engineering, and production to improve production scheduling. Then it analyzed the entire range of molds it was making and found that 85% of them could be built with standard off-the-shelf bases. So it decided to standardize its entire product line and only offer those sizes. It also standardized the process of developing bids for customers' jobs and found it could reduce bidding time by 90%. The company also improved coordination with its supplier of mold bases to ensure that it could always get immediate delivery on the mold bases it required. Defective quality resulted in the need for frequent reworking of molds, which also delayed deliveries. The company made a major commitment to eliminate the need for reworking by improving quality. It introduced a comprehensive quality training program based on Deming's 14 points to upgrade the skills of its people. Therefore, in trying to improve punctuality, it actually enhanced the values of coordination, standardization, quality, and development of people as well. The focus on values enabled C & J to cut its delivery time by 50%.

Values Are the Keys to the Five Engines

Each component of a business consists of many types of activities. By raising the quality of performance on these activities, we release the potentials of the component and turn it into an engine of growth. Each value can be applied to all of the five components. Quality, accuracy, orderliness, and punctuality are as important in finance as they are in production. Innovation applies to designing systems, developing advertisements, and raising capital as much as it does to improving technology. Therefore, raising performance on even one value across the board can have a tremendous impact on all five components of the company. Every value is a window of opportunity for raising overall corporate functioning, just as much as a new market or a new product.

When Waltz Brothers was on the verge of bankruptcy, the owners focused on values to turn their business around. One of the keys to their success was the value systematic functioning. When the four cousins took a close look at their business, they realized that they were spending so much of their time on routine operational tasks that they really had no time left to manage the development of their business. They also saw that many important tasks were not being done very regularly or reliably. They decided that one way to improve the performance of their company dramatically would be to run the company much more systematically. So they reviewed all five components of their business and improved the systems for budgeting and cost control (finance); workforce planning, recruitment, and training (people); inventory control and scheduling (organization); quality and maintenance (technology); and sales planning and customer service (market).

Values Raise the Quality of Corporate Energies and Elevate Work

Values are the most powerful way to release and harness the company's latent, unutilized energies for growth. The process of energy conversion which we described in Chapter Four takes place in every company. But in most companies, it occurs primarily at the level of physical energy and physical work—which is the lowest and least powerful level of functioning. Values upgrade the quantity and quality of energy available by harnessing organizational energies—the power of authority, freedom, systems, coordination, and communication—and psychological energies—our interest, excitement, enthusiasm, pride, emotions, innovation, and inspiration. Values elevate our work from the level of mere physical activity to the level of organized efficiency, emotional involvement, and mental creativity. Values also focus and multiply these energies more effectively. They refine the lenses and generate more efficient transmission and utilization of the available energies.

AMRE was just about the only very fast-growing company we visited that has been able to manage rapid growth without a lot of wear and tear on its people. In fact, no matter how hard we tried to get AMRE employees to complain about the pressures of rapid growth, invariably they started talking about how enjoyable it has been to work for the company. Bud Lane joined AMRE as national production manager after 25 years with another company in the industry, "because I wanted to work hard and have fun. Its been the most exciting experience of my life. The growth is fascinating, exciting. The first two weeks I was here, at least 100 times I heard people say, 'I love this company.,"

AMRE has been able to make a smooth transition from small scale to high growth, which many other companies in the home improvements industry have failed to do. A commitment to powerful corporate values has enabled AMRE to expand rapidly without feeling the stress and burnout so often experienced by other fast-growing companies.

This is a company that believes in standardizing and systematizing everything. The forms and procedures used in every office have been standardized, so that the company can operate a highly decentralized operation and yet maintain uniformity and control. "If we had 44 offices operating 44 different ways, we would go crazy," says founder Steve Bedowitz. "We are great believers in standardization. We want everything done in the same way in every place. Everything should be kept simple. You can build a large, profitable company by keeping it simple." The emphasis on organizational values like standardization and systematic functioning has enabled AMRE to operate very smoothly and to grow without stress and strain.

Yet despite the effort to organize and control, AMRE is a very lively and enjoyable place to work, because the standards and systems are there to make work easier and more pleasant. Along with these organizational values, the company has developed another very powerful value, which continuously releases the psychological energies of its people.

AMRE is as much committed to development of its people as it is to its standards and systems. The company implements this value through a wide variety of programs for training salespeople and managers, continuing education of employees, and promotion from within. "We promote from within," says Rob Levin. "That's important for people to know. People want to know where they can go within the company. Personal growth is very important. It is a great source of pride to walk through the offices and see people who started as accounts payable clerks now in supervisory positions. Internal growth is important."

By constantly taking efforts to upgrade the skills and job opportunities of its people, AMRE has established a close linkage between the growth of the company and the growth of its people. Bedowitz explains: "What will keep people excited and happy is to keep the company growing. As long as we continue to grow, the people will see there is room for them to grow." Not surprisingly, the company has virtually no turnover of administrative employees.

THREE TYPES OF VALUES

The accompanying list offers some of the most important corporate values, but it is not exhaustive. These values are divided into three categories, according to the primary type of energy which the value generates when it is implemented. Implementing values in the first list releases greater physical energy. Work becomes brisk and precise. It proceeds on schedule without interruption. Implementing values in the second list upgrades the functioning of the organization. People, departments, and activities function more smoothly and interact more harmoniously. The organization becomes alive and dynamic, responsive, and adaptable. There is a sense of competence and momentum. The psychological values release the emotional and mental energies of people in the company, customers, vendors, and even the general public. These values make work exciting and rewarding. They generate pride and dedication. They motivate employees to go the extra mile to serve and please the customer. They can also invoke an intensely positive attraction or loyalty from customers—like the intense loyalty of many Macintosh users to Apple Computers.

Physical	*Organizational*	*Psychological*
Cleanliness	Discipline	Pleasing the customer
Orderliness	Accountability	Respect for the individual
Punctuality	Standardization	Innovation
Regularity	Systemization	Decisiveness
Safety	Authority	Growth of the individual
Efficient use of money and materials	Coordination of depts.	Loyalty
Quality of product	Integration of levels	Service to society
Quality of service	Communication	Integrity
Max. utilization of time	Cooperation (teamwork)	Creativity
Max. utilization of space	Freedom	
Care of equipment		

VALUES PROPEL GROWTH

Our interest in values is far from academic. Values have everything to do with energy, the five engines, and the energy conversion process. Therefore, they have everything to do with growth, especially rapid growth, and with doubling or tripling your company.

In earlier chapters we asked you to analyze the five components of your business and the energy flow in your company to help you answer the question "Where are we?" Values represent a third and final piece of the picture. To evolve the most effective strategies to accelerate the growth of your company, you need to know where it is with respect to values as well. In the next chapter we will examine specific strategies to raise the level of value implementation. But first, think about the values in your company: (1) How many of the values listed above are really important to your company? Which are the strongest? Which are the weakest? (2) Which values have helped propel the growth of your company? Which ones have a direct impact on sales? on profitability? on motivation? (3) How successful are you in actually implementing these values on a day-to-day basis and maintaining a high level of performance on them?

SUMMARY

- The greatest potentials for the growth of any company are generated by a commitment to high corporate values.

- By values, we mean the qualitative goals which the company strives to achieve in all its activities.

- Values release and direct energy, motivate people, generate profits, and promote nonstop expansion.

- Values are the key to energizing the five components.

- Values raise the quality of corporate energies and elevate work to a higher level.

- There are three types of values—physical, organizational, and psychological—which differ in the level and intensity of the energy they release.

RATING CORPORATE VALUES
Instructions

The following exercises are designed to assist you in evaluating the actual extent to which important corporate values are implemented by your company. If you are directly involved with work in only one division, office or department of the company, you may wish to answer the questions with respect to that area, or for both the company as a whole and your area of work. In answering the questionnaires, it is important to distinguish between how important the value is to the company and how well it is actually being expressed in work. These questionnaires focus on the level of implementation, not the level of importance.

Part 1 contains a detailed set of questions on two fundamental corporate values, orderliness and punctuality. These questions have been made quite specific and detailed in order to illustrate how these values apply to virtually every level, department, and activity. Each questionnaire consists of ten statements. Evaluate how true each of these statements is for your company (division, office, or department) on a scale from 0 (low) to 10 (high) as shown. You may score the statements with any whole or decimal number, for example, 2, 3.5, 6.7, 9.

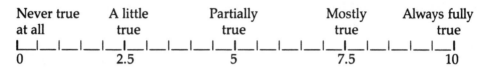

Never true	A little	Partially	Mostly	Always fully
at all	true	true	true	true

0   2.5   5   7.5   10

After completing each questionnaire, add up a subtotal score for this value. The maximum score is 100.

Orderliness

1. Are the offices clean?
2. Are the offices orderly in appearance?
3. Are desk drawers, file cabinets, and shelves orderly?
4. Can people always find a file or paper immediately when they need it?
5. Can all files/papers used by someone be easily located by others in their absence?
6. Do all files conform to a common system of order?
7. Are things frequently lost or misplaced?
8. Are records of phone numbers maintained in an orderly, logical manner?
9. Is work carried out according to a clear order of priorities or on a first-come basis?
10. Do people plan out their entire day's/week's activities in advance?
    Subtotal for orderliness:

Punctuality

1. Do people arrive at work at the appointed time ?
2. Do people return from lunch and authorized breaks on time?
3. When a meeting is called, do people come on time?
4. Does the company keep its time commitments to customers?
5. Is routine work completed when it is due?
6. Do people reply to letters and phone calls promptly? (10 = same day for letters and one hour for calls)
7. Do people maintain their records/accounts to date?

8. Are bills paid on time?

9. Do people complete reports on time?

10. Do people complete meetings/discussions on time?

Subtotal for punctuality:

Part 2 consists of a list of 30 corporate values with a brief note on some of the most important areas in which each value applies. In this section, you will be giving only one score for the value. Therefore, this score should represent the general level of value implementation of each value. The notes are intended to assist you in thinking in broad terms about how the value applies to many different areas, levels, departments, and activities so that your answers will be more comprehensive and representative.

Rate your company (division, department, or office) on each value on a scale from 0 to 100%. Begin this exercise by transferring your subtotal scores from the two questionnaires in Part 1. These will help you in evolving a relative scale for the other values. Try to formulate a comprehensive and representative rating for each value *based on the actual level at which it is implemented in the company at the present time.*

1. Orderliness: (post answer from page 93)
2. Punctuality: (post answer from page 94)
3. Cleanliness: of offices, production and warehouse facilities, equipment, customer service areas, raw material and finished product inventory, closets, bathrooms, and so on.
4. Regularity: of meetings, reports, sales calls, performance reviews.
5. Efficient use of money and materials: in purchase of raw materials, parts and supplies, production, shipping, transport, research, and so on.
6. Quality of product: in terms of functionality, value, reliability, repeatability, life span, packaging, presentation, safety, and so on.
7. Quality of service: in terms of timeliness, reliability, suitability, value, repeatability, courtesy, and friendliness.
8. Maximum utilization of time: of senior management, middle management, supervisors, other employees, technical staff, customers, and vendors.
9. Optimum utilization of space: in offices, files, showrooms, warehouses, production facilities, and so on.
10. Optimum utilization of plant and machinery: in production capacity, offices, retail outlets, vehicles, and so on.
11. Maintenance of equipment: in terms of frequency, quality, cleanliness, care.

12. Safety: in offices, warehouses, production and research facilities, vehicles, for employees, vendors, and customers.

13. Discipline: in adherence to company policy, rules, systems, procedures, schedules, standards, ethics, and so on.

14. Freedom for initiative: to make suggestions, develop plans, make decisions, carry out or modify actions, and so on.

15. Accountability: of individuals, departments and divisions for performance, results, problems, and so on.

16. Standardization: in terms of forms, files, procedures, reports, performance evaluations, equipment, training, recruitment, orientations, communications, and so on.

17. Systematization: in sales, marketing, customer service, accounting, research, production, engineering, estimating, recruitment, training, promotions, communications, coordination, reporting, and so on.

18. Coordination: horizontally between departments in terms of plans, activities, and systems.

19. Integration: for smooth operation vertically between different levels of the organization in terms of plans, decisions, priorities.

20. Communication: up, down, and sideways within the company, with customers and vendors, in terms of openness, frankness, clarity, frequency, accuracy, timeliness, and brevity.

21. Cooperation (teamwork): among individuals, departments, divisions, branches, and so on.

22. Pleasing the customer: in terms of promptness, courtesy, friendliness, thoughtfulness, anticipation of needs, meeting unreasonable demands, and making happy.

23. Respect for the individual: in establishing rules and policies, design of systems, making decisions, executing instructions, and so on in terms of people's health, safety, self-esteem, feelings, and opinions.

24. Decisiveness: in solving problems, planning, executing plans, in terms of speed and commitment to decisions once made.

25. Developing people (personal growth): through education, training, increasing responsibilities, promotion, flowering of capacities.

26. Loyalty: to and from suppliers, customers, and employees.

27. Service to society: community welfare, environmental protection, development of products and services that meet real physical, social, or psychological needs.

28. Integrity: honesty with employees, customers, vendors, government, etc.
29. Innovation: improvements in marketing, research, production methods, systems, financial management, human resource development.
30. Creativity: in terms of new products, new ideas, new systems, new production methods, new applications of technology, new methods of financing, new marketing strategies.
31. Harmony: the overall atmosphere of smooth and harmonious interaction between people, departments, divisions, systems, activities, rules, and policies within the company and between these elements and the external environment, customers, vendors, community, laws, and so on.

Chapter Eight

PUTTING VALUES TO WORK

There is a direct relationship between the growth of a company and the degree to which it implements values in its work. Hard work is the foundation of business. A small, local business, such as a machine shop or retail store managed and operated by the owner, can exist and grow primarily on the basis of physical energy and effort, that is, hard work. But as soon as a business begins to expand beyond these narrow limits, physical energy and effort are not enough. To increase in size, the company finds it has to increase in quality too. It has to provide a product or service that is good enough to attract more customers. It has to be faster in producing goods or serving customers than its local competitors. The company must be able to attract and keep good employees, which means making their jobs more pleasant and satisfying and creating opportunities for their growth. As the company becomes larger and more complex, work has to be better coordinated to avoid confusion and duplication of effort. People must learn to work together smoothly as a team. The growth of a company beyond the minimum size necessitates the development of such corporate values as quality, service, punctuality, employee satisfaction, coordination, and teamwork. In other words, values propel growth.

Take any company and add or increase its values and watch it grow. That is what happened to Robert Ross's company, Ross Incineration Services, 30 years after he founded it, when his children bought the business and added a value to it.

The elder Mr. Ross is a physically big and powerful man with lots of energy, a self-made man like a great many other entrepreneurs, capable of hard work and untiring effort. When he built his first waste incinerator in Grafton, Ohio, back in the late 1950s, there was very little public awareness or concern in this country about the dangers or consequences of environmental pollution. So there was relatively little demand for the services he offered. It took nearly 30 years for the company to reach $1 million in revenues. When environmental issues started to emerge as an important national issue in the late 1960s and throughout the 1970s, Ross was happy for the business it generated for his company. But when the federal government began strictly regulating the hazard waste industry, Ross felt stifled by the mass of new legislation and resented the burden of cumbersome, bureaucratic procedures which the new laws imposed. By this time, his son, Gary Ross, and daughter, Maureen Cromling, had become very active in the business. Unlike their father, they were able to accept these changes and could fully appreciate the importance of the new regulations and recognize in them a great opportunity for the company. This prompted them to make two very crucial decisions. First, they bought the company from their father. Second, they made environmental compliance the number one value and priority in the company.

At a time when many generators and disposers of hazardous waste were using all their ingenuity to find ways around the regulations or to minimize their impact, they decided to implement every new regulation to the fullest extent possible and even go beyond the dictates of the law where public safety would justify it. In doing so, they raised necessity to the level of an ideal.

This effort was extremely laborious and expensive. It involved major investments to upgrade their physical plant. It also involved a complete revision of the systems for handling waste, training employees, tracking shipments, documentation, and recordkeeping.

At first, neither their employees nor their customers could understand the need for these radical changes. Both complained of excessive documentation. But as more and more cases came to light of bad or irresponsible waste management by generators and disposers around the country, Congress pushed through more stringent regulations and the Environmental Protection Agency demanded stricter enforcement by the industry. Generators were held responsible for any violations of the law by those who disposed of their waste materials.

Ross was well prepared for these changes. Large chemical companies felt confident that Ross was a safe and reliable company that would comply with all regulations in disposing of their wastes. Ross's incineration facility was one of the first in the United States to be approved under the Environmental Protection Agency's rigorous licensing procedures. Ross is the only facility in the state that is not monitored by a full-time, on-site state official. During the first five years after they purchased the company from their father, revenues rose eightfold.

By focusing on implementation of a psychological value, Ross was able to elevate the level of its work and the level of service to its customers. It no longer provides merely a physical mechanism for disposal of waste. It also provides legal and psychological security to its customers that their waste is in safe hands. The value raised both the quantity of energy (volume of work) and the quality of energy (from physical to mental) in the company. Adherence to a value enabled Ross to prosper in the new regulatory environment.

TRANSITION TO RAPID GROWTH

The relationship between values and growth can be seen in companies of every size and stage of development. Each time a company makes the transition to the next higher level in terms of the size, scale, or complexity of business, it has to increase its implementation of values significantly to maintain high performance. Success on a larger scale and at a higher level of the business world is directly and proportionately related to the level and intensity of value implementation.

Most fast-growing companies are companies in the process of transition. They have grown beyond the limits achievable on the basis of purely physical energy and work. They have discovered or at least begun to discover—sometimes almost too late—the importance of corporate values as a means to raise the quality and quantity of energy for continued high performance.

The personal commitment of the founder or CEO may be enough to ensure high performance on values in the early days of a small business, but as the company grows, personal example and enforcement are not enough. That is what Paul Maestri found out after he took his company public in late 1986.

P.A.M. is a company that shot past the entrepreneurial stage so quickly that it is hard to mark the transition point, growing from $5 million to $75.8 million in eight years. Until then, the founders, Paul Maestri and Bob Weaver, had managed the company on their own. They personally dealt with the customers and handled every complaint. They kept in close contact with their drivers and were always available to discuss any problems that might arise. Customers were satisfied. Employee morale was excellent.

After the company went public, Weaver retired and Maestri decided to hand over management to a group of seasoned executives. He brought in a team of experienced, senior managers from one of his competitors and gave them complete freedom to manage day-to-day operations. Then followed "the most miserable, the most difficult time" of Maestri's life. The new management team put tremendous pressure on the organization to increase freight volume and expand the fleet. They shifted the focus from quality to quantity, selling price more than service. They distanced themselves from the drivers and took on an "I don't know you" attitude. Within six months service failure rates rose alarmingly, and customers were vocally complaining. Once satisfied employees were threatening to go on strike. Employee turnover increased dramatically. Suddenly profits started to fall.

In growing so rapidly, the company had abandoned some of the basic values that had made it successful in the past. As Maestri put it, "We got away from the customer and the driver." To save the situation, Maestri replaced the entire senior management team and came back to manage the company full time. He also hired a new president, John Karlberg, who understood the importance of people and service. Together they took steps to restore and institutionalize the values of people and service and put P.A.M. back on the path of growth. They brought down service failures to below 1%. They gave special training to the telephone dispatchers to teach them how to listen to the drivers and respond to their needs. Regarding service, "Now we are dealing more with the quality concept to develop long-term relationships with our customers," says Karlberg. "The customer is willing to pay a premium price for high-value service." Regarding people, Maestri explains, "We've gone back to our original values. The drivers know we care. We give them a fair shake. They all know they can come to me." Morale improved. *The company began to grow rapidly again.* Management's new goal is 30% annual growth until revenues reach $250 million.

The difficulty encountered by P.A.M. in maintaining its values while it grew is quite typical of companies making the transition from an entrepreneurial to a professionally managed company. The way in which they handle this challenge very often determines whether they make that transition at all. P.A.M.'s problems were a direct result of its growth. When the company was smaller, the founders could personally instill and enforce the values they believed in. But like many founders, they had never created an institutional foundation to ensure that the values would continue in their absence. Therefore, Maestri had to return to reestablish the values. Management now realizes that this will not be enough to make the values permanent. "We need to articulate the culture of the company," Karlberg explained. "We have a way to go finding our culture and putting it together. We need to articulate our mission, so our employees know that we want to be perfect." Culture and perfection are a matter of quality, that is, values. Instilling those values and making them permanent is an essential condition for nonstop growth.

GROWTH THROUGH VALUES

Linear Technology is one of the few fast-growing companies we studied where the process of institutionalizing values has been taken quite far. Linear has a number of pronounced values which it not only believes in, but also works very hard and systematically to implement. Quality of product, quality of service, reliability, and punctuality (on-time delivery) top the list. "Even in starting the new company," founder-president Robert Swanson explains, "we had the ideas about quality and reliability. We started out a little idealistic—the best product, the best quality, the best reliability, and on-time delivery. From the beginning we were and still are doing that. We have generated a quality and reliability image that is a reality." The company has developed specific quantifiable standards for product quality and service response time, as well as annual goals for raising those standards. It also has created an unusual structure to monitor and enhance performance on these values. There is a single department headed by a vice president responsible for both product quality and customer service and empowered to cross all departmental lines to ensure that these two values are enforced.

At a very early stage the company put in a quality assurance system designed to meet the most stringent requirements of major customers like Ford. The system is so good that Linear became the first company in its product category to get line certification from the U.S. military on the very first inspection. The company's quality assurance program is a self-sustaining, fully documented system more commonly seen in companies 10 to 100 times its size. Linear tests all its products not only to ensure that they meet the product specifications, but to determine whether they will work in a very wide range of different applications for which customers may try to use them. The quality program works so well, because it is understood and supported by every department of the company. "Everyone here has bought into the QA program," says Paul Chantalat, Quality Assurance manager.

The company really specializes in on-time delivery. The normal lead time for the production of one of their analog chips is 14 weeks. To reduce this time, they have developed a staggered inventory strategy. The company manufactures chips to various stages of completion where they await conversion into a wide variety of finished products. One of the key response times is the time it takes for their sample products to be tested and approved by the customer, which in some cases can be as long as one or two years. By introducing good systems for collecting data and monitoring the test performance of their chips, they have been able to provide key test information to their customers along with the samples. This system has enabled Linear to reduce product qualification time by 50%.

Most fast-growing companies are still in the process of acquiring distinct corporate values and institutionalizing them in every activity. Their success in bringing these values down and making them real in their daily operations will be a critical determinant of how fast and how far they will grow in the future.

SUSTAINED SUCCESS

In researching major corporations with a long history of rapid growth and high profitability—companies that consistently rank among the largest, most profitable, and most admired in their industries such as American Express, Anheuser-Busch, Coca-Cola, Delta Airlines, DuPont, General Mills, IBM, Merck, and Northwestern Mutual Life Insurance—we found that they were invariably companies with a very strong commitment to a wide range of high corporate values and that this commitment was put into practice in virtually every activity they perform.

Year after year Northwestern Mutual is the best performing and most admired company in the life insurance industry. The company insists on top quality in just about everything it does. Two closely related values, teamwork and communication, occupy a special place. The company has interdepartmental committees whose primary purpose is to ensure effective communication and teamwork between different parts of the organization. When Northwestern recruits new people, the most important thing it looks for is not intelligence, education, or experience, but whether this person can work effectively as a member of a team. Periodically the company conducts confidential surveys asking employees to evaluate the ability of their peers, subordinates, work groups, and even their supervisors to interact well with others and function effectively as members of a team. Based on the survey results, they formulate training needs for *every individual* and conduct training programs on a wide range of interpersonal and communication skills. Northwestern believes that its commitment to these values not only makes people feel the company is a wonderful place to work, it also goes a long way to explain why Northwestern leads the industry every year on a long list of performance and productivity measures.

INSTITUTIONALIZING VALUES

Northwestern Mutual is a 100-year-old company. But it need not take a century to raise your company's values to the level Northwestern has attained. It is possible for any company to increase the implementation of values dramatically by following a systematic process. Think about the ratings you gave to your company's values in the exercise at the end of the last chapter. Which values can be strengthened to accelerate its growth? Making values permanent is not an easy task, nor one that can be accomplished by hard work or constant proclamation alone. Values become permanent when they become an integral part and parcel of the way the company carries out all its operations. The process of institutionalizing values requires five essential steps: commitment, standards, structure, systems, and skills.

Commitment

Making a firm and genuine decision to implement a value and then remaining committed to that decision through thick and thin is serious business. Its a funny thing, but as soon as companies make that commitment or say they have, life has a way of knocking on the door to test just how serious they really are. That is what Walt Stinson found out at Listen Up when he announced a new customer policy—satisfaction guaranteed or your money back. One customer came in and bought a $15,000 public address system for his bar in Aspen, Colorado, and brought it back saying he was not satisfied with the quality of the sound it produced—six months later! Walt gave the refund. Another customer, who had bought a $500 car stereo system and a car burglar alarm system, came back to report that the stereo had been stolen and demanded a free replacement because the alarm system had not prevented the burglary. When asked if the alarm system had failed to operate properly, the customer replied: "No, it operated all right, but it did not stop the robber!" Walt replaced the stolen system.

Think about the values of your company. Is senior management fully committed to those values? Middle management? Other employees? Think about values the company would like to implement better. Is the company really and fully committed to improving performance on them? If you are a divisional, department, or branch manager, are you committed to improving value implementation in your area of responsibility?

Standards

Commitment is absolutely essential, but by itself it is not enough. Bob Cavalco learned at Bang & Olufsen that values are too vague and abstract to direct people's actions effectively. Many companies say they are committed to service, on-time delivery, good communication, employee satisfaction, and a host of other high values. But what do they actually mean by these words? Probably each one means something different. Even within a company, these words mean different things to different people.

Cleanliness is a key value behind the success of McDonald's in attracting middle-class Americans to its restaurants. When the company tells its employees that cleanliness is a value that must be maintained at all costs, what does that mean? To answer that question, McDonald's has developed detailed written standards of cleanliness for its restaurants, which specify exactly when and how tables, floors, counters, sinks, skillets, closets, windows, utensils, yards, driveways, sidewalks, and just about everything else should be cleaned.

When most airlines say their flights departed on time, they mean they took off within 15 minutes of the scheduled departure time. Delta's standard is 5 minutes. American Express's standard for replacing lost cards is 24 hours, anywhere in the world.

To ensure that everyone understands the same thing when we speak of a value and to give a very clear guideline against which to evaluate our performance, values should be defined in terms of simple, quantifiable standards of performance. Virtually any value can be measured against a standard of one type or another.

Merck has been voted the most admired corporation in America on the last three annual surveys by *Fortune* magazine. Merck is very strong on values such as product quality, service to customers, technological innovation, systematic functioning, coordination, and development of people. But the company is really outstanding on one value, credibility with its customers, which means physicians and pharmacists. Every medical representative, as their salespeople are called, is taught the principle of fair balance. In speaking with physicians about the drugs which Merck produces, the company insists that their representatives accurately and objectively present both the positive and negative characteristics of each drug. Merck has clear standards for evaluating the credibility of its sales representatives. Periodically it conducts surveys asking physicians to rate the quality and accuracy of the information which the representatives provide them.

The top management of Northwestern has measured the clarity and effectivity of its communication with employees by conducting a survey asking employees how much confidence they have in information coming from above. Innovation can be assessed by the number of new ideas, strategies, programs, products, or patents generated. The number of complaints received is an index of service quality.

We have witnessed groups of senior managers trying to formulate standards for very simple, mundane activities in their companies. It is not long before they discover that creating standards is hard work and quite time-consuming. Managers down the line and on the front lines can play a very constructive role in formulating standards. Those who participate in establishing standards for values are much more motivated to achieve the value in their work.

Then who should make standards? In our experience, the best results are obtained when senior management sets the broad, overall standards for the company—such as reducing product development time by 50% or completely eliminating safety-related accidents—and then allows operational managers or personnel to formulate the standards for individual tasks or activities that are needed to meet the overall corporate standard.

To be effective, standards should be simple, clear, quantifiable, measurable, and achievable. The last adjective is quite important. Standards that everyone knows cannot be achieved will not release energy and motivate people. Even if your ultimate goal is to reach a very high level of perfection, it is better to set an interim goal which everyone can believe in, rather than shooting for the ultimate when it does not appear achievable. Once the interim standard has been reached, it can be revised upward toward your ultimate goal. Standards are most effective when everyone buys into them and feels a challenge to achieve them, not when they are used as a means of pointing out the inadequacies of people's present performance.

Every value applies to literally hundreds of activities in a company. Standards can be developed for assessing performance on every value for every activity. At least the most important ones should be covered. Are there quantifiable standards for measuring implementation of key values in your company on every important activity?

Structure

Who is responsible for implementing values in your company? Or, rather, is the responsibility of each person for implementing key values clearly defined and understood? Structures define responsibility and authority. They tell us who is in charge of which department, which activity and which value. A structure can be a department, a committee, or an individual job description.

Linear Technology has specific departments for quality assurance and customer service, each headed by a manager, and both presided over by a vice president of quality and service. But the task of implementing quality and service is certainly not left entirely to these three people. These values are far too important and require far too great an effort for a few key people to implement them on their own. Every department at Linear is partially responsible for achieving high quality and service. The product engineers have accepted as their responsibility to design chips that can be manufactured with relative ease and little rejection. The field service engineers are responsible for monitoring performance of the chips in the customers' products and reporting back quality problems that need correction. The production engineers have a responsibility not only for quality but for on-time delivery and quick response to customer inquiries regarding the status of their orders as well.

At SAS everybody assumes responsibility for getting flights off on time, even the baggage handlers and maintenance crews. The same is true of every value. To raise value implementation to a high level and keep it there, the responsibility of each person and department for the value should be clearly defined, preferably in writing.

Has your company clearly defined the responsibilities of each department and position for implementing key corporate values?

Systems

When Walt Stinson decided to commit Listen Up to the value of customer service, he really did not contemplate what was in store for him. His commitment was genuine. He established clear standards for service in key areas. He took personal responsibility on himself to monitor customer satisfaction and personally reply to every complaint. He assigned responsibilities to his managers and their subordinates for providing good service. But still something more was needed. He found he did not have the systems that were required to make his commitment a reality. For example, the service department set a standard of responding to customer inquiries about the status of a repair job within 30 seconds. That is pretty fast compared with the industry average of several hours and sometimes several days. But the systems Listen Up had in place were not adequate to provide that level of service. A new computerized tracking system had to be developed and introduced that could instantly generate a status report on any pending job. The new system brought down response time to less than 1 minute, probably a record in the industry.

Systems are essential both for achieving high performance on values and for monitoring that performance. When Jan Carlzon established the goal of 100% on-time departures, a computer terminal was installed on his desk to enable him to monitor corporate performance on the value punctuality. A few years before the recent uproar about late airline departures, we sat in on a typical top management briefing at Delta Airlines, which starts at 9:30 A.M. and lasts all of 5 minutes. Every morning some 30 executives gather in a conference room to listen to reports coming in from stations around the country on the company's on-time departure rate and other key performance indicators for the previous day's operations. This simple system enables them to monitor value implementation and take immediate corrective action where necessary.

Merck has elaborate systems to support its commitment to credibility. All advertisements and product literature have to be reviewed and approved by a committee prior to being used. Virtually every piece of paper that goes from the company to the customer is monitored to ensure that the information given is correct.

Does your company have in place all the systems it needs to achieve high performance on key values and to monitor that performance on a regular basis? Do all those systems function as smoothly and swiftly as they should? If not, achieving and maintaining your standards may be very difficult. What practical steps can you take to improve your company's systems for value implementation?

Skills

You can have all the good intentions in the world, clear standards, responsible people, and magnificent systems, but without the right skills it may all be for naught. At least that is how we felt recently when we visited Dallas to deliver an executive training program and checked into a palatial Dallas hotel for more than a princely price. Before retiring for the night, we ordered coffee for 6:30 A.M. Due to the change in time, we were up an hour early and glad for the extra time to prepare for the meeting. So we called room service to advance our order. Sure enough the coffee arrived five minutes later—good system. At 6:30 A.M. there was another knock and another pot of coffee—bad system—which we politely refused. Five minutes later there was a call from room service—quick follow-up, we thought—to inquire why we had refused the second pot. After we explained the circumstances and expressed our understanding of the matter, we were taken aback by the caller's response. "Next time, sir, please do not change your order!" Here was a truly magnificent building, with beautiful rooms and excellent systems to serve, and yet the staff had not been trained not to blame customers for the company's mistakes. Just one small skill was missing.

There are literally hundreds of skills needed to achieve high performance on even one value—physical skills, technical skills, organizational skills, interpersonal skills, and managerial and psychological skills, too. Northwestern Mutual analyzes the training needs of every manager and employee, because the company recognizes the importance of continuously improving the interpersonal skills of its people to support the value of teamwork.

Merck's salespeople have the best reputation among physicians for the quality of service and accuracy of their presentations, because Merck has a training program that has become a model and standard for the pharmaceutical industry. New sales representatives spend 10 weeks studying basic medical subjects and must score at least 90% on weekly exams. This is followed by three weeks of training in presentation skills. The next 6 months are spent accompanying experienced salespeople on live sales calls. After nine or ten months, they get to go out on a call by themselves. But training is not over. They must still attend regular sessions to improve their knowledge and skills further. "Training is our obsession," says Jerry Keller, a vice president of Merck's U.S. drug division. "People who come to us from other companies can't believe we have this kind of program."[1]

If your goal is to achieve high values and nonstop growth, you cannot afford to omit even one small skill. Sounds difficult? It is. That is why high performance and nonstop growth are not a lot more common than they are. It's difficult, but certainly not impossible or beyond the reach of those who really want it—and there are no shortcuts to long-term success.

Think about all the skills your company needs to achieve high performance on key corporate values. Does everyone have the skills they need to fulfill their responsibilities for the value? What additional training should be done to upgrade skills for value implementation?

GETTING THERE FAST

The process of value implementation outlined in this chapter is comprehensive. Any company can apply it to raise performance on any value to the highest level. But in practice we see that most companies that have achieved high performance on values are such companies as American Express, Delta, Merck, and Northwestern Mutual, which have been around for quite a long time. Does high-level value implementation have to take decades?

Fortunately, it does not. It is possible to vastly accelerate the normal process of value implementation through a systematic effort. Jan Carlzon and Ben Thompson-McCausland employed this process to raise performance suddenly and dramatically on values in two older companies. Fred Smith followed the same method to raise Federal Express from ground zero to the leader of a whole new industry in a little over a decade.

If you really want to see and feel the power of values to generate and release energy, you need only visit the Federal Express hub in Memphis on any weekday night. The place is overflowing with intensity. The company has many high values that contribute to this atmosphere—service, development of people, systematic functioning, and others—but unquestionably the one that reigns supreme is being fast and on time, that is, punctuality.

Literally everything at Federal Express moves fast—parcels, planes, people, paper, even stairways, one of which had just been moved a few days before our arrival as part of the constant rearranging and redesigning that has continued nonstop for the past 16 years to keep up with the fast movement of the company itself.

Information moves fast at Federal Express, too. Fred Smith was not only quick to recognize the latent demand for faster parcel delivery, he realized also that customers are almost as concerned with getting fast and accurate information about their packages as they are about getting the packages themselves very quickly. At Federal Express people really believe in the direct relationship between values and profits: time and quality equal money, that is, the less time and fewer errors, the more profit.

All five stages of value implementation discussed earlier in this chapter are clearly evident at Federal Express.

Commitment

There are visible signs everywhere of Federal Express's commitment to speed. Every night more than 100 planes fly into Memphis from all over the country between 10 P.M. and 2 A.M. to unload some 800,000 packages for transshipment, wait for them to be sorted, and then fly back to where they came from with a fresh load of packages to be delivered. The last scheduled arrival is a DC-10 from Los Angeles carrying 15,000 packages. If that plane is more than 30 minutes late, it could miss the sort. That means 30,000 unhappy customers—15,000 who sent the parcels and 15,000 who wait to receive them.

As part of its commitment to on-time delivery, the company will go to virtually any length to get those 15,000 parcels to their destinations. The company has rented up to 30 Lear jets to fly the packages that missed the Memphis sort out on time. Another expression of the company's commitment: it maintains five extra planes fueled and on runways around the country ready for use in an emergency, although they are called into use less than 1% of the time.

Standards

Smith's standard for punctuality is clear and unambiguous—100% on time. "We're not far off from that now for a transportation company. We're at an unbelievable level. But I think that through the application of technology we can reach a point where we probably will never get to 100% in my life time, but we can get to 99.9%." In 1988 Federal Express achieved an on-time rate of 96%. "Today with one million packages a day, we feel that a 92% service level would put us out of business—that's a lot of failures," says Ted Weise, senior vice president of ground operations. "Even though our service level is now between 96 and 98%, the competition is up to between 88 and 90%. That is how important the 100% goal is." For 1989 it revised its standard upward to 98%, and you know what happens when the company achieves that.

On-time parcel delivery is only one of the company's many standards for punctuality. In the customer service department, there is a standard that phones must be answered within 20 seconds. The actual answering time is tracked by computer and is posted on the bulletin board every day. The day we visited the department, the actual average time was 11 seconds.

There are strict, very strict, standards for departure and arrival of flights too—within 3 to 5 minutes of scheduled time. "Our job in aircraft maintenance is to get every plane off on time. Our standard is 100%," says Paul Benbrook, senior manager of aircraft maintenance.

Structure

Who is responsible for punctuality at Federal Express? You guessed it—"Everybody is responsible," says Benbrook. That starts right from the top of the company and goes all the way down. Last fall the company announced to its employees that unless Federal Express achieves the 98% on-time delivery standard in 1989, the management of the company, including the CEO, will not take bonuses. That demonstrates both management's commitment and responsibility. But accountability does not stop at the top. Benbrook adds, "Every manager is accountable. Even the line mechanics come out to watch the aircraft take off on time." If a plane is 5 minutes late, it has a major impact on service. Pilot Everett Hicks explains how he and his fellow pilots are responsible for achieving the company's values. "We have to explain every minute of delay—delays due to fueling, paperwork, crews, maintenance. We run the most on-time airline in the world." What is true for the pilots is equally true for every station and branch sorting operation. Accountability goes all the way down the line—to the end. If a parcel destined for New Jersey mistakenly lands in Atlanta instead, the error can be traced back to the individual container checker at the hub who was responsible for ensuring it got on the right plane.

Systems

Systems are a very big part of the reason for the phenomenal growth of Federal Express. Working systematically and through systems is itself a core value of this company. Performance against the company's standards is tracked constantly and broadcast on a continuous basis over in-house TV monitors located throughout the company. A sorter in the hub can read on the screen how many packages were sorted the previous day and how many were delivered on time. A service quality indicator report is published weekly. The report monitors a wide range of performance indicators—damaged parcels, missed pickups, invoicing errors, everything. "It records the absolute number of failures, not percentages," Roger Podwoski, managing director of service systems administration, explained. "It's a subtle but important difference. The customer doesn't care about percentages. He only cares about his package. Our corporate objective is to improve the absolute level of service while growing at 30% per year. Otherwise, no management bonuses this year. That's our commitment!"

These systems involve plenty of hardware and software. They all center on six of IBM's largest mainframes that constitute the information hub of the company. These computers are linked with an incredible number and variety of computer terminals for customer service, maintenance, sorting, parcel tracking, and scheduling. "Information systems hold many companies back," says Jim Barksdale, the firm's chief operating officer. "We have been able to grow our systems with the growth of the business. We recognized early that good information is just as much a part of the product as the package."

To understand the magnitude of the company's achievement, consider that in 1988 the volume of packages it handled increased by 51 million in a single year. That is more than the total volume of packages handled by the company in 1983, that is, equal to the entire growth of the company during its first decade in business.

The heart of the computer operation is COSMOS, which consists of 100,000 computers in offices and vans around the world. Info Week selected this system as one of the top ten strategic information systems in the country. Every pickup is entered into the system and automatically relayed to a Federal Express courier, who receives direct instructions on DADS, a digitally assisted dispatching system. A terminal unit is housed in every truck. When the courier enters a customer's premises for a pickup, he or she enters the parcel into a hand-held supertracker terminal, which is used to scan the airbill number and then slides back into a slot in the truck and immediately transmits the information back to COSMOS. From that moment, through delivery of the parcel to its recipient by another courier, the location of the parcel is tracked continuously by the central system. The DADS unit saves the couriers a lot of time by eliminating the necessity of having them call into dispatchers for instructions. "This system has really energized people," according to courier Greg Cooper. "Now we have more time to spend with our customers. It has increased the quality of service."

The zip code sorter is a system used in the hub, which provides immediate feedback to parcel sorters regarding their productivity. Even though compensation is not linked in any way with data generated by the system, the feedback has had a significant impact on individual sorting rates.

COSMOS also provides direct information to the customer. When a customer calls Federal Express for a pickup, the customer service representative has access to 72 different computer screens of information to answer any questions that may be raised. A caller asking for a parcel to be delivered to a major city may be informed that a parade is scheduled in the destination city the next day, which may prevent delivery of the parcel.

To support punctuality and reliability in the aircraft service division, a computerized maintenance system has been installed. The system informs each airport service station around the country of the repair and maintenance operations to be carried out on each company plane the next day, so that work can be planned well in advance and completed on time.

MCIDAS is the acronym for the company's computerized weather system, which is similar to the one used by NASA for space flights. Federal Express uses the system to reroute its planes to avoid delays due to bad weather. Its 92% accuracy is significantly better than that of the U.S. Weather Bureau.

Training

However impressive the company's systems may be, no company can achieve 96% or 98% reliability without a tremendous commitment to training. Such high on-time performance depends on people in dozens of departments who must have literally hundreds of different skills for decision making, planning, forecasting, scheduling, coordinating, communicating, and executing work at all levels of the company. "We have always recognized the significance and importance of training," says Chief Personnel Officer Jim Perkins.

The company has many programs to support the value of punctuality. New couriers undergo a three-week program including two weeks of classroom training and one week riding with an experienced courier. Customer service representatives receive a total of four weeks initial training to master the complex computer information system. Their training also includes role playing, enunciation, phraseology, handling irate customers, and stress management. After completing the course, the representatives are monitored regularly and retested twice a year. All senior managers in customer service must take the same program and spend a minimum of four hours taking live calls twice a year to stay in touch with customers.

There are many other elements that contribute to the company's high performance on values such as punctuality and service. They are all part of the Federal Express system. "We have institutionalized the idea of 100% service through communications, awards, discipline, systems, everything," says Stephen Rutherford, managing director of human resources analysis.

The company is constantly being energized by its commitment to high corporate values—or as Ted Weise described it, "by a fanatical urge to do it better." According to Weise, "To achieve the last 5% in terms of quality of performance requires as much effort as achieving the first 95%." That commitment and that effort continuously release fresh energies in this company and continuously propel its growth.

EVERY VALUE IS AN OPPORTUNITY

Federal Express institutionalized the process of value implementation during the first decade of its existence. Its ability to achieve such high performance on a range of values has enabled it to keep growing rapidly long after most fast-growing companies have leveled off or slowed to a crawl.

Remember, ten years ago Federal Express was only a $160 million company, described as "the fledgling venture that everyone said would never get off the ground."[2] Six years before that it did not even exist. Five years later it crossed $1 billion. Ten years later it was described by *Barron's* as "a triumph of free enterprise." We would prefer to call it "a triumph of values."

The process Federal Express followed is essentially the same as that which C & J Industries, Waltz Brothers, SAS, and London Life employed to energize themselves for rapid growth. It is a process which any company of any size can employ to double its rate of growth or profitability in a relatively short period of time.

What are the values of your company? It sounds like an innocent enough question. Individuals have different values—why shouldn't companies? But when we refer to corporate values, we are talking about the fundamental elements of successful organizations. The emphasis and relative importance may change, but the values themselves are universal. Review the list of 30 values found in the previous chapter. Which company can say that it does not believe in or does not want to attain high performance on them all?

Every corporate value represents an untapped potential for every company. Each of them is capable of an almost infinite development. There is no such thing as too much quality or service, innovation or teamwork, so long as it remains in relative balance with all the other values. There is no company that cannot grow by implementing the values on this list. There is no company that can say it has discovered all the treasures and utilized all the opportunities which even one of these values offer.

Three Strategies

Then where should we start? Which values should we raise first? Is it more effective to concentrate all your efforts on improving one value or to work on all of them simultaneously?

In our experience there are several effective strategies that can be employed to utilize values as a springboard for rapid growth and doubling profitability. Three different approaches are outlined here. Any company can double its profits in 12 to 24 months using one of these three approaches.

1. Raise Performance on Every Corporate Value by 5 to 10%.

The most powerful way to grow a company is to develop each component and element in a balanced manner. Focusing on the development of many values simultaneously ensures the greatest balance and harmony and generates the maximum results. However, it is also the most difficult strategy to execute, because it requires concentration on many things at once. Incremental progress on many values does not seem as dramatic or significant as sizable progress in one or a few areas, but this strategy generates the maximum results.

2. Implement One Value to the Highest Possible Level That It Can Go

This approach has the advantage of being very clearly focused on a single goal. Focusing on one value is easier and more dramatic. But raising performance on any value throughout the company requires improving performance on many others as well, so the focus is not as narrow as it may seem. The power of this strategy comes from applying the one chosen value comprehensively in every major and minor activity and raising it to the highest conceivable level in all these areas. If you are working on only one value, it is best to choose one that is centrally related to your business and that is rated weakest of the important values.

3. Implement Three Values to Double Their Present Level

This strategy is our favorite. It has some of the advantages of both of the others. It is more balanced than focusing on 1 value and easier to execute than focusing on 30. We recommend selecting three values which are relatively weak and, therefore, possess the greatest potential for improvement. Preferably, one value should be chosen from each of the three categories—physical, organizational, and psychological—listed in Chapter Seven. When we say double the level of their implementation, we are speaking figuratively. Doubling refers to something midway between a 10% increase referred to in the first strategy and the highest possible level referred to in the second. For example, if you have scored the company 60% on a value across the board, doubling would be raising it to 80%.

To facilitate implementation of this strategy, we recommend that the initial effort to improve each of the three values be started three months apart, that is, start on one value now, another three months later, and the third six months later. But once you have started improving a value, it is important to maintain and continue making improvements during successive periods when you are also working on the other values.

ACTION PLAN FOR VALUE IMPLEMENTATION

1. Rate your company on all 31 corporate values using the questionnaire at the end of Chapter Seven. Better still, customize the questionnaire to cover all activities that are specifically important for your business.
2. Ask other executives, managers, and employees to rate the company (division/office/department) on these values and compare their perceptions with your own.
3. Conduct discussion groups to examine these differences in perception and arrive at a consensus as to where the company really stands on each value.
4. Identify specific areas or issues on which implementation of each value should be improved. The issues should cover all five components of the business, all departments, all levels of the company and all activities. If you have chosen strategy 1, then you should identify major issues for each of the 30 values. If you have chosen strategy 2, then you should identify every major and minor issue related to the one value you are working on and pursue each in full detail. For strategy 3, focus on all major and some minor issues related to all three values.
5. Set clear overall targets for raising the value on each of the issues identified within a specific time frame.
6. Assign responsibility for working on each issue to a group and specify the level of authority the groups will have for taking action.
7. Each group should analyze their issue and identify specific actions required to improve performance on the value through the five stages outlined in this chapter—commitment, standards, structure, systems, skills.
8. Each group should act where authorized or make recommendations for approval at a higher level on how to implement the value through the five steps.
9. Regularly monitor performance of the groups and the company as a whole on implementation of the values on all issues.
10. Administer the value questionnaire after 6, 12, and 18 months to measure overall progress.

11. Write a detailed Action Plan listing the actual steps you propose to take to raise value implementation in your company/division/departments.
12. Estimate the impact on your revenues and profits of carrying out the actions listed.

SUMMARY

- The real power of values come from implementing them in every corporate activity.

- The implementation of values can be institutionalized in a company by a five-step process: making a real commitment to the values, setting clear quantifiable standards, assigning responsibility for achieving the values, creating the right systems for achieving and monitoring performance on them, and training for all the necessary skills and attitudes.

Chapter Nine

ENERGIZING YOUR PEOPLE: AN INEXHAUSTIBLE RESOURCE

In the preceding chapters, we have looked at companies from three different perspectives. First, we looked at the anatomy of a business, the five components—people, technology, market, capital and organization—without which no company can come into existence, survive, or grow. Then we looked at corporate physiology, the process by which companies generate and release energy, harness and channel it, and convert it into practical results to achieve their goals for growth and profitability. Finally, we looked at how by focusing on corporate values, companies can raise the process of energy generation and conversion to peak levels for maximum growth and maximum profitability.

We said earlier that the five components are the engines that propel the growth of any business and that each of them contains within itself hidden and untapped powers and potentials which any company can utilize to accelerate its rate of growth dramatically and increase its profitability. Each of the five engines consists of an ascending scale of lesser and greater powers. Some companies tap one or a few of these powers to a considerable extent but ignore the rest. Other companies release many of them, but to only a very limited degree. The full development of each engine is achieved by harnessing all its powers, just like the full development of a company requires the balanced development of all five components.

Many of these powers are quite well known. Yet we still say they are hidden, because most companies recognize only a small part of their potential and utilize only a tiny fraction of their power. If, as psychologists say, one utilizes only a small part of one's intellectual capacity in normal life, it is equally true that companies use a very meager portion of the resources at their disposal. In the next five chapters, we look at some of the hidden powers of the five engines and at practical stategies that can be employed to release them in your company.

In this chapter we will explore the varied powers of the engine people. In virtually every fast-growing company we have visited, we heard testaments to the enormous power of people. "People have made this company grow," says Robert Dobkin of Linear Technology. "People are #1," says Randy Angelocci of AMRE. Since the goal of this book is to generate rapid growth in your company, we begin with the engine that has propelled most fast-growing companies to where they are today. The next chapter explores the powers of the engine organization. If people have been the greatest driving force for growth, organization has unquestionably been the engine that has most commonly stalled and retarded the growth process. Organization is the Achilles' heel of most growth-oriented companies. Strategies to unleash the powers of the other three engines are presented in subsequent chapters.

The powers of people are most dramatically expressed in revolution—the Boston Tea Party, the storming of the Bastille, the flower power of the 1960s. In these rare moments of inspiration (or exasperation), some of the latent powers that lie hidden below respond to an idealistic call and explode upon the placid surface of social life.

Suppose for a moment that a force of this intensity could be released and constructively utilized by an organization for its growth? That company might arise phoenixlike out of nowhere and generate revolutionary shockwaves in its industry—just as Apple Computers emerged out of its garage and grew against all odds into a tremendously innovative, competitive and profitable business. Or it might spring out of a dream and create an entirely new industry overnight—as Federal Express created the overnight delivery business. Or it might suddenly rocket from the middle ranks of obscurity to become the undisputed leader of its field and soar on into the future opening one new vista after another, year after year, decade after decade, commanding a preeminent position in its field world-wide—the way IBM rose from fifth to first in the punchcard machine industry during the Great Depression, then moved into computers, where it has reigned supreme for four decades. Each of these three companies has grown phenomenally by unleashing the powers of people. Yet, however dramatic and impressive these examples may be, they are partial and inadequate, for even these great corporations have tapped but a little of the hidden potentials of this engine.

TEN POWERS OF PEOPLE

It was not too long ago that the individual was looked upon by industry as a physical resource to be utilized like any other material resource to the maximum of its physical capacity for work. Labor was regarded as a commodity like oil, a source of physical energy. Over the last century, we have come to realize that men and women possess a productive potential that extends far beyond the limits of the their bodies and *physical energies*. We have seen in Japan a nation that has generated a formidable productive power by releasing and harnessing the *social and cultural energies* of its people—which are expressed as dedication, patriotism and loyalty to the company and the national economy. The progress of the United States over the last 200 years can be traced back to the unique ability of this country to awaken and release the *creative energies of the individual* and to become a nation of entrepreneurs seething with more creative energy and activity than any other in the world.

Thus we can identify three types or levels of energy in humans—the physical energy of their bodies, the social energy of a common member of the group, and the psychological energy of the unique individual. Every human being possesses these three levels of energy in some measure. Every company taps and utilizes these different energies to some extent. Our aim is to release all these energies to the maximum extent possible and channel them to achieve maximum results for your company.

The extent to which these energies are tapped and utilized for work depends on three other important factors: attitudes, skills, and values. For each of the three levels of energy—physical, social, and psychological—there are attitudes, skills, and values that determine how much energy is released and how effectively it is channeled into work. These attitudes, skills, and values depend directly on the way we recruit, train, motivate, and direct the activities of our people. Together they combine to generate a multitude of powerful levers for energizing your company through people. This chapter examines ten graded powers of people. Let us begin with the known and the obvious and explore the ascending powers of people.

Physical Energy

What is the first thing you look for when you recruit new people? In the old days when railway contractors were hiring labor to lay tracks across the country, the bosses naturally looked for the biggest and strongest men available to cut the timber and lay the gauge. Few jobs these days demand that type of physical size or strength, but the physical health and energy of a person is just as important as it ever was. Yet it is surprising how few companies consciously look for energy when they recruit new people. Try thinking creatively, being enthusiastic and inspiring other people when you have a 102-degree fever, and you will understand the importance of physical energy.

That energy is the foundation for all physical work. The more abundant it is, the more lively and resilient the work. When that energy is lacking, work becomes a drag and a strain. It slows to a crawl and leads to frustration, errors and waste. Add a little burst of fresh energy and work that was grinding picks up and is easily accomplished. Recruiting people with high levels of energy and good health makes everything a company does that much easier and more successful. How are you going to have a high-energy company without high-energy people?

The first thing that struck Neal Amarino when he joined Vipont Pharmaceuticals was "the energy of the people. There is a different feeling . . . an excitement . . . an air of expectation about what is to come." Many of the fast-growing companies we have seen go out of their way to look for people with the energy needed for quick action and nonstop change. AMRE looks for high-energy salespeople. Linear Technology wants chip designers who are not only technically qualified, but who have the energy and persistence to push their designs all the way through and make sure that they get translated into products. "In order to make these products successful, you just have to pour your energy into them," says designer Tom Redfern. "We look for people whose designs are translated into production, not just those that like the work they do," says Carl Nelson. "Did he get his products out into production? Does he have the energy and drive to make things work?" Gartner Group even selects computer industry researchers for their energy level.

According to Jim Perkins, chief personnel officer, from the beginning Federal Express "attracted people with a very high energy level." High energy starts at the top with the management team, says Fred Smith:

> You have to put high-energy people in the key positions. You've got to have an enormous amount of energy . . . The watchword at FedEx is action. God knows you can get a lot of people who can identify problems. The trick is to find that one jewel who can solve one. That's why you need that high energy level, a penchant for action.

Compensation

Getting energetic people is the first essential step. Getting them to express that energy in work is the second, and that has a lot to do with compensation. There is a great deal of truth in the old adage, "You get what you pay for." We have seen companies invent many clever ways to get more from their people than they give, but very few prove more resourceful than their people in maintaining a fair balance between work and rewards.

Federal Express wants every employee in every department to go that extra mile to cut an extra minute off delivery times. The company pays well across the board for that effort. "Our people concept is simple," Perkins says. "If you take care of the people, they will deliver the service efficiently with a smile. We believe that the profits will somehow come as a result of that." Couriers in major markets earn between $30,000 and $40,000. "We review our pay structures constantly," says vice president of hub operations, Karl Birkholz. "You can lose key people by insensitivity. We share the profits with all employees. We even treat part-time employees the same as full-timers in terms of the benefits they receive—medical, profit-sharing bonuses, and so on. This policy has really reduced absenteeism and turnover." In a company that employees about 18,000 part-time people, that policy represents a sizable commitment.

For compensation to release people's physical energies for work, it must be perceived as fair. We have been in companies with high absenteeism, high turnover and low morale that never seem to make the connection between pay and performance. Even when companies realize they are losing people because they pay poorly, many think, "Why should I pay more when I can always get new people to take their place?" The real cost in terms of money and management time spent in recruiting and training new people almost always exceeds the savings from keeping salaries low. But the real cost is in morale and the energy output of those who accept low pay.

Compensation should be *perceived* as fair, which means it is not enough that it *is* fair. Some companies offer low pay and excellent benefits that more than make up for the low base. But offering good benefits along with low base pay usually does not work. Employees tend to look on base salary as the measure of their worth and bonuses and profit sharing as something extra, based on their performance and the company's. Other companies offer excellent benefits but forget to "sell" them to employees, who often do not fully realize the value of what is offered unless it is fully explained. Rich Pagliari of Elizabeth Carbide in Pennsylvania explained how he was losing skilled workers to his competitors who offered higher base salaries, only to have many of them come back to reapply for their old jobs after they realized that the benefits Elizabeth offered were far superior. Now Pagliari educates all his employees about exactly what the benefits package contains and what it is worth to them.

Pay and Performance

Beyond fairness, there are higher dimensions to compensation, which can release many times greater energy than equal pay for equal work. These dimensions are linked with people's social aspirations to rise in life and their psychological aspirations for personal growth, of which income is taken as an outward expression. Although these dimensions are more rightly categorized higher in the progression of powers, they are discussed here for the sake of completeness.

Compensation releases a lot more energy when it is tied directly to performance. Many successful companies have gone through periods when their top salespeople earned more than their top executives. Aggressive 30-year-old salespeople at Gartner Group take home an average of $100,000 to $150,000 a year. Gartner's sales people receive a fixed salary that represents roughly 35% of their pay. The balance two-thirds is based on sales performance. The company says its salespeople outsell competitors 2 to 1.

But even more interesting is the pay package for the information researchers creating useful ideas in the bowels of Gartner's research division. "We pay more for analysts and get high-quality people," says senior vice president of sales, Rick Smith. Analysts' pay is based on 65% fixed salary and 35% performance-related bonus, which is directly linked to the financial success of the information services which each analyst works on. Gartner's rationale is that a researcher paid on the success of the information services he or she produces will be much more attuned and sensitive to customers' needs.

High pay is not confined to high-tech industries. AMRE is only too happy when a commissioned salesperson reaps an executive-sized paycheck. "The first thing we do to energize our people is make sure they have a chance to make a lot of money," says Bedowitz. The top AMRE salesperson last year earned $140,000, and the average was around $55,000 to $65,000. "A salesperson should make a minimum of $40,000 a year or he or she probably shouldn't be here." Randy Angelocci, vice president of sales, says, "Our salespeople are on straight commission. They have no limits. That brings out the best in everybody. The salespeople love the challenge of being able to make whatever they can."

Share the Wealth

The greatest power of compensation is released when the growth of the individual and the growth of the company are very closely linked with one another. If there is one belief that fast-growing companies hold in common, it is the dictum, "Share the wealth." This principle has had a lot to do with Expeditors International's explosive growth over the past five years. Every branch manager has invested personally in the local branch company he or she manages and receives, in addition to salary, 22% of the pretax operating income of the office, to take home and/or distribute to employees as an incentive. One implication of this arrangement is that if the branch office fails to collect payment from a customer, 22% of the loss comes out of the manager's incentive pay. Dave Lincoln, controller, stressed the importance of this system: "We haven't lost any key people that we wanted to keep. The reason is the branch compensation program. If you are successful, you are rewarded. We reward those who have produced."

A point often comes in the growth of a privately owned company, when the founders are tempted to take their company public to raise additional capital or simply to capitalize their own assets in the company. A less common motive, but one that can have considerable impact on the future performance of the company, is the ability of public corporations to offer stock options to employees that may appreciate rapidly as the company grows.

Many private corporations that do not need the capital may still benefit immensely from opening up ownership to a larger number of employees. When Vipont Pharmaceuticals started to grow rapidly in the early 1980s, the company was not in a position to offer lucrative salaries to attract top talents. So it coupled a modest pay package with an aggressive stock-option plan that has made many employees shareholders and some of them quite wealthy. Today 30% of the shares are owned by Vipont employees. Michelle Morgan, director of Marketing at Vipont Pharmaceuticals summed up a feeling frequently expressed by people in these companies: "Sharing in the profits, we not only make money for shareholders, we also make money for ourselves. This has had a big role. It gives people a common goal and purpose."

"It is no secret," says Linear Technology's Robert Swanson, "successful companies . . . share the wealth. We drive our people here. This is a big time business with big money to be made. Financial rewards are a big part of what this company is about."

Until two years ago, every Linear employee owned stock in the company. Every employee was given 100 shares of stock at the end of his or her first and second year with the company. "We wanted everybody to have a piece of the action." Last year the company funded a profit-sharing program based on salary, in which everyone participates as well. It also gave bonuses to both hourly and salaried employees. Linear's vice president of Operations, Brian Hollins, says, "Profit-sharing has been a very important incentive. We give stock options which make people feel like they have a piece of the rock."

When Gartner Group was founded, one third of the equity was set aside for distribution to employees other than the founders. "Typically the entrepreneur is sole proprietor and over time he might provide some equity shares to key people," Gartner explained. "But we allocated a third of the equity from day one to a broad spectrum of partners beyond myself. That's a big chunk of equity that was reserved for people who had nothing to do with founding the company." At the time of our study, virtually every analyst in the company was a shareholder.

Think about the structure of compensation in your company. How effectively does it release the physical energies of your people for hard work? Does it sufficiently motivate them to perform at peak levels of enthusiasm? Does it create a direct and proportionate link between the financial success of the company and the financial rewards for your people?

Exceptions to the Rule

How simple the world would be if everything were that simple. But there is a corollary to every good principle, and a good corollary often contradicts the principle it is intended to modify. Such is the case with "share the wealth." Good compensation is not only or always energizing. There are at least two fairly common situations in which it can also be deenergizing. The first is a well-known phenomenon in fast-growing public companies which have done exactly what we have described so far in this chapter. It is the phenomenon of satisfaction. Some people who join a company before or during the early stages of its takeoff reap such enormous financial rewards from being in the right place at the right time that they become satisfied and level off.

Most of the fast-growing companies we have investigated have either had that experience or are now in the midst of it. They find they have promoted people to high-level positions at an early stage who either do not have the skills to support the further growth of the company or do not have the drive to make it happen, because they are satisfied. One CEO was frank enough to raise the question as to whether he or any of the original founders were really competent to take the company to the next plateau. Another expressed his frustration at not being able to motivate his second-level executives to take up part of the burden of energizing the company for further growth.

Yet in most cases we found that the loss of motivation was not entirely or even primarily due to the enormous rewards. There are many senior executives of fast-growing companies who have become millionaires in their early thirties, yet still enjoy their work immensely and feel highly motivated to make the company grow further. Very often the problem is not too much money, but too much stress from an underorganized organization or too much pressure and too little freedom from an overbearing CEO. Sometimes it is simply because the demands of growth have left no time for the executive to acquire the skills needed to keep up with it. Any of these situations can be remedied, if the people involved recognize their source and are willing to make the effort.

The second exception to the principle of paying more is not so easily resolved. The corollary states: if a person is paid more than his capacities or his sense of responsibility justify, he may not only level off but even become a disturbing and troublesome influence in the company. We have seen this phenomenon time and again at every level from senior executives to clerks and laborers. Yet surprisingly few managers recognize the danger. When a person is paid more than their abilities or commitment justify, some individuals work that much harder to compensate and justify the higher pay. But others consciously or unconsciously justify it not by working harder, but by finding real or imaginary grievances against the company and its management. They complain and foment discontent among their colleagues. We once asked a personnel consultant to think back over all the cases he could remember of problem employees and ask himself whether they were individuals who were paid more or less than they probably deserved. To his own surprise, he replied that virtually all were paid too much.

Training Energizes

Think of the last time you attempted a task for which you lacked the necessary skill—cooking a meal if you are not a cook, calculating your family's tax returns, struggling through a computer program you have never used before, typing a letter when your secretary was out sick, or trying to figure out how the new phone system works. You are asked to interview a job candidate and feel awkward or uncomfortable, because you have never been trained in how to conduct an interview. You are asked to make a presentation before a large group for the first time. You are asked to develop a strategic plan and are ashamed to tell your board or your boss that you do not know how. Life can suddenly become frustrating, annoying, grating on the nerves, even terrifying.

Now think of the last time you were taught or taught yourself a new skill. You took a day off to read the software manual and understand how that program works. In half a day you are up and running and humming along like a pro. You read the instructions for the phone system and discovered to your surprise that the world is rational after all. The system does more than you ever dreamed of. You took a course in interviewing or presentation skills and learned enough small tricks the first day to feel relaxed and fairly proficient. *Learning a new skill is energizing.* It can even be exhilarating. Exercising a skill in which you are competent generates a sense of confidence and mastery. It makes any work enjoyable, even exciting.

Now think of all the people in your company who have never been trained to do all the things they are doing. How much agony could have been avoided? How much energy could have been released by creating a structured situation where learning generates a sense of accomplishment and mastery, instead of frustration and failure? Think of all the people even now who are doing tasks for which they do not possess all the knowledge and skills needed to do it perfectly and feel good about their work, even if they will not admit it out of pride or insecurity. A tremendous amount of energy can be released in these people by giving them training to make the exercise of their skills perfect and enjoyable.

Dave Gray is a middle-aged middle manager at Nedlloyd Lines' London office. When Rick de Rooy was transferred from San Francisco to become CEO of Nedlloyd's U.K. operations, his predecessor described Gray as a troublesome, pessimistic, complaining type who was a thorn in everyone's side, a poor worker and a bad manager. Six months later de Rooy met his predecessor at a corporate gathering and their conversation came to Gray. The previous CEO was surprised to hear that Gray was still with the company. But he was downright shocked to hear that de Rooy considered Gray one of the company's best motivated and most productive employees. De Rooy went on to explain that over the last six months, he had reassigned Gray from his administrative position to assume responsibility for installation and operation of the company's new computerized information system, a job for which Gray had absolutely no prior training or experience. When we met Gray a few months later, we found an exuberant and enthusiastic individual behaving like he had just had a wonderful time on his first date with a beautiful girl. He had just completed a training course on the new computer system and could not say enough about how much he loved the company and his new job. Learning a new skill has that much power.

Dave Gray's experience is one instance of a truth that IBM has known for decades. Last year while we were at Marriott's 1,500-room resort hotel in San Diego for a conference, half the hotel was filled with IBM production workers and managers being retrained for positions in marketing. A total of 10,000 IBM employees went through the program. IBM spends more on corporate training for its people than the entire budget of Harvard University—$750 million or 1.5% of sales last year—and probably generates more professional managers than all the business schools put together. Ex-IBM people occupy high positions in both mature and fast-growing companies in virtually every industry, because the company trains its people so well.

Embassy Suites Hotels is rated extremely high by consumers for quality of service and the efficiency and courtesy of their staff. A guiding principle of the company is that minimum wage employees possess the ability to perform well in higher-level positions, provided they are given proper training. "Historically hotel managers have believed that minimum-wage workers aren't smart or ambitious," says president Harvey Feldman. "With training and experience, they all have the curiosity and intelligence to go beyond making beds."[1] Embassy Suites has a pay system that is based on skills to encourage continuous training. The company offers a variety of skill courses and awards pay increases to those who pass them. Thus, the company mobilizes two powerful levers—compensation and training—for releasing greater energy from its people.

Training not only energizes people. It makes good financial sense too. A few years ago Motorola substantially increased its investment in training production workers on quality and problem solving. Overall the expenditure on training rose to $90 million, equal to about 2.6% of payroll or close to 1% of sales. The results have been dramatic, says the company's training head, Bill Wiggenhorn. "We've documented the savings from the statistical process control methods and problem-solving methods we've trained our people in. *We're running a rate of return of about 30 times the dollars invested.*"[2]

Three Levels of Skills

As there are graded levels or methods of compensation, there is an ascending gradation of skills that can release and direct the expression of people's energies. The first level consists of physical skills (e.g., driving or typing) and technical skills (e.g., product knowledge, repairing a product, operating equipment) that release and direct people's physical energies. Interpersonal skills (e.g., selling, negotiating, communicating, motivating) and organizational skills (e.g., systematizing, coordinating) are of a higher level and are more powerful energizers. The highest level skills are mental (e.g., managing, planning, problem solving) and psychological (e.g., understanding and judging people, giving attention, pleasing others). Although the interpersonal, organizational, and higher-order skills possess a greater capacity to release and harness energy, for purposes of completeness, we refer to them all at this point in the progression of powers for energizing people.

Which skills should we train for? Train for every physical, technical, interpersonal, organizational, managerial and psychological skill required to be the very best in your business.

How much or how often should we train our people? As much and as often as possible, and keep on training them. There is no more powerful way to energize your people and your company for nonstop growth.

Run down a quick checklist in your mind. Just list all the problems—big ones and small ones—that you encounter in day-to-day business with your employees, your managers, your customers, and your vendors. Nothing is too small for the list. If you scrutinize that list, a vast majority of those problems can be traced back to someone who is not properly educated or trained. Take basic things like documentation, for instance. Listen Up was being constantly harassed by its inability to maintain accurate inventory records. No matter how often the inventory was recounted and set right, it quickly got out of balance again. On investigation the company traced a major part of the problem to the fact that nearly 25% of the sales receipts filled out by its salespeople contained errors, so the inventory system was continuously being fed erroneous information. What the company needed was not a new inventory system, but better training on basic documentation skills for its technically qualified sales staff. Physical skills are that critical to every business.

Think of the best salesperson in your company. Think of other salespeople who perform at an average or below-average level. What would be the impact on the profitability of your company, if every average salesperson could be raised to 80 or 90% of the level achieved by the best and if every poor performer could be lifted to the level of today's average? Wayne Puntel of Audio Craft runs one of the most profitable retail chains in his industry. He completed the exercise described at the end of this chapter and was shocked by the answer he came up with—a potential 100% increase in profitability. Actually, during the next six months Puntel's profits soared 40%. What about your company?

Now suppose you completed the same analysis for your production workers, design people, marketing, finance, and managerial staff. What would the impact be on their energy and morale? What would be the impact on corporate revenues and profits? Double, as for Audio Craft? Or a 30-fold return on investment, as for Motorola? Or more?

No Time for Training

As we went from one fast growing company to another, we were somewhat surprised at how uncommon formal training programs are and how seriously their absence has retarded the growth of these businesses. Time and again we heard people say, "There is no formal training," and in the next breath remark, "My biggest fear looking at our growth is how are we going to continue to get the types of people and the numbers we need." In our surveys of American and European companies, a shortage of skilled people and no time for training were among the most frequently cited characteristics of rapid growth.

Companies that continue to grow over long periods of time put in place the training systems needed to generate highly skilled people from within, rather then remain dependent on the whims and fluctuations of the marketplace. Otherwise, sooner or later they discover that the pace of growth outstrips the availability of qualified and experienced people. Federal Express had such systems in place from day one. "The easiest thing that management can do is put training on the back burner," says Birkholz. "But training should be right up front ahead of everything else. I am only as efficient as my people make me." Every new employee goes through an extensive training program. To provide a high quality of training effectively and efficiently, the company utilizes interactive video. This enables employees to learn at their own pace and guide themselves through learning sessions simply by touching the screen. The same method is used for constantly updating the skills of more experienced people. Flight crew members are required to complete a training course every time they change positions on a plane. Normally the course requires about 21 days of training time. By putting the course on interactive video, that time is expected to be reduced to 16 days. If Federal Express has found ways to train its people while in the process of growing from zero to more than $4 billion in 16 years, other fast growing companies can too, and need to if they really want to keep growing.

One common attitude regarding training is summed up in the words, "We cannot train the people we need. Our business is unique. The only way for people to learn our business is to spend two or three years on the job and learn it from the bottom up." In a country where we train physicists to smash atoms and physicians to give us new livers and hearts, it is surprising how many companies believe that their business is unique. Yet the most successful companies in every industry are companies that believe that they can teach virtually anyone their business, given the time, interest, and minimum capacity.

If you have been thinking that yours is a business that defies formal training, think about this. The fundamental principle of education is that it is possible to teach the next generation in a few years the essence of what the entire society or world has learned about a subject over many centuries. The fundamental principle of formal training is that it is possible to teach any capable person in a relatively short period of time the knowledge and skills for a job which others have acquired through long years of work experienced—if not completely and 100%, then at least to the point where they will be functionally competent with a minimum of on-the-job experience. Formal training is not only much faster, it is also more complete and comprehensive in scope than learning from experience. When you learn from experience, you learn only about those things which are presented to you, not about all the other problems or solutions that are possible; and you learn only from those who are physically near you, not from all those who have acquired knowledge on the subject who you do not know or cannot meet.

Even on-the-job or apprenticeship training can be much more or less energizing, depending upon how it is done. Many companies look upon a long apprenticeship training as an indispensable tradition, when often it has degenerated into a dead habit. Kennedy and Bowden Machine Co. found that this is exactly what had happened to their apprenticeship training program for toolmakers. "The apprentices were demotivated. They were never given tasks beyond their capacity, which means beyond what they had already done before. They were getting all the grunt jobs that nobody else wanted to do," Ray Kennedy explained. Under heavy pressure to speed up deliveries, Kennedy assigned each apprentice to an experienced toolmaker and asked the toolmakers to provide the apprentices with challenging tasks that were within their level of competence to perform. Kennedy said, "I walked around the shop and was really surprised at the work the apprentices were able to do under supervision. I myself probably would not have had the confidence to assign those tasks to such inexperienced people. But the toolmakers knew what they could do better." The attitude of the apprentices changed dramatically overnight. They felt stimulated and challenged. Employee turnover stopped. The result was a vast increase in the productivity of the shop, a steep fall in overtime costs and better on-time delivery to customers. Kennedy released some of the latent capacity that was in his people all the time.

Buzz Szitas is chief financial officer at C & J Industries. Recently Buzz stood up in front of a few hundred members of his industry and told them: "You have probably never heard this from a financial person before, but my advice to all of you is to go back to your companies and spend a lot more money on training your people. The returns are really phenomenal." Buzz speaks with conviction, because he speaks from experience. When Harold Corner was engineering C & J's turnaround, he hired a director of human resources and carried out an in-depth analysis of the skills required for every job in the company. The director then compared the job requirements with actual skill levels of employees and developed a training needs analysis for each individual. He found that most of the skills needed could be acquired through courses at the local community college at very low cost. This aggressive training program has enabled C & J to grow from 185 to 325 people over the last two years.

Physical Values

In Chapter Seven, we classified corporate values under three different categories according to the dominant type of energy which they release when implemented. Among the physical values are listed cleanliness, orderliness, punctuality, regularity, safety, quality, and several others. When an individual or a company focuses intently on the implementation of any of these values, a tremendous amount of physical energy is released.

Cleanliness

There is something about cleanliness that defies explanation. With rare exception, companies which sustain high rates of growth and high levels of profit seem to have an obsession with cleanliness. It is not a matter of industry or even country for that matter. We have observed the same phenomenon in India and Indiana, in computer manufacturing and shoe making. Anheuser Busch, Coca-Cola, Disney, DuPont, IBM, Intel, Marriott, McDonald's, and Merck are just a few of the companies that have lost all sense of proportion when it comes to cleanliness.

Paul Maestri insisted on cleanliness even back when the company was operating out of a trailer and doing repairs under an oak tree. Today you could almost eat off the floors in P.A.M.'s repair shops. The company's 700 trucks and 1,500 trailers are maintained the same way. Everything is immaculate. The same is true of the offices. Everyone is expected to leave their desk clean every night. How do people respond to cleanliness? Nancy Johncox, one of P.A.M.'s four original employees says, "It gives people a sense of pride. It makes the drivers feel like professionals."

"Cleanliness has been a value at Federal Express since the very beginning," says Carole Presley, senior vice president of marketing and corporate communications. "It generates a feeling of security and confidence. You have to work hard at it every day." That effort releases energy.

But even more striking and more inexplicable is what we have observed in companies which make an effort to improve dramatically the level of cleanliness in their facilities. People get energized and money pours in. That is what happened to Listen Up when Walt Stinson ordered a wholesale cleaning of all the company's showrooms, offices, and warehouses a few years ago. "The whole company got charged up, energized. And quite unexpectedly we received a lot of money from different sources which we really needed at the time but had not counted on receiving." Sounds ridiculous? Why not try cleaning and see.

Examine any work area where quality is poor, accidents frequently occur or morale is a problem. Chances are it is also dirty. When Iacocca took over at Chrysler, the company's plants were seething with every variety of trouble—labor unrest, gambling, prostitution, even a murder. And they were filthy too!

A few years ago we met a consultant who specializes in turning around near-bank-rupt companies and making them solvent again. What is the very first thing he does when he goes into a new company? He has the entire place painted and made spotlessly clean. Imagine spending precious dollars on painting the walls when creditors are knocking at or down the doors. But it works for him.

Orderliness

Orderliness is another physical value with a great power to energize work and people. Remove a little orderliness and watch what happens. Work gets bogged down and loses momentum. You spend time searching for a file or an object and end up exasperated or exhausted. Add a little orderliness to a chaotic situation, and it feels like a breath of fresh air. People relax and cheer up, and work flows more smoothly. Orderliness has a greater power than does cleanliness, because it requires mental as well as physical effort to put things in a rational order. How many companies have we been in where a salesperson cannot find a product brochure for the customer or the service technician cannot locate a repair manual he needs to fix a machine.

An inspector from the U.S. Department of Transportation, who asked the service manager for the maintenance file on one of P.A.M.'s 700 trucks, was virtually speech-less when it was produced in less than 30 seconds from a well-ordered filing system. That is how unusual orderliness is in the companies he visits. "Cleanliness and orderliness help to coordinate work. They are good for morale. They also give a good impression to the customer," says P.A.M.'s manager of vehicle maintenance, Roy Strode. From the office of the chairman and CEO down to the level of the repair shop, from the files to the secretary's drawers and the executive's briefcase, orderliness is hard to come by. Install it where it is absent and energy flows.

Safety

Safety is another powerful value that can release abundant physical energy, but that also has the capacity to release higher energies as well. Safety requires a clean and orderly environment, as well as well-timed and disciplined actions. It takes a lot more effort to maintain an accident-free environment than it does to maintain a clean and orderly one, but the resulting release of energy is even greater. One of the strategies that Waltz Brothers employed to energize their company for a quick turnaround was to focus on improving safety in the plant. They established a safety committee on which every employee in the company was asked to serve for three-month periods. The committee got everyone actively involved, brought down the accident rate to almost zero, and benefited from lower insurance charges.

Some companies, like P.A.M., have made safety into a real motivator. P.A.M. presents safety awards to drivers who maintain accident-free records. Those that go a year without any accident join an exclusive club called "Randy's Rangers" and get diamond rings. Each additional accident-free year, another diamond is added to it. When new trucks are purchased with more comfortable driver compartments and other improvements, the rangers are first to get them. The most energizing thing about safety is that it says to employees "we care." That releases not only physical energy, but psychological energy as well.

How much energy does your company release in its people by implementing values like cleanliness, orderliness, and safety or other physical values? Why not increase the level of commitment and implementation to raise corporate energies to their peak?

Social Recognition

Physical energy, material compensation, training on physical skills, and implementation of physical values form the foundation. By themselves they can be great sources of energy. Yet by comparison with what lies beyond, they are limited, the least powerful of the hidden potentials of people. But if this foundation is not properly laid, it is difficult for the higher powers to emerge and express in work. Physical energy and skill ensure that the people have the basic capacities needed for work. Fair compensation provides the motive for expressing those capacities in work. Physical values raise pride and precision in work to a far higher level.

But the individual is more than just an animated and intelligent machine functioning independently of others. Each person has a social personality that responds to attention and recognition from others, that cares—whether we admit it or not—what others feel and think about us, that wants to be accepted and appreciated, that is motivated to equal or excel with reference to our peers, that aspires to be more than it is today. Companies that recognize the social needs of their people and create opportunities for the fulfillment of those needs release powerful energies in their people, energies that material incentives alone cannot bring out.

The simplest way to tap these energies is to create an external standard by which people can evaluate their own performance. Regardless of the level of compensation, people like to feel that they possess the competence to do a good job. Yet surprisingly often they have no clear indication of how they are performing at all, because no one has ever told them or created a measure by which they could assess themselves.

Jerry Kowitz, the owner of Jerry's Audio chain in Phoenix, was quite dissatisfied by the performance of one of his salesmen and took great efforts to try to improve it through training programs and frequent personal discussions. In spite of these efforts, the salesman continued to perform far below the level of his peers. After some time Jerry started posting a list on the bathroom wall every week of the sales made by each salesperson. To his great surprise, in a few weeks the poor performer started improving. He rose from the bottom to the middle ranks and then to within the top 25% of the sales force. Perplexed by this sudden change, Jerry called him in and asked for an explanation of his remarkable improvement. The salesman replied: "I was really quite satisfied with my earlier level of performance. I was making enough money to be comfortable. But when you started posting that list, I just could not stand to see my name at the bottom week after week."

Some time ago, Walt Stinson introduced a salesperson of the month award at Listen Up. The award consisted of a bonus and a letter from Walt to the salesman's family informing them of what a great job the salesman was doing. For the first nine months the same salesman won the award every month. Then Walt decided that writing home every month to the same family had become a little redundant, so he stopped sending the letters. The salesman later complained how disappointed he was when the letters stopped going home. "You just don't know how much it meant to me and my family to get that letter every month. It made them proud and me happy."

If a list on the wall or a letter home can have that much impact, how much more powerful can be awards and celebration programs that generate widespread social recognition for high achievement. As AMRE grew bigger, management found it more and more difficult to keep in touch with people through informal means. So the company has established a host of social programs to recognize and reward high performance, including a President's Club, plaques and diamond rings for top salespeople, and awards and prizes for production and administrative personnel. The firm also goes to considerable expense to bring together employees and their spouses—some 1,300 people last year—from offices around the country once a year for a lavish annual Christmas party.

The recognition and celebrations at AMRE are not just hype. They reflect a basic philosophy and understanding. Bedowitz explains:

> Ideas and organization are worthless without the people to carry them out. People got us to where we are today. People are going to take us to where we will be tomorrow. Our value is to take care of the people . . . One of the keys to our long term success is that we have fun and we encourage our people to have fun. We look at the better performing offices and see that they are the ones that are having more fun. If the

receptionist isn't smiling, we know there is a problem in the office. We try to make sure that everyone has fun. We like to think we are a family.

Entrepreneurs are often the independent type. Some have difficulty appreciating just how important social recognition can be to their employees, little realizing how much they appreciate the nod of recognition from the board of directors, the smile of appreciation from their own family members or even a complimentary word from their own subordinates! The power and appeal of that recognition are so great that every year a good number of highly successful business executives are lured by it to accept honorary posts as presidents of industrial associations, so that they can tour the country and lobby in Washington without pay on behalf of their own competitors, while their own businesses suffer from neglect back home! That is the power of social recognition.

Career Paths

We referred in Chapter One to the close relationship between the growth of a company and the opportunities which it creates for the growth of its people. Companies that take conscious efforts to help their people are the ones that grow the fastest, the farthest, and the longest. Linking personal compensation to corporate profits is one way in which this is accomplished. Creating opportunities for continuous promotion and career development is another.

Federal Express excels at helping people grow. "I think the best thing we do for our people is the program of promotion from within," says Perkins. "Those promoted from within understand the culture and have been able to grow with the company. There is a tremendous amount of pride. Employees realize that they can achieve their personal objectives by helping the corporation achieve its objectives." The company never looks outside for people until it has conducted an exhaustive search for qualified company employees. More than 85% of the jobs are filled in house.

Searching for talent among 65,000 employees is no easy task. If you visit the Memphis hub late in the night, you will find employees glancing at the bulletin boards that list job opportunities in the Federal Express organization. Any qualified employee is free to apply for any job. The company also has a system called PRISM, which enables a manager to access information about an employee from any computer terminal. Via the terminal, the manager can update employee information or even effect a promotion. The idea is to eliminate the burden of paperwork, which often spoils performance appraisal systems, so proper attention is given to employee career development.

Employee expectations can be a serious deterrent to proper career planning. How many talented performers are promoted to managerial positions before either they or their supervisors realize that their talent for sales or production does not necessarily mean that they have the talent to make good managers. To minimize this problem, Federal Express offers a course on what it is like to be a manager. Any aspirant to a management position can take the course and decide if being a manager is really what he or she wants. After taking the course, some decide that it is not and save both themselves and the company frustration down the line. Even if the path to management is barred, there are always opportunities in other departments. In fact, Federal Express sometimes moves people around to introduce variety and reduce the burnout from job monotony. Customer service agents can apply for anything from an hour a day up to two years full-time work in other departments for a change of pace.

Organizational Values and Skills

Organizational values such as teamwork and communication bring out higher-level energies, both because they demand considerably greater effort and skill to establish and maintain and because they appeal to deeper-seated sentiments in people and generate more intense satisfaction. The effort required to implement physical values is partially physical, that is, based on hard work, and partially organizational, that is, based on discipline, systematic functioning, coordination, and so on. The skills required are also partly physical—knowing how to clean a window without leaving streaks or how to design and manufacture a product properly for quality and reliability—and partly organizational—knowing how to organize information or design an effective system.

By comparison, the effort required to implement organizational values is primarily organizational or social—dealing with groups of objects, activities, departments, systems, and people. It is also partially psychological—instructing, guiding and motivating people. The skills required for implementing organizational values are of a higher order. They are not only organizational, but also interpersonal and psychological, for example, giving a suggestion, receiving an instruction, and understanding people's attitudes and motives and the dynamics of group interactions.

Implementing organizational values is also more rewarding and enjoyable. When communication and cooperation between people, departments, and levels of the company are better, people feel closer, more united and harmonious, more secure and more identified with the organization. These values touch deeper springs of energy in people and generate greater intensity.

Teamwork

Implementing organizational values has the power to release and channel great energy, regardless of how large or how small your business may be. John Stoneback, CEO of J & M Incorporated in Cleveland, is a zealous proponent of teamwork. John founded his precision machining company 23 years ago. Until 3 years ago, J & M had sales of just a few hundred thousand dollars a year, but was profitable enough to make John quite comfortable. Then John's daughter and son-in-law joined the company, and suddenly the little nest egg was not big enough any more. So John decided to expand his company. One of the main instruments he used was teamwork.

Stoneback implemented teamwork through all the five stages outlined in the previous chapter. First, he made teamwork the first and highest priority—*commitment*. He got all his people involved in improving the company and working together in partnership—*structure*. He introduced a profit-sharing plan that gave his employees a concrete sense of ownership in the company and a 40% share of the company's net income. He also conducted a survey asking his people to rate each other on their spirit of cooperation—*systems*. He drew up a plan to develop the interpersonal skills of every manager and supervisor and conducted training programs on team building. As a result of all these efforts, absenteeism decreased dramatically, while productivity, quality, and on-time delivery improved. Over the last three years his company has grown 5.5 times in size to $1.5 million and has business in hand that could double its size again over the next two years.

Bill Hockenberger is president of Precision Grinding and Manufacturing Corporation in Rochester, New York, a $10 million company with 125 employees. Over a three-year period Bill struggled to put together a management team that really worked. In the process he made three separate attempts to bring in people who could work together and he failed three times. Finally he hired two psychologists to assist him with the task of building a solid management team. They started working with the management team and later extended their efforts to include other managers and supervisors. Bill believes that this successful effort is directly responsible for his company's 25% increase in revenues and 50% increase in profits over the last year.

Teamwork was also the engine that propelled the growth of Elizabeth Carbide over the last one year. The company employs 170 people and has sales of $13 million. In recent years it opened several new production plants. A year ago, owner Rich Pagliari became concerned that the growth was having a negative impact on morale and people relationships. "As you get bigger, communication becomes a problem," says Pagliari. So he sent 21 managers and supervisors to a Dale Carnegie course on team building and made efforts to improve communication and cooperation within and between his three plants. During the year his company's sales and profits both grew by another 25%. Pagliari attributes it directly to the team-building effort.

All the evidence suggests that high levels of teamwork and rapid growth go together. In our survey of U.S. companies cited earlier, high energy and high levels of teamwork were the two most common characteristics reported during periods of rapid growth. In addition, 76% of companies surveyed reported that during the period when teamwork and cooperation were at peak levels in their company, the company was also growing very rapidly. In other words, *teamwork is not just a characteristic of rapid growth, it can generate that growth.*

Communication

Communication and teamwork go together. They are both powerful energizers. Communication is a key value at Federal Express, where a corporate television network—*system*—has been established to facilitate rapid and direct communication between top management and every employee of the company about new products, competitive information, policies, plans, and so on. One feature of each 30 minute to 1-hour TV show is a live phone-in segment in which employees' questions and comments are answered by senior executives—*structure*. There are also daily 5- to 7-minute newscasts that relate current company news. Fred Smith explains the company's *commitment* to communication this way:

> We try to empower our employees by keeping them well informed. But just as important, by listening to them. We've found that they have really terrific ideas about ways to improve productivity in their jobs, and about shaping policies that affect them. But we've also found that the company must provide the opportunity for employee input or we'll never benefit from it. So we've developed a variety of channels for listening to our employees.

For example, Federal Express conducts an annual employee attitude survey, which is a vital tool for helping managers discern potential problems in their work groups. Within six weeks after survey results are distributed, managers must meet with their staff and develop an action plan for dealing with every problem. Problems surface and problems are solved through survey feedback. The company's Guaranteed Fair Treatment policy is also designed for surfacing employee grievances. Any employee that is not satisfied by the response of his supervisor can pursue a path of appeal that ultimately leads to Fred Smith. Smith and Barksdale meet every week to review cases, many of which are referred to a board of review composed of the employee's own peers and empowered with the authority to overturn management decisions.

In-house studies at Federal Express have shown that employee morale is linked directly with quality of service. Stations with the highest service-performance records are those that have high morale, low absenteeism, and few accidents.

Real communication takes place only when people fully understand the why and wherefore for the instructions they receive and are given an opportunity to respond with questions or comments. At Federal Express "We explain to our employees why we do things," Perkins says. "Our employees understand and are motivated beyond the point where they perform activities just because the boss said do it. They understand why they are asked to do something."

The Mirror Approach

When Paul Maestri came back to restore the values at P.A.M., communication was at the center of his strategy. He reopened the direct lines of communication with his drivers and made himself personally accessible to deal with serious grievances. But even more important, he took steps to institutionalize this value at lower levels of the company through appropriate standards, structures, systems, and skills.

Maestri selected a new operations manager, Randy Berry, who was the very embodiment of the values Maestri believed in, particularly the value of teamwork. Berry understood the importance of listening to the drivers and started out by conducting training programs for all P.A.M. dispatchers to teach them the importance of listening and to provide them with the skills to do it effectively. For 30 to 60 days at a time, the drivers' only link with the company is over the phone. So Berry trained the dispatchers to listen carefully to the drivers' tone of voice and mood on the phone. Whenever the dispatchers detect the slightest problem, they have been trained to ask the drivers whether they need any help. Berry explains:

> You have to be a good listener. You have to listen to hear—not listen to argue. When we lost that approach for ten months, we had no lateral control of the drivers. The new management pressed the dispatchers for higher volumes and *didn't care about the people—only the results*. We weren't picking up and delivering on time. Driver morale went down and turnover increased. The dispatchers were not routing the drivers to ensure that they got home to their families every three weeks. The dispatchers were not relating to the drivers as people. I told the dispatchers to treat the drivers the way you would want to be treated yourself. Earn their respect. The general attitude of the drivers to the customers depends on how he feels about the company. It's a mirror image. The best way we can service our customers and be on time is to treat drivers well and see they feel good about P.A.M.

Berry also changed the *structure* of his department, assigning each driver to a specific dispatcher regardless of which territory the driver moved through, instead of shifting responsibility from one dispatcher to another as the drivers moved to different parts of the country. This fostered closer and more personal ties. In addition to defining a clear structure of responsibility and accountability from the dispatcher all the way to Maestri and to imparting the *skills* needed to make it work, P.A.M. also put in new *systems* to foster better communication. A voice mail system enables drivers to call in and leave or receive messages without tying up their time on the phone waiting for their dispatcher to be available. The result of focusing on teamwork and communication has been a dramatic reduction in P.A.M.'s problems and a fresh burst of energy and rapid growth.

THE HIGHER POWERS

The first seven strategies have focused on releasing the physical and social energies in people for maximum productivity and involvement in work. We now come to the third and highest category, strategies designed to bring out the psychological energies of every individual and encourage each of them to grow personally through their work. These strategies have the power to take any company to the top of its field and keep it there for decades.

Individuals are more than just physical workers or members of the group. They each possess their own unique talents, capacities, skills, aspirations, values, ideas, attitudes and feelings. The truly people-oriented company is not the one that treats everyone alike, even in a family sort of way. It is the company that recognizes the uniqueness of every person and provides ample opportunities for each individual to express that uniqueness creatively in their work—for their personal growth and for the growth of the company.

Recruiting for Higher Capacities

Recruiting people with good physical health and energy energizes the company's physical operations. Recruiting people with cheerful, expansive, outgoing personalities and good interpersonal skills energizes the company's relationships with its customers and vendors and relationships between people and departments within the corporation. Recruiting people with higher levels of education and mental energy energizes the company's creative activities in research, marketing, strategic thinking, organizational development, and other areas of innovation.

It is true that only a small part of what is taught or learned in college has even the faintest application in business. But it is also true that education builds up the personality of the individual. Mental training in critical analysis of problems, exposure to a phenomenal range of information on a wide variety of subjects, stimulation and development of mental faculties by the effort to learn, and development of skills acquired for oral and written communication of ideas and information broaden the scope and intensify the energy of personality of the educated person. Therefore, recruiting for education, even when it does not bring with it greater practical knowledge or job-related information, almost always brings greater capacity of the person for understanding, problem-solving, adaptability to change and personal growth. These are great resources.

Many companies recognize the irreplaceable contribution of education to the capacities of their people and encourage their employees to continuously seek further and higher levels of education throughout their careers. One medical representative we interviewed at Merck, Sharp & Dohme was in the process of acquiring his third masters degree since joining the company. AMRE not only encourages education, but has made it in some sense mandatory for its sales force. Every salesperson is required to read at least one book a month and submit a summary of it to management.

Unfortunately, not too many CEOs act on their own understanding of the importance of continuing education. Yet, those who do have acknowledged it as among the most important management decisions they have made. When Listen Up started to grow explosively, Walt Stinson realized that the business was growing beyond his capacities to manage. He made a decision that perhaps very few could bring themselves to. He decided that however much it might slow down the company's short-term growth, he was going to take time off to complement his technical background with an MBA, so that in the long run he would be able to keep growing as the company grew. After completing the MBA, Walt commented that, apart from proposing to his wife, it was the best decision he ever made.

Many other executives have expressed similar sentiments about their decision to attend a course to augment their knowledge and skills. Buzz Jensen, founder of Sound Advice in Phoenix, was feeling intimidated by the numbers on his company's balance sheet, because he did not have any formal training in accounting. So he enrolled in a night-school course on accounting for nonfinancial people and felt absolutely exhilarated by the sense of competence and accomplishment it gave him. Gary Ross, chairman of Ross Incineration Services, and Bill Cromling, president of Ross Transportation, expressed similar feelings after enrolling in a Dale Carnegie course to help them improve their interpersonal skills and ability to communicate with their people.

Experience

Generalizations risk sounding simplistic or self-evident, but our observation of fast growing companies prompts us to make one. Companies that are able to grow rapidly and sustain high rates of growth for considerable periods of time are companies managed by people who have been through it all before. Companies that encounter innumerable problems in the course of their growth are usually those who are unable to anticipate the demands of growth and provide for them in advance, because management lacks the previous experience to know what is coming.

Before founding AMRE, Steve Bedowitz worked for one of the largest construction companies in Texas and ran his own advertising agency, which gave him a broad exposure to the operations and problems of other growth companies. Robert Levin came as a CPA with nine years experience in the wholesale end of the home improvements business, which gave him a good understanding of inventory management and financial controls. This experience has enabled them to visualize the company's future growth, anticipate its needs in advance, and act to provide for them in time.

In 1985 when Bedowitz and Levin saw that business would double in a short period of time, during a slow period they decided to put in the next layer of management they would need six months down the line. If they had not done so, they figure they would have lost one year's growth. At the time of our visit to the company, they had recently recruited a new manager to head up the introduction of a new product group before the product had even been identified and at least half a year before it would be introduced into the market. That is the value of the experience they gained before starting the company.

Both education and experience have their place. The best strategy is to *recruit for education and experience wherever both are available, recruit for experience first wherever you desperately need it to get started or sustain growth, and recruit for education first wherever you are building for a bigger and better future.*

Managerial and Psychological Skills

To be an effective manager you have to understand people and how to motivate them. You have to understand organization and how to develop it. In fact, you have to understand all five components of the company—how they work, how they interact with and depend on each other, and how they can be energized. How many managers really qualify for their jobs on these criteria?

Many talented salespeople have been promoted to managerial positions, because they were the best in sales. Many engineers have been promoted to become managers of R&D or production, because they were technical experts. Many accountants have become controllers and even chief financial officers, because they were excellent accountants. Many senior executives have reached their positions, because they have been with the company for a long time and know all about its operations. All these people may possess a high level of knowledge and technical skill in their particular fields of specialization. But what exactly does being a dynamic sales person, a talented designer, a good production engineer, a brilliant accountant or a long-time employee have to do with understanding and motivating people? The same applies even to the CEO. On many occasions in the privacy of an executive office, we have heard CEOs ask questions like "What is my job?" and "Am I really qualified to run this company?" and "How do I learn how to be a good CEO?"

Regardless of whether it is the job of the production superintendent or the sales manager or the CEO, being a manager requires a wide range of skills that are not physical or technical in nature. A manager needs a host of mental and psychological skills like planning, prioritizing, analyzing and solving problems, goal setting, scheduling, exercising authority, decision making, time management, seeing work from a wider perspective, listening, coordinating, understanding, and judging people, which he or she may have acquired in the course of his or her specialized job or through long experience, but equally likely not at all. That is why IBM requires every manager in the company, including senior executives heading large divisions, to undergo a minimum of 40 hours a year of nontechnical training in interpersonal and managerial skills.

John Kaiser of Expeditors International has recognized the challenge which he and his company face as it continues to grow:

> It is difficult to find well-trained professionals in this industry. We try to educate our people and ourselves. We've tried to broaden our horizons. *Our challenge is not to know the business better, but to manage it better*. We are very much aware of a need for greater managerial sophistication. I am not sure that our present staff could run a $500 million company. We hope that as managers we will be able to grow. If you are top management, you have no one to nurture you. Possibly some of our younger managers have a better chance at running the company as a $500 million business, because they have formal education. When you get this big, it may be necessary to have both experience and education.

Earlier, we cited several examples to document the obvious importance of experience in managing a business. But what happens, as in Expeditor's case, if experienced people are not available in your company's specialized field or in the numbers required to fuel further growth? Our response is—*if you cannot find experience, create it*!

Accelerated Management Development

Small entrepreneurial companies suffer from a perpetual shortage of skilled and experienced managers to fill the new positions they create as they grow. Fast-growing midsized companies are continuously hampered and constrained by a lack of talented managers to fill their growing ranks. Nor does this situation exist only in companies up to a few hundred million dollars in size. Among the largest and most admired companies in the United States, there are many whose single greatest limitation to growth is a shortage of competent managers. Yet despite this fact, surprisingly few, even today, act on the truth that IBM proved half a century ago—any capable individual can be made into a competent manager through appropriate training.

Suppose just for a moment that every managerial position in your company could be filled by a person with the managerial competence of the CEO or senior executives? What would that do to the performance of your business? What would be the impact on product quality? service? punctuality? morale? decision making? revenues? profitability? Where would your company be today and a year from now if it possessed managerial expertise of that caliber? Think about it.

These questions are not as academic or utopian as they may at first seem. Ask yourself: What is the difference between a highly experienced senior executive and a young, well-educated MBA occupying a junior managerial position in sales, marketing, or product development? What does the experienced person have which the others lack? Three things: information, skill, and values. The experienced senior executive has acquired a tremendous amount of information about the industry, the history of the company, competitors, technology, and the like. The experienced person has also by sheer passage of time and practice acquired a range of skills in understanding, communicating and motivating people, analyzing and resolving problems, managing time and materials, and so on. Finally and most important, over the course of many years the executive has learned by experience the importance of corporate values like cleanliness, orderliness, punctuality, systematic functioning, coordination, respect for the individual, integrity, and so forth.

The question is whether these qualifications of the senior executive can be acquired all or in part through formal training. Information? Most certainly. Our entire educational system is geared up to cram us brim full of information, relevant or irrelevant, on virtually any subject under the sun. Just because the information which the senior executive possesses is not taught in any business school, does not mean it cannot be taught formally by the company itself. Skills? Most surely. If physicians can learn how to operate on the brain in medical school and aspiring actors and actresses can learn how to portray any emotion in drama classes, then basic managerial skills like problem solving, planning, decision making, delegating, giving instructions, negotiating, and managing time can be acquired through formal training—and they are by many people. Then what about corporate values? Definitely. Cultural and social values have been taught for millennia at home and by the church. The importance of corporate values like cleanliness, speed, teamwork, and service are being taught every day—only not to everyone, and not systematically.

Now suppose every young manager in your company could acquire in a year or even two the information, skills and values possessed by your senior executives to the extent of 90%, 80% or even 70%. How much more efficient, dynamic, energetic and profitable would your company be? How much greater would be its potentials for growth in the immediate future? Certainly to speak of a mere doubling or tripling of sales or profits grossly underestimates the potential this represents for most companies. Yet, the cost and effort required to build up that competence is well within the means of most companies to accomplish at their level. And if they do, they will certainly not be at that same level very long.

This is the guiding principle behind Federal Express's management development programs, which it first introduced in 1976, and the Leadership Institute which the company established to accelerate the development of managers to keep pace with the growth of the company. Federal Express has even conducted research to determine the profile of the successful manager and leader in its corporate environment. This program has enabled the company to promote relatively young managers to vice presidential positions.

Pygmalion Effect: The Power of Attitude

Education, experience, and managerial and psychological skills are tremendous strengths. Yet as great as these powers are, every CEO, every executive, every manager and supervisor possesses a capacity infinitely more powerful, which they can utilize without cost any time they choose or all the time, if they choose. This capacity by itself is enough to energize any business to double its performance. It is the power of personal attention.

Educators and psychologists have given a lot of thought and study to this power, because it is so important to the process of learning and personal development. They have even coined a phrase to describe it, the Pygmalion effect. The name is derived from George Bernard Shaw's play, *Pygmalion*, which formed the basis for the Broadway musical *My Fair Lady*. In the play, two linguistic experts, Professor Higgins and Colonel Pickering, successfully undertake an experiment to instruct a poor common flower girl, Eliza Doolittle, how to speak and conduct herself as a lady and member of the aristocracy. After the miraculous transformation has taken place, Eliza remarks with some bitterness to Colonel Pickering:

> The difference between a lady and a flower girl is not how she behaves, but how she's treated. I shall always be a flower girl to Professor Higgins, because he treats me as a flower girl and always will, but I know I can be a lady to you, because you always treat me as a lady and always will.[3]

In other words, our attitude and attention have the power to create in other people or bring forth from them capacities no one ever imagined they possess.

About 25 years ago two social scientists conducted an experiment in an elementary school to test for the Pygmalion Effect. They told the teachers in the school that they had developed a test which could identify late bloomers, poorly performing students with a high aptitude who would flower as high performers in later years. Actually the test was a measure of IQ. At the beginning of the school year, they administered the test, went back to their offices and randomly selected the names of 20% of the students in each class. Then they informed the teachers that these students were late bloomers. Eight months later they went back and measured the IQ of the students again. Guess which students showed the largest increase in IQ? Those whom the teachers had been told were late bloomers.

This experiment shows that the expectations or attitude of the teacher toward the students had a significant impact on the students' performance and even on their intelligence! Over the last quarter century, the same experiment has been administered in many different settings, including a training institute for welders in Sweden. Here the instructors were informed that their test would identify students with an innate talent for welding! Sure enough at the end of the year, the students which had been randomly identified had made the most progress.

If the power of attention can raise the IQ of young students and improve the skill of welders, it can improve the performance of every employee in your company. You as a manager, as an individual, possess that power and can exercise it to bring out the hidden potentials and develop the capacities of your people. Your managers and their subordinates also possess that power and can in turn use it to help their own people flower. In fact, if you look closely at companies that continue to perform at high levels year after year, you will find that these are companies which knowingly or unknowingly believe in the power of attention and encourage their managers to shower it on their people for the growth of those people and the growth of the company.

Federal Express's Karl Birkholz describes just such an attitude: "One thing that has helped us throughout all this pressure of rapid growth has been an undying dedication to making sure we pay attention to the needs of our people. . . . You have to teach your managers to know your people. The better you know them, the better you can motivate them. That is the manager's job." Jim Riedmeyer, former senior vice president of air operations, put it this way: "My job is to make sure that *everyone* who works for me is successful."

But, you may say, I am always and forever giving attention to my employees. True, but *there is a subtle and important distinction that should be made between taking interest in employees for the sake of accomplishing work and taking interest in them for their own sake as individuals.* That is the difference between social recognition and personal attention and the reason why personal attention is so much more powerful. Far greater power emerges when we shift the focus from the work to the individual and shift the motive from getting things done to just plain giving attention to another human being. *Attitudes have extraordinary power. Changing an attitude can release phenomenal energy.*

Psychological Values

Every industry and every economy goes through phases of growth and recession. Most every company goes through similar phases of expansion and contraction or leveling, and the large majority disappear after some time. Based on past trends, out of every 100 companies started this year, fewer than 20% will still be in business five years from now; and of those 20%, only 20% will be in business five years later.

Yet despite these facts, there are companies that not only survive Great Depressions, major and minor recessions, economic cycles for the nation and their industry, but continue to grow through it all, year after year, decade after decade, even when their industry is in a tail spin or the economy is in a dive. That is because these companies have succeeded in tapping and releasing some of the deepest springs of human energy—the energy generated by commitment to psychological values like respect for the individual, personal growth, harmony and service to society.

In 1932 when 25% of the work force was unemployed and companies were casting off workers as unwanted liabilities, Tom Watson made a commitment to every IBM employee guaranteeing them their jobs as long as the company remained afloat. That commitment to a high corporate value powerfully energized people throughout the company from the production floor to the sales counter and drove the growth of IBM from fifth to first place in its industry within seven years. Respect for and commitment to the individual are so powerful.

Personal Growth

Even more powerful is commitment to the value of personal growth for your people. Much of what we have been discussing in the last part of this chapter relates to the personal growth and development of people, not so much in the external sense of the term—which is commonly understood as increased compensation and promotions—but in a deeper, more inward sense—which relates to the development of their physical, social, mental and emotional capacities.

Personal growth of this description occurs all the time in work. It takes place unconsciously and very gradually. Each new experience, positive or negative, broadens and deepens the personality. Each new skill acquired increases our sense of competence and self-esteem. But this unconscious process is usually so slow and sporadic that the amount of energy generated is not significant. The process can be accelerated and magnified by a conscious corporate effort and programs, so that individuals are continuously acquiring new mental and psychological skills, being exposed to new learning experiences, and being given opportunities to grow by taking on challenging responsibilities like Dave Gray at Nedlloyd.

Unleashing the Creative Powers of Individuality

In this chapter we have been examining strategies to release people's physical, social, emotional, and mental energies in work. The greatest of these energies is the inner urge or aspiration in each person to develop his or her own unique individuality. It is that energy that provides the driving force for the entrepreneurial spirit that has made this nation so creative and productive. Presently organizations are so structured that one or a few people at the top release the creative energies of their individuality, while tens, hundreds or thousands of other people are only permitted or encouraged to express the lesser energies of their personalities.

Imagine the impact on your company if these creative energies, which lie within every person, could be released in all or many of those who presently follow the dictates and execute the inspiration of one or a few leaders? Then instead of the company being propelled forward by the force of a few people at the top, it could develop 10, 100, or a 1,000 engines of growth powerful enough to propel it to 10, 100, or 1,000 times its present size. That possibility is the essential truth behind the concept of "intrapreneurship"—creating entrepreneurs within corporations—but so far it is more an idea than a reality in American enterprise.

The keys for that achievement are right attitude and freedom. The attitude required is one of genuine, deep appreciation for the incredible creativity and resourcefulness of the human being and the willingness to give people the freedom to express that endowment. Individuality can only flower in an atmosphere of freedom. Companies that function from above downward through authority may be very efficient, but they can never match the vitality and intensity of a company that releases even a little of this ultimate power. Glimpses of this power can be seen in companies like Apple Computers during the first flush of its growth. Any company that succeeds—even to a small degree—in sustaining an environment where every individual has an opportunity to flower can plan to double itself, not once or on occasion, but every year.

ACTION PLAN FOR ENERGIZING PEOPLE

Use the strategies listed here to develop Action Plans to unleash the powers of your people. Estimate the impact which these actions will have on your company's revenues and profits over the next three years.

1. Recruit people with a high level of energy and good health.
2. Review your wage and salary scales and ensure that the compensation for every position is not only fair, but perceived as fair. Wherever necessary, educate people to understand the true value of the company's benefits package.
3. Link compensation directly with performance for every job.
4. Introduce profit-sharing or equity programs to make your people "owners" of the company.
5. Develop the physical and technical skills of your people through formal training programs.
6. Raise implementation of physical values such as cleanliness, orderliness, and safety to the highest possible level through appropriate standards, structures, systems, and skills.
7. Recruit people with the right types of personality to work well in your company and implement its values.

8. Establish formal and informal programs to give social recognition to high performers in every department, not just in sales. Every day make it a point to go out and find someone doing something right and recognize it.

9. Develop the interpersonal and organizational skills of your people through formal training programs.

10. Define clear paths for career development in the company and put in place an effective performance appraisal system to evaluate people's performance and help them to acquire higher level abilities.

11. Implement organizational values such as teamwork and communication to a very high level.

12. Recruit people with the highest possible level of education and experience.

13. Develop the managerial and psychological skills of your people through formal training and personal guidance.

14. Give greater personal attention to the people you work with (not to their work) and encourage them to do likewise with their people.

15. Implement psychological values such as respect for the individual, personal growth, freedom, and harmony to the highest possible level.

ANALYZING SKILLS

1. Make a list of several high-, low- and average-performing salespeople in your company on the form that follows.

2. Evaluate each person on three criteria: selling skills, knowledge of products/services, and motivation. Rate each person on each criteria on a scale from 0 to 100%.

3. Now calculate the total effectivity score for each sales person by multiplying the percentage scores on the three criteria; for example, if selling skills = 70%, product knowledge = 75%, and motivation = 80%, total effectivity score = $0.70 \times 0.75 \times 0.80 = 42\%$.

4. Utilizing the strategies discussed in this chapter, develop an Action Plan for raising the score of the low performers to the present average level, raising the scores of the average performers to the present level of the highest, and raising the score of the highest performers by 10%.

5. Estimate what would be the impact on the sales and profitability of the company if this plan is implemented.

6. Repeat a similar analysis of the knowledge, skills, and motivation of your managers, production workers and supervisors, administrative, finance, marketing, and research personnel.

PROFIT PLANNING

1. Review your answers to the questions on people at the end of Chapter Two.
2. Identify the practical steps you will take to raise the performance of your company/division/department on this component.
3. Develop a detailed action plan for carrying out these steps.
4. Estimate the growth in your company's revenues and profits that can be achieved by applying the ideas presented in this chapter to energize people and convert it into an engine for growth.

SUMMARY

- The engine that relates to people has the power to propel any company to the top of its field.

- Most companies tap but a small portion of the energies and potentials of their people.

- Releasing the powers of people is accomplished by tapping their physical, social, and psychological energies through appropriate strategies for recruitment, training, motivation, and value implementation.

- The ultimate power for the growth of any company is to release the creative energies of the individual.

ANALYZING SKILLS

Name	Skills	Knowledge	Motivation	Total Score	Remedial Actions To Be Taken	Impact on Profit Plan

Chapter Ten

TAPPING THE GREAT
SECRET: ORGANIZATION

What is the greatest invention of all time? The wheel enabled men and women to transport heavy loads and travel long distances. The sextant permitted ships to leave their coastal routes, venture out into the uncharted oceans, explore new continents, and open up worldwide sea trade. The printing press served as the impetus for universal education. The steam engine ushered in the Industrial Revolution. The electric bulb, the locomotive, the automobile, the telephone, and the computer have all played revolutionary roles in the development of civilization. But the greatest invention of them all is something without which virtually all these other discoveries would be rendered almost useless. That "something" is organization.

If the component "people" has been perceived as the greatest engine of growth by many companies, organization has been perceived as the greatest obstacle and constraint to that growth. Organization is the least appreciated, least admired of the five components. Almost everyone seems to be against it. There are outspoken, zealous advocates of the importance of people, market, technology, and even capital. But being antiestablishment, antibureaucracy and antiorganization has become respectable and even fashionable. Yet the fact is that organization contains the deepest secrets and greatest unutilized potentials for the rapid growth of your company.

Organization is the power that brings the other four components together, unites them and makes them productive. Without some type of organization, people cannot work together toward a common goal, money cannot be productively invested, technology cannot be developed or applied on a large scale, and markets cannot develop beyond the level of barter trade between individuals. We tend to regard

151

technology as the real driving force for the evolution of society from the primitive to the modern era. But the entire development of civilization has actually been made possible by the evolution of larger, more complex, more efficient, and more innovative types of organization.

In Chapter Two we described how two American entrepreneurs with a small amount of capital started a business in Brussels in a low-tech industry which is thousands of years old and utilized unskilled hourly wage earners to build up a global network of consumer service centers. There was nothing extraordinary about the market they tapped, the technology they utilized, the people they recruited or the financial resources they invested. The real power that has propelled the phenomenal growth of Minit International is organization. Organization enabled this company to create a new delivery system to meet an ancient need. Organization enabled the company to expand the scale of what had previously been a tiny localized business into a global operation. Organization enabled it to revive a dying industry and convert it into a rapidly growing and very profitable field of activity.

This organization consisted of a highly decentralized management and supervisory structure; detailed standard operating procedures to define every major and minor activity of the service centers, sophisticated management information systems for centralized monitoring of performance by service units, regions, and countries; and close coordination of every activity in the chain of production from procurement of raw materials and fabrication of service center machinery to recruitment and training of supervisors and workers. Minit International put in place the right structure, systems, and well-synchronized activities to expand almost effortlessly around the world.

ORGANIZATION: THE LEVER

What is the essential difference between the CEO of a $1 million company and the CEO of a $1 billion or a $50 billion company? The CEO of the larger company is not 1,000 times bigger, more intelligent, or more experienced than his or her $1 million counterpart. Then what enables the one CEO to produce 1,000 times more revenues and perhaps 1,000 times greater profits than the other? Organization. Organization enables an individual to extend himself or herself infinitely in space and time, to perform thousands of actions simultaneously, and to accomplish work on a scale that is impossible for any individual or group of individuals, no matter how large their number, to accomplish without it.

The Greek philosopher Archimedes once said, "If you give me a lever that is long enough and a fulcrum to rest it upon, I can lift the earth." Organization is such a lever and fulcrum. With it any company can rise to the top of its industry locally, nationally, or even internationally. The one technology that is most essential to nonstop growth is the technology of organization. Organization is a tool box filled with powerful levers that can elevate and energize market, people, technology, and capital to unimaginable heights. The aim of this chapter is to explore the secrets of some powerful instruments in the organizational toolbox.

Think of a time when it was the most fun to work in your company. More than likely it was a time when the organization you had in place was well suited to the size and nature of your business. When organization is right, work is expansive, smooth running, and enjoyable.

WHAT'S WRONG WITH ORGANIZATION?

If organization is as wonderful as we say it is, why then is it so maligned and misunderstood? There are five reasons. The first is because of the five components, its powers are the least visible and its actions the least dramatic, while its inadequacies are highly visible and its failures to act are directly felt by everyone. Few people are conscious of its powers, though everyone benefits from them. Organization is not something physical like people, money, a product or a customer that can be seen or touched. When it is most effective, it is least noticed and felt. On the other hand, because it is so pervasive and so essential, when it breaks down or malfunctions, everyone knows it and feels it and everything grinds to a halt.

The accusation most frequently raised against organization is that it stifles individual initiative and creativity. But, in actuality, organization is the most creative of the five components. Creativity means to combine things in new ways to generate new results. Organization is constantly creating new combinations of people, actions, systems, capital, technology and market needs. In fact, without organization the full creative potentials of the other four components could never be realized. The most creative organizations bring out the greatest creativity from the other four. At the end of this chapter we return to the issue of how to make your organization most alive and creative.

What, then, of the bureaucracy that encumbers our operations, demotivates our people, turns off customers, and blissfully disregards new technology? Bureaucracy is all too real and pervasive. But bureaucracy has nothing to do with any inherent deficiency in the powers of organization. It has everything to do with the inadequacies in the way we use those powers. Just like the typewriter we curse at for typing the wrong letter or the computer program we blame for not behaving as it should, even though we have not read the manual, we reproach organization for our imperfections. When organization breaks down, the first impulse of every entrepreneur and many managers is to throw it to the wind and act on inspiration or impulse.

That brings us to the third reason that organization is held in disfavor, one that strikes even closer to home: most companies and most managers are not very good at it. We have lots of motivating leaders, brilliant technocrats, financial wizards, and marketing geniuses, but not too many entrepreneurs and executives who are really masters of the technology of organization.

The fourth reason that organization is so often disparaged is that it has no defenders, no constituency, and no special interest group lobbying for its needs, because no one has been made responsible for it. Most companies can clearly identify one or more persons or departments responsible for the development of the other four components—market, finance, technology, and people. But what about organization? Who in your company is responsible for organization and its development? In a vast majority of companies the answer is "no one" or "everyone," which usually amount to the same thing. Sure, many companies have departments responsible for administration or management information systems, which are important elements of organization. But these areas represent only a tiny portion of the component.

The final reason is that, to a large extent, organization is a free resource. It requires relatively little or no investment in comparison with the returns it gives. Most companies are so preoccupied with caring for their "interests" that they ignore their greatest opportunities. If every company had to pay a licensing or patent fee for organizational technology, as it does for computer software, perhaps this powerful software would be much better utilized.

For all these reasons most companies think of organization more like Achilles' heel than Archimedes' lever. This is especially true when companies are growing rapidly. It is relatively easy to increase production to meet increased market demand. The addition of new people during rapid expansion is usually a manageable task, even when the numbers are large. But most companies find that building up an organization while growing rapidly is like trying to repair an aircraft in midair. That is why so many of the negative characteristics of rapid growth reported in Chapter Five directly relate to organization, or rather the absence of adequate organization—chaos and confusion, breakdown of systems, internal conflicts, poor coordination and poor communication. Learning to make your organization grow rapidly and properly is the single greatest challenge faced by companies aspiring to nonstop growth, and it is one of the most valuable skills that a manager or a company can acquire. As a senior executive of one fast-growing company put it, "Nobody has yet addressed the fact that as we go to the next level of size, we have a major problem in managing this organization."

HOW DO ORGANIZATIONS GROW?

People grow by releasing greater energy in themselves, improving their knowledge, acquiring new skills, changing their attitudes and committing themselves to higher values. How then do organizations grow?

It sounds like a simple question. But all the problems companies face with building an organization arise from the fact that the real process by which organizations grow is something of a mystery. It is easy to describe the growth of an organization as the creation of new positions, new departments, new divisions, or new layers of management. That is simple enough. We can visualize it. We can depict it on an organizational chart. But that is a very superficial conception and a dangerous one. For the moment we imagine that the only thing we have to do to make our organization grow is increase the number of positions, our organization begins to lose power and degenerate into a bureaucracy. Growth in size is not the same thing as growth in power and creativity—either for the physical body or the organization.

Our goal is to generate greater energy, productivity and creativity from the organization, not to lose what we already have. Where then is that energy to come from? How does an organization grow more efficient and effective, more powerful and creative?

THE THREE BUILDING BLOCKS

The mystery of organization arises from the fact that we are so familiar with its basic elements, we take them for granted. To acquire mastery over the powers of organization, it is necessary to approach them freshly with the innocence and curiosity of a child discovering something wondrous for the first time. Only then do their real potentials clearly emerge.

In this chapter we propose to look at the organization of your company and determine how suited it is to achieve the company's growth and profit goals. We begin by looking at the fundamental principles upon which every organization is based and from which it derives its powers and potentials. Our objective is to identify the untapped powers, the gaps, and missing links which when supplied will give greater energy, life, and creativity to your organization and your company.

Organization consists of three basic subunits:

1. *Positions*. The basic subunit of organizational structure is the individual job position. Positions are grouped together to form teams, departments, task forces, offices, regions, divisions, and so on.
2. *Activities*. The basic subunit of functioning is the individual act. Hundreds of individual acts are linked together to form major and minor activities, such as purchasing, recruiting, production, estimating, sales, advertising, meetings, correspondence, accounting, and so on.
3. *Systems*. Systems are the subunits that connect positions with each other, activities with each other, and positions and activities together.

The key to the growth of organization lies in understanding how each of these subunits develops and how they interact with one another to form an organic whole, which is capable of life, growth, and creativity. To understand how organizations grow in power and effectiveness, we must first understand how jobs, activities, and systems grow.

ANALYZING YOUR JOB

Structure answers the questions: Who is responsible? and Who has authority? The structure of a company consists of many individual positions ranked in orderly relationship to one another. Let us begin by looking at your job and asking some basic questions.

Are Your Responsibilities Clear to Yourself and Other People?

Each job consists of certain responsibilities and a certain measure of authority to carry them out. The clarity of those responsibilities has a major impact on how each individual performs as part of a greater whole, the organization, and how the organization performs in relationship to the individual. When Marty Wiegel, CEO of Wiegel Tool Works in Wood Dale, Illinois, asked himself this basic question, he realized where a lot of his frustrations and problems originated. He and two other senior executives all had responsibility for dealing with customers and coordinating their needs with the estimating, engineering, and production departments. As a result, these departments were receiving independent and often directly contradictory instructions from the three people at the top. Whenever one of the three executives complained to a department manager that something had gone wrong, the manager blamed poor performance on the conflicting priorities established by those above, or on the lack of cooperation from other departments, which were functioning according to different priorities set by one of the other executives. Each of the three executives held each other accountable for the confusion. Once Wiegel became fully conscious of where the problem lay, he redefined his own job and that of the other executives to eliminate the ambiguity and confusion. Setting right this tiny component of his organization helped Wiegel to increase sales 27% from $4.5 million to $5.7 million and to raise profits by 40% in one year.

Of course, such basic ambiguities never occur in larger companies! A few years ago we called one of the nation's largest banks to negotiate a loan for an $80 million industrial project in India. When we asked the switchboard operator to connect us with the department responsible for industrial investment in foreign projects, we were connected to the real estate division. From there we were passed from department to department—a total of at least ten by our then bleary-eyed reckoning—before we finally reached the appropriate executive in the right department, who belatedly expressed great interest in our proposal. Contrast this with a similar experience we had at IBM, when we called to discuss a proposal for collaboration with India, where IBM does not even operate since its withdrawal in 1974. The switchboard operator immediately connected us to the appropriate vice president, whose secretary informed us he was home sick and promised to get back to us shortly. Within 24 hours we were meeting with the one individual in the company most qualified to discuss our proposal, the former general manager of IBM's India division.

This is not a discussion concerning switchboard operators—which might merit a book of its own. It is about the clarity of structure in your company at all levels from the CEO and management team down to the lowest-level supervisor; from corporate headquarters out into the stores, offices, and plants; among departments, branches, regions, and divisions. It is not enough that you, your close associates and subordinates understand who is responsible for what in the company. For structure to support smooth functioning, that clarity should extend to everyone. How many companies can pass the test which Wiegel and the bank failed? How much frustration and confusion are generated, how much energy is wasted by a mere lack of clearly defined jobs—energy that could be converted into greater sales and higher profits? Think about your job, the jobs of senior executives and department managers. How many pass the simple test for clarity?

Does Authority Match Responsibility?

If a job description does not already exist for your position, make a list of your major responsibilities. Now list the actual levels and types of authority assigned to your job. Do they match? Do you have the authority to carry out all the responsibilities? Think about the jobs of the people who report directly to you. Do their responsibilities and levels of authority match? Problems frequently arise in areas where lower-level managers are responsible for meeting schedule deadlines, yet are dependent on higher-level approvals at various points in the process. In one company project management was running an average of six months behind on a multitude of large projects to expand the production facility. When called to task for the delays, the manager pointed out that virtually every project was awaiting clearances and approvals from senior executives who were in meetings all day and unavailable to their subordinates.

Contrast this with the amazing achievement of Bajaj Auto Limited of India, which constructed a new $180 million motor scooter plant in 18 months—a credible accomplishment in any country, a miracle under conditions in India! Rahul Bajaj appointed a single executive engineer as sole responsible and fully empowered authority for the project and met with him just once a month for a progress report. As the project neared completion, the biggest constraint became the inability of the local government to get approval and allocation of funds for a new telephone exchange to service the plant. To meet the schedule, the executive engineer constructed the government facility at company expense and was reimbursed after the plant was commissioned. That is the power of a proper blend of authority and responsibility.

To what extent do responsibilities and authority match in your company?

Are You Sure You Are Doing What You Should Be Doing?

An important distinction needs to be made between the responsibilities assigned to a position and the actual tasks carried out by the person in that job. For example, the CEO of a small company or the vice president of a larger firm may accept responsibility for personally replying to all customer complaints. But that does not necessarily mean Bill Marriott personally writes or types each letter himself. Yet more than one CEO and executive we have met interpret the responsibility in that way. Are you sure you are carrying out your responsibilities through tasks appropriate to your level in the organization?

Job Analysis

Ask virtually any senior executive to carry out a thorough analysis of the way they actually spend their time, that is, the physical tasks they perform, not the responsibilities they are in charge of. For each of those tasks, ask whether it could be performed more cost effectively at a lower level of the company without sacrificing quality. The answer in many cases is "Yes." Now split those tasks into their component parts and ask whether any of the components could be carried out just as well or better and more cost-effectively at a lower level. The answer is almost always "Yes." After moaning and groaning about the arduous nature of the exercise, executives usually come back smiling and say as one dedicated and hard-working vice president did, "I never realized before how much time I could save. I can free up 50% of my time for the design and construction of our new production facility." A vice president of marketing found he could free up 25% of his time from administrative tasks to go out and meet the company's *Fortune* 500 customers.

The same type of rationalization can be done at every level of an organization from top to bottom. It is most effective when it starts at the very top and moves down level after level. What are the savings in terms of efficient use of people that can be achieved by this one strategy? A few years ago, Ford Motors asked white-collar workers in some units to list all the things they do in a month, rank the duties, and stop doing the bottom 20%. This analysis has saved the company hundreds of millions of dollars a year.

By analyzing jobs, established companies usually discover, as did Ford, that they can do more work with the same people or the same work with fewer people. On the other hand, young growth-oriented companies usually discover that they are trying to do too much with the existing people and that key responsibilities needed to sustain high rates of growth cannot be properly handled without adding new positions at one level or another.

How about you? How can your company, your department, or your career grow, unless you can find ways to accomplish more work more effectively in the same amount of time? The first exercise at the end of this chapter outlines a ten-step process to analyze and expand your job and the jobs of your people.

DELEGATION AND INTEGRATION

Job analysis is a powerful tool for the company to improve organizational efficiency and for the manager to grow in personal effectiveness. It also reveals part of the process by which organizations grow.

When a manager succeeds in improving her effectiveness and taking on higher responsibilities by delegating less important tasks to people at lower levels, she makes individual progress and rises in the organization. That is the process of personal growth. When the manager succeeds in creating a capacity in people at a lower level to do the same work with the same skill and quality under her guidance and authority, the organization progresses. That is the process of organizational growth. In other words, *an organization grows when it is able to carry out a higher level or a wider scale of activity at a lower level of the organization.*

The process of expanding jobs is commonly referred to as delegation. Most people think of delegation as transferring a task or responsibility to a subordinate, but that is only half the story. Delegation becomes fully effective only when the tasks undertaken at different levels are properly integrated with one another. *Integration means to harmonize the activities of all the levels so they work together smoothly to achieve a common purpose.* When delegation is accompanied by integration, the company is able to continuously push tasks to lower levels to improve efficiency, while ensuring that the activities carried out at different levels stay in harmony with one another. Integration is the real foundation for the growth of organization because it enables organization to transfer tasks continuously to lower levels and yet at the same time ensure a common direction to activities carried out at different levels. Integration is the most powerful of any organizational values. The key to integration is effective delegation.

FOUR RULES OF DELEGATION

Delegation is one of the most important activities an organization must manage to grow. A failure in this area can absolutely stop the growth process, as it has for many companies, or lead it quickly to crisis or ruin. Yet, regardless of whether you speak to the CEO or executive of a $1 million company or a $1 billion company, the responses are surprisingly similar.

Few managers will quarrel with the idea of delegating physical tasks. But the heart of delegation is delegating decisions, that is, responsibility and authority. That is a different matter. Many sincere executives genuinely believe that no one else can make the decisions they are making with equal or near equal effectiveness. In most cases they are probably right. But delegation does not mean just putting decision-making responsibility into someone else's hands. It means building up the capabilities of the organization, so that someone at a lower level can assume the responsibility with equal effectiveness.

When asked to identify the first step in effective delegation, most managers respond: "Find the right person." We disagree.

Institutionalize Your Skills

The first step in effective delegation is to identify the knowledge, guidelines, or thought processes that you utilize in making a decision and create a system for evaluating alternatives. By this process, the individual imparts his or her personal capacity to the organization. He institutionalizes his skill.

The CEO of a very profitable and fast-growing industrial leasing company once told us that at $18 million, his company had reached the limits of growth possible for it. His rationale was that he was already spending 16 hours a day at the office, a good part of it reviewing lease proposals prepared by his staff of qualified MBAs, and there simply was no more time in the day available. When asked whether any one else in the company could approve the lease proposals, he immediately ran off half a dozen very convincing examples of wrong recommendations made by his staff that could have led to disastrous consequences had he not reviewed and overturned them.

After listening patiently to his description of the process, we confronted him with the following challenge: "We believe it is possible for *you* to create a system that will not only make decisions as effectively as you do, but actually more effectively, because it will ask all the right questions all the time, whereas you ask most of the right questions most of the time." The CEO accepted the challenge. Six months later he reported that his company was again growing rapidly and as profitably as before. According to his own assessment, he had succeeded in creating a system that actually did a better job than he did of evaluating lease proposals.

As Jan Carlzon of SAS put it,

> A leader is not appointed because he knows everything and can make every decision. He is appointed to bring together the knowledge that is available and then create the prerequisites for the work to be done. *He creates the systems that enable him to delegate responsibility for day-to-day operations.*[1]

Most managers never think of asking how their counterparts in larger companies are able to manage much larger operations than they without sacrificing the quality of decisions. It never occurred to the CEO of one mold manufacturer that he could create a system for estimating the cost and price on new jobs until he heard three of his competitors talk about the systems they had developed to delegate estimating and keep growing. The CEO of a 30-unit hotel chain, who felt he had reached the limits of growth possible for his company, was surprised to learn how Willard Marriott had solved the same problems 25 years earlier. The real limitation is attitude. The moment we give in to the suggestion—whether our own or someone else's—that we are the only ones who can do it right, we put a lid on our own growth, both personal and corporate.

Harry Patten had a real knack for identifying rural properties suitable for development into homesites and he used to fly in his corporate plane to view every potential site for acquisition. That was all right at a time when Patten Corporation's activities were confined to a handful of offices in New England. But how could the CEO of a fast-growing company spend all his time roaming the country to identify new sites and still manage the growth of his business. Patten analyzed the critical variables that go into selecting good sites, trained others to understand his approach, and institutionalized the process of evaluating and acquiring new properties. Today there are over 50 specialists in offices throughout the eastern and midwestern United States selecting sites for the company. Patten institutionalized his skill so that both he and the organization could grow . . . and grow they did—from $11 million in 1985 to $116 million in 1988.

Identify the Right People and Train Them

Now is the time to find the right people and give them a thorough training in how decisions should be made. The CEO of a $150 million company once remarked, "Delegation? I have no problem at all in delegating. My only problem is that when delegation fails, I have to take back the task again." Delegation usually fails for one of four reasons: the right person is not selected, the right system is not in place, the right training is not given, or the rules, guidelines, and expectations of the person delegating are not properly communicated to the person receiving the charge.

Who is the right person? First of all, the right person is one who has the *ability* to undertake the work—the right knowledge, skills, and capacity for acting according to the guidelines you have established and through the system you have created. Second, and equally important, the right person is someone who has the *time* to undertake the work—whose present job is not so demanding that additional work results in burnout, errors, or lapses in other areas of responsibility. It sounds obvious enough. But very commonly delegation breaks down, because we pass tasks on without first assessing what will be the impact of the additional work on the beneficiary. In other words, you cannot effectively rationalize your own job without also analyzing the jobs of those who report to you and making it possible for them to rationalize their jobs as well.

Delegate and Monitor

Paul Maestri learned this rule the hard way. When he brought in the new executive team and delegated authority, he walked away and never looked back, that is, he delegated without any type of monitoring or control. Delegation without control is abdication. Effective delegation requires a feedback system to monitor performance on a regular basis. As Karlberg explained it, "One of the problems we had when the new management team came in was that there were no systems in place to measure the performance of delegation."

The importance of monitoring sounds obvious, but this is shaky ground. Very often monitoring is the door through which managers, knowingly or unknowingly, take back the decisions they have given away. The real issue is—"What should I monitor?" That brings us to the fourth important rule.

Monitor the Results, Not the Actions

How many times have you heard a manager say—or perhaps heard yourself say—"I delegated the responsibility, but he is doing it the wrong way"—meaning he is not doing it the way the manager would have done it. That is not delegation. Delegation means to instruct someone in what result you want to achieve and then leave that person free to determine the best way to achieve that result. The result may be both quantitative and qualitative, for example, reduce production costs by 10% without sacrificing quality. As long as the result is achieved, hands off! As Carlzon said, "The result-oriented leader does not dictate the methods for achieving the results . . .[2] Many executives struggle with this principle. But unless it is followed, delegation almost invariably is reduced to second-guessing.

Delegation Requires a Psychological Effort

This is the crux of the matter. Bruce Phelps, CEO of Fulton Tool Company, summed up the problem of delegation wonderfully: "The real problem of delegation is to stop doing a thing after you have delegated it!" As Steve Bedowitz candidly remarked, "The hardest thing is not being hands on everyday." The hardest part about delegating is to stop wanting to do what you know that someone else can do in your place.

The CEO of a $500 million manufacturing company complained: "I keep telling my executives to make decisions and act. But at every weekly production meeting, they ask me what I think. Then I ask a few questions. Before you know it I have reversed or seconded their decision and the responsibility is back in my lap." After some thought the CEO added, "I guess the truth is I really like to make the decisions."

Delegation requires many skills—in judging people properly, in communicating with them, in creating effective systems, and so on. But delegation also requires a psychological effort to give up what you have delegated—to grow and let someone else grow too. Fred Smith knows what that effort is like:

> I've tried to give people who are in positions of authority lots of freedom, so they can be creative. That's the hardest thing to do, because it takes a lot of discipline. You want to insert yourself in lots of things, where you don't have any business getting involved or where you want to protect people from themselves or to protect the organization from the people. You've got to give people some degree of right to fail.

DELEGATION AND CORPORATE GROWTH

Everyone likes to be considered indispensable. But being indispensable puts a limit on our growth, because the company can never afford to take away from us what we already know and do well. Which means, in that measure there is no opportunity for us to learn new things, acquire new skills, and master other fields of activity. The really indispensable executive is the one who constantly makes himself dispensable, so that others can take over his job and he can grow onward and upward.

Delegation is not merely an important management skill by which managers improve their efficiency and accomplish more work. It is part of the process by which companies evolve to higher and higher levels of organization. Through delegation, the structure of the company is constantly changing, even when the positions and titles remain the same. Delegation enables the CEO, the management team, and managers at all levels to redefine their jobs and the acts which they perform continuously. Delegation, at the micro-level of the individual job and task, enables a company to instill a culture of perpetual change that ensures freshness and prevents the organization from becoming old, static, and bureaucratic. *A perpetual process of delegation enables a company to keep growing perpetually.*

Delegation is a natural process, but it does not always happen naturally and by itself. And it cannot happen at all, unless there is someone to whom to delegate. The pressure to maintain high earnings to satisfy the board of directors, investors, or analysts on Wall Street prompts many growing companies to delay adding people until serious symptoms begin to manifest themselves. The ability to recognize when new positions are needed and to add them in time is essential for continuous growth.

THE JOB OF MANAGEMENT

There is one other important reason why delegation is difficult for many CEOs, executives, and managers. They do not know what they should be doing, if they stop doing what they are doing now. It comes back to the question we have heard so often: "What really is my job, anyway?"

Fred Smith has answered the question very clearly in the negative sense of defining what the job of a manager is not. At Federal Express's management course, he tells first-line managers:

> If you think that management is moving this piece of paper from one side of the desk to the other, or being a megaphone for upper management, or signing your name for some performance review, you better start looking for a job. Because we're going to automate that right out of existence. We can't afford to have a nanny for every 15 people in this company. *What you are employed for is to bring your intellectual energy to some sort of business problem.* To make the cost of what we do less, or the value of what we do more for the customer. When we put that on the line to people, *we go a very long way toward keeping the organization energized.*

If pushing paper, being a megaphone, or signing a performance review is **not** management, then what is? To answer this question, we have to distinguish between two types of management: operational management of the existing business and developmental management of corporate growth. Smith is saying that his operational managers cannot afford to be doing mere physical tasks that can be delegated to a lower level or a system. But what about higher-level managers in the company?

The real responsibility of higher-level management is not operational. It is developmental. The primary responsibilities of the management team are to direct their attention toward the development of each of the five engines of the business in order to release their untapped potentials, that is, development of people, identification of new opportunities in the market, evaluation of new technologies, examination of innovative financial techniques, and most important, accelerated development of the organization.

Review the list of tasks you perform. How many executives, even of multibillion-dollar corporations, really dedicate their time and energy to developing these five engines? If your goal is to grow rapidly and profitably, the job of the CEO and senior executives must evolve to the point where developing the business is their main responsibility, if not their sole occupation. But that is only possible when all levels of the organization develop in unison. Delegation is an important key to that development, but it is not the only key.

For the next key, we turn to another basic subunit of organization, the act.

ANALYZING ACTIVITIES

Energy expresses, in work as movement, as action. The faster and smoother the action, the greater the energy it generates and expresses. The energy and speed of movement on the streets of New York can be quite startling to first-time visitors. That is raw, unorganized activity—people moving hurriedly in all directions, bumping into one another, each pushing to further his or her individual goal without regard for the others and without a common plan or direction. Peak-performing organizations achieve a similar speed and energy, but without the haste, waste, and confusion. They harness the energy and organize the action, so that it flows smoothly, quietly, and harmoniously without friction.

The individual act is the basic subunit of corporate functioning. Each step performed by an individual in carrying out a task in fulfillment of a responsibility of his or her job is a mental or physical act. These acts are linked with other acts in a chain to generate activities. Organization is the capacity to carry out several different activities at different times or different places in such a way that they serve a common purpose. Anything that increases the capacity to conduct activities efficiently and effectively increases the power and productivity of the organization.

We began our examination of job positions by asking some fundamental questions about your job to show that jobs are capable of continuous development and that that development in turn enables the organization to grow. Like jobs, activities can be continuously improved too. Each improvement releases fresh energy and makes the organization more effective.

The approval of new drugs for medicinal application is a very laborious and time-consuming process in the United States and in most European countries. The Dutch subsidiary of a huge multinational pharmaceutical company was averaging 32 months to obtain government approval for sale of new drugs in the Netherlands. The company accepted the long period as the inevitable result of government bureaucracy. In the course of reviewing major activities in the company, a consultant examined the drug registration process and came up with a surprising conclusion. He reported that in spite of the slow government procedure, it would still be possible to reduce the registration period from 32 months to 21 months. He argued that in the process of receiving potential new drugs from the company's overseas headquarters and evaluating them for possible marketing in Holland, the company was carrying out many actions successively that could be equally well performed simultaneously. He also pointed out that while the government reserved the right to 90- and 120-day response times to submissions by the company, in the past the company had failed to issue reminders to the government, even when responses had been delayed over 150 days. The management of the drug company finally became convinced that the reduction in time was in fact achievable and calculated that by getting new drugs on the market nearly a year earlier, the company would earn additional net profit of more than $500,000 from each new drug it introduced. A week later, the head of the pharmaceutical division happened to meet his Dutch counterpart from Merck. On inquiry, he learned with amazement that Merck's average registration time was only 16 months and that on two occasions it had done it in 6 months!

If that is the potential improvement that can be obtained on an activity so dependent on the government, how much greater is the potential in the hundreds of strictly internal activities in your company? The type of activity analysis applied by the pharmaceutical company for an administrative process can be applied to any research or manufacturing process as well.

Today many manufacturers are analyzing their product development activities to reduce the time from initial conception to putting a new product or new model on the market. Honda has cut the development time on new cars from five years to three. AT&T has reduced development time on its phones from two years to one. Hewlett-Packard has cut to less than half the time it takes to bring new printers to the market. Other companies are accelerating the time from receipt of order to delivery of finished product. General Electric has brought down delivery time on its circuit breaker boxes from three weeks to three days. Motorola has cut the time for delivering new electronic pagers from three weeks to two hours.

Think about some of the important activities in your company or your department. How much scope is there to improve the quality or reduce the time required for completing each activity? What would be the impact of such an improvement on the service to customers, efficiency, revenues, and profits? What would be the result on other activities of the company of accelerating performance on just one major activity?

These achievements are triumphs of organizational innovation. They have been brought about by a minute analysis of every step in these key activities. They involve changes in the way activities are conceived, executed, and linked together and in the way responsibilities are allocated to different positions and levels of the organization. But to raise performance on any corporate activity to the maximum possible level, a rationalization of individual acts and a reallocation of responsibilities is not enough. A third essential element is required, the third basic subunit of organization, systems.

SYSTEMS ANALYSIS

Systems are the mechanism which an organization uses to link activities with each other and to link activities with positions. Activities involving thoughts and decisions are linked together through management information systems and manual or computerized decision-making systems, like the ones referred to under the section on delegation. Physical activities are linked together through standard operating procedures, which define a series of physical tasks to be carried out, like the ones Minit International employs for the operation of its service centers, regions, and national subsidiaries.

Systems possess an amazing power of expansion. Systems supported the expansion of Minit International from one service unit in a Brussels department store to thousands of units worldwide. Systems enabled Compaq computers to reach the *Fortune* 500 list faster than any other corporation in history. Compaq grew from $111 million in 1983, its first year of operation, to $1.2 billion in 1987. At the time it was founded, Compaq put in place systems that would enable it to grow exponentially without slowing down or looking back.

Systems possess the power to carry out activities much more quickly, precisely and regularly than individuals can perform them on their own. Herein lies their tremendous power to energize an organization. The productivity of an organization is determined by the extent to which routine and recurring physical activities are systematized as standard operating procedures.

Systems are not dead or mechanical devices. They derive their power directly from corporate values like orderliness, punctuality, standardization, coordination, and so on. Think for a moment of the last time an important decision or action was unduly delayed in your company. What was the impact on corporate energy? We have seen the morale of an entire company sink to a low ebb because a performance review system introduced to improve morale was running six months behind schedule. Speed up that process and what is the result? Everyone gets energized.

Systems are usually associated with drudgery, bureaucracy, and monotonous repetition. But the companies which are the most creative and fun to work in are very often those which have converted systematic functioning into a fine art. The high level of customer service and the genuinely friendly and relaxed manner of Marriott hotel employees are a direct result of the systems the company has in place to make everyone's job easier. Contrast the experience we described in the palatial Dallas hotel, when we asked room service to serve coffee an hour earlier, with this one from the Marriott O'Hare:

> It was the hotel's fault from beginning to end. We ordered breakfast for 8:15 A.M. to be ready for a seminar starting at 8:45. Our breakfasts did not arrive on time and we were getting a little nervous. At 8:20 we called room service and they promised to send them up immediately. At 8:22 A.M. there was a knock at the door. As the door opened, a smiling waiter said, "I am extremely sorry your breakfast is late. It is on us."

The impact was profound. The waiter was simply carrying out a company standard, which is written on a card in the room. "If your breakfast is late, it's on us." Think about what is happening here. In a split second, the customer's tension and the employee's anxiety are eliminated by a system. The employee, who probably had nothing to do with the late breakfast in the first place, can maintain his cheerfulness, because he is supported by a system.

Time after time we have found that in companies which have built up basic systems to support smooth-running routine activities, people are more relaxed and cheerful and enjoy their work more. AMRE is a dramatic example. Virtually every recurring activity has been reduced to a system at AMRE. It is a hard-hitting, fast-growing company where people like Bud Lane are really enjoying themselves. "I never had it so good. I'm working twice as hard, but I love it. I go home at night feeling good."

Systems have been the key to AMRE's nonstop growth. As the company has anticipated its people's needs six months down the line, it has always tried to build its systems with plenty of extra capacity to accommodate future growth. Trying to bring your systems up to date after the fact is "like trying to build an airplane in the air. We've never had that problem. We build it on the ground," says Ward Richardson, vice president of management information services. The other thing AMRE has done is to keep the systems simple so that they are easy to understand and easy to operate. Richardson adds, "We keep our systems as simple as we can, so that people can interact and work with the systems, so they don't learn to hate them."

AMRE is not only a fun company to work in, it is a creative one too. "I've never been in a functionally freer creative environment than here," Richardson exclaimed. "The creativity has been tremendous." That creativity is made possible because the organization at AMRE is continuously evolving. Not only do jobs continuously change, the systems do too. "Systems constantly have to be changed," says Bud Lane. "Steve [Bedowitz] is constantly saying in staff meetings, 'Just because you did it this way a year ago, doesn't mean that it works now. What have you done recently to streamline your systems?' "

As individual jobs constantly evolve in a growing organization, systems can be constantly improved in their functioning to carry the organization to higher levels. As jobs grow by adding on and shedding specific tasks in an incremental manner, systems grow by continuous refinement and innovation. Even relatively minor improvements can energize a simple activity.

Computerization has had a major impact on the growth of P.A.M. Recently the company added a small modification to its computerized dispatch system. It introduced a 13-digit alphanumeric code for each consignment, which classified the shipment in terms of one way or round trip, the type of equipment required, the pickup and delivery location, and other factors. The code improves communication between the solicitor who takes the customer's order and the dispatcher who arranges for pickup. It enables dispatchers to utilize the equipment at their disposal more efficiently by easily sorting shipments by the type of equipment needed and the location. It also enables the driver to identify key facts about each shipment at a glance and serve the customer better. The estimated savings from this small innovation will be several hundred thousand dollars a year.

Systems are like atoms. They contain tremendous latent energy. The more refined the improvements, the greater the power released. Federal Express recently introduced a peelable bar-coded label that its couriers use to affix an airway bill number to their delivery records, instead of writing out a number by hand at the point of delivery. The cumulative savings generated by eliminating 3 seconds from each transaction works out to 417 hours per day, or roughly $2 million per year.

Even in a company as committed to systems as Federal Express, evolving new and better systems fast enough to sustain maximum rates of growth has been difficult. Says Smith, "The brake on the company's ability to meet the demand in the market has been systems. Today organization is not just people in boxes. It's the way you align against business problems. The development of strategic information systems, which is an integral part of that organization, is probably the biggest brake on what we can do."

Think about the systems in your company. How effectively do they perform their allotted tasks? What have you done lately to streamline your systems and build them up for rapid growth? The second exercise at the end of this chapter is an analysis of your company's key systems. The future of your company depends on the constant development of new and improved systems to carry out activities faster, better, and more efficiently.

ORGANIZATION: TOO MUCH OR TOO LITTLE?

Organization is absolutely essential for the existence and growth of any company. The fast-growing companies referred to in this book could never have grown as rapidly and as large as they have if they had not expanded their internal organizations to keep pace with their external expansion.

Yet we read constantly these days of how large companies are attacking what they perceive as excessive organization by slashing red tape, reducing the number of management layers, and decentralizing decision making. So much has been written and said on the dangers of bureaucracy and complacency that even small and midsized firms that lack the minimum structure needed for survival and growth have developed an aversion to adding new people and more systems. Some entrepreneurial-style managers take such great efforts to prevent the growth of organizational weeds that the flowers stop growing too. How can you tell whether you need more organization or less?

Does your company suffer from any of these symptoms: inability to respond aggressively to opportunities and changes in the external environment; slow decision making; poor communication or coordination; or declining speed, quality, or productivity? If so, the company may have too much organization—or it may have too little! For the symptoms of both are often the same.

The bureaucratic, overorganized company is very slow to respond to opportunities and changes in the external environment, because senior executives are out of touch with the field and their own front-line operations. Its decision making is slow, because too many people and steps are involved in getting approvals. Communication and coordination are poor, because the company has become segmented and fragmented into isolated departments and divisions. Speed, productivity, and quality decline, because authority is vested in managers who are too far removed from the activities they are responsible for directing.

The understaffed, underorganized company is slow to respond to opportunities and changes in the external environment, because senior management is so preoccupied by fighting fires and maintaining existing operations that it has no time to think of the future. Its decision making is slow, because there are too many decisions to make and too few people to make them. Communication and coordination are poor, because there is no time, no system or no person responsible. Speed, productivity, and quality decline, because people and systems are not adequate to handle the volume of work.

The symptoms of excessive organization and inadequate organization can be very similar, because in both instances the organization is not suited to the present needs of the company. Any company can assess the suitability of its organization by applying the basic tools to any problem.

APPLYING THE BASIC TOOLS OF THE TRADE

What does your company do when something goes wrong? In many companies, the first impulse is to blame somebody. Yet in most cases the real culprit lies elsewhere—a job that is not clearly defined, responsibility that does not match authority, systems that are inadequate, or an activity that needs to be streamlined. To diagnose the problem properly, you have to return to fundamentals.

General Electric's success in reducing delivery time on its circuit breaker boxes from three weeks to three days dramatically illustrates the power of analyzing organizational problems at their roots. The strategy GE employed involved analyzing and making improvements in all three subunits—the systems, the activities, and the positions.

A team of manufacturing, design, and marketing experts was assembled to analyze GE's entire $1 billion circuit breaker business. The team started by recommending a change in structure. It consolidated operations from six manufacturing units into one. It then analyzed the 28,000 parts used in making 40,000 different sizes and shapes of circuit boxes. By standardization, the number of parts was reduced to 1,275. A new computer system was introduced, which automatically programs factory machines when salespeople enter new orders. This eliminated an entire activity of referring all new orders to the engineering department. The number of layers of plant management was also reduced to facilitate quick communication and decision making. In addition, a new structure was created consisting of teams of workers that were invested with the authority and responsibility previously exercised by managers at a higher level. Fortune reports: "Everything those middle managers used to handle—vacation scheduling, quality, work rules—became the responsibility of 129 workers on the floor, who are divided into teams of 15 to 20. And what do you know. The more responsibility GE gave the workers, the faster problems got solved and decisions made."[3] These changes have enabled the company to increase pro- ductivity by 20%, reduce costs by 30%, and bring down the backlog of orders from two months to two days.

Think about the problems and constraints facing your company. How many of them can be resolved by restructuring jobs, refining systems, or streamlining activities? How can you make your business grow and double profits by applying these basic tools of organization?

THE REAL POWER OF ORGANIZATION

Thus far we have been looking at the basic subunits of organization and the way they fit together and interact to accomplish the company's work. We have also looked at some of the ways in which these subunits develop and how that development improves the functioning of the organization.

But the true source of organization's energy and creativity does not lie within any of these basic subunits. They are just the building blocks. The real energy of organiza- tion is generated by the relationships created between the subunits. The real creativity of organization lies in its ability to link these subunits—people, activities, systems, materials, and time—together in ever new, more complex, more effective combina- tions. *The real power of organization arises from its capacity for coordination and integration of people, activities and systems.* Coordination and integration are two of the advanced tools of organization.

We said earlier that the development of jobs increases the level of integration in the organization by linking higher and lower levels closely together, so they act as a single whole, and shifting actions from higher to lower levels. The development of systems increases the level of coordination in the organization by linking separate activities and separate systems together as part of a greater unified whole.

The power of coordination and integration can be most dramatically illustrated by their absence. Departments and divisions isolate themselves into duchies or mini-em- pires as they did at Chrysler before Iacocca arrived. When Iacocca joined Chrysler, the company had all the pieces in place, but they were not working together with one another. Production was not speaking with engineering, engineering was not listening to what sales tried to tell them the customers wanted. Management and workers were completely at odds. Talented middle managers were stifled by a top-heavy bureaucracy of executives out of touch with the front lines. As a result in spite of its enormous resources and technological competence, the entire company—a $12 billion operation—came to the brink of bankruptcy. Iacocca broke down the barriers that divided divisions, departments and levels of the organization from one another, opened up communication, streamlined and accelerated new model development activity, and put in the systems needed for effective coordination and control of the giant company. These measures not only saved Chrysler and returned it to profitability, they also provided it with the organization it needed to more than double in size over the next five years.

Coordination of activities can generate a powerful impetus for growth. East Asiatic Company is one of the last of the giant trading houses of Europe. The company was founded in 1871 by a Danish merchant seaman who bought a shipload of teakwood lumber in the kingdom of Siam and sold it in Europe. Throughout the decades the company diversified into many different fields, but still maintained its timber business. In the early 1980s EAC's timber operations consisted of 26 activity centers throughout the world, buying, selling, warehousing, and distributing lumber. Not infrequently, these highly decentralized timber centers ended up competing against one another for the purchase of timber from a supplier or sales to a customer. In 1983 the company made some changes to improve coordination and integration of its worldwide timber activities. It reorganized the timber division geographically and introduced new systems to coordinate closely the activities of each center with the other centers. As a direct result of improved coordination, profits of the division, which had been flat throughout the early 1980s, grew by 30% a year for three years in a row.

In our survey of U.S. companies, there was a significant difference in the level of coordination reported by the most successful and the least successful companies. The larger and more profitable companies reported closer coordination in all areas: between sales and marketing, marketing and research, research and production, and production and sales.

The power of coordination and integration can be demonstrated at any level and in any part of an organization. Bang & Olufsen operates three machine shops at its production facility on the Jutland peninsula of Denmark. Until recently the shops were each headed by a manager who reported independently to the vice president. In early 1987 a new position, director of machine shops, was created to coordinate activities of the three departments. Within the first six months, productivity of the three shops increased by 25%. Per Kysgaard, the director, explained: "We really did not do anything much. We just talked about improving coordination between the shops. The response has been tremendous."

COMPREHENSIVE COORDINATION

Organization has been a key factor in the phenomenal ninefold growth of Linear Technology over the last five years. The company has a lean, simple structure with clear functional areas and clear lines of authority. When the work goes well and when there are problems, everyone knows who is responsible.

But the real power of Linear's organization arises from its commitment to the value of coordination in virtually every one of the company's departments, activities and systems. In Chapter Two we described how Linear fosters close coordination among its chip designers, production engineers, sales force, and customers. Responsibility for that coordination is built right into the job description of the design engineer. "The designer knows his job is more than design," says Robert Dobkin, vice president of engineering, who encourages his designers to get out and talk with customers—which he refers to as "sending out our crown jewels"—and to be actively involved in all areas of production where problems arise. It is the designer's responsibility go out with the sales force to learn what customers need, to move with the chips he designs right through the production process and work closely with production engineers to iron out any production problems, and to deal directly with customers who encounter problems in utilizing the chips in their products. Many companies have problems getting their design engineers to design products that are producible. Very often the problem is attitude, "a natural antipathy between designers and manufacturing," as one engineer put it. That is not a problem at Linear. "Our design engineers recognize the importance of the manufacturing component," says Brian Hollins, vice president of operations. "They are very good at following the product through the production process." In this way the designers are not sheltered from quality and reliability problems.

Coordination does not stop there. Linear has created an entire cadre of field application engineers (FAEs) to accompany the sales people on visits to customers to improve the linkage among design, production, and sales. There is also an FAE coordinator, whose responsibility it is to report back opportunities and problems from the market to the designers. The coordinator's reports go to engineering, marketing and senior management. To generate quick responses to problems, the coordinator is authorized to interface directly with people in all departments without going through the respective vice presidents.

The same attitude and effort can be seen in other areas. Every week the company conducts a production control meeting to ensure close coordination among design, production, quality control, sales, and finance. "If this meeting didn't take place, you could plot the decline of the company on a graph," says CEO Robert Swanson. The meeting is run by the production control manager, PCM, who reports to the vice president of finance rather than to the head of production. This results in better coordination between inventory management and cost control and gives the PCM greater freedom to press for responsiveness from the production team.

The production control meeting is also a good example of how Linear fosters the value of integration. The meeting is attended by 25 top managers including the CEO and senior executives. It gives top management direct access to information from middle management. It also gives middle management direct access to the highest level of decision making, which is one of the reasons for the company's great responsiveness to new needs and new situations.

THE ULTIMATE SECRET

Freedom is the essential condition for creativity. The individual grows only in freedom, but organization is based on the principle of order and stability. The ultimate measure of an organization is its ability to give people freedom without losing its cohesiveness and effectiveness. *The proper balance of self-discipline and freedom provides the stability and creativity needed for endless expansion.*

Linear has developed its own formula for freedom and discipline. It has raised the value of freedom to a high level in some areas. It gives a remarkable latitude of freedom to its designers to decide what type of products they want to develop. "Freedom to design what you will is the key," says design director Tom Redfern. Yet in other areas it is run strictly according to the book, with no latitude for deviation. "I run a two-headed monster," says Swanson. "The design guys have a lot of freedom, because they need it. The rest of the company runs with an iron fist."

Freedom and discipline are not mutually exclusive. Rather they make each other possible. Freedom without discipline is chaos. Discipline without freedom is tyranny. *The ultimate secret is to arrive at a delicate balance between the two. The company should provide freedom for entrepreneurial energies and newly emerging ideas and initiatives to sprout and develop, unencumbered by excessive organizational constraint. At the same time, it should fully organize all established areas, systematize every routine and recurring operation, so that those activities can proceed smoothly and effortlessly, leaving the best minds and the greatest energy free for creativity and innovation.*

Yet Linear still has challenges to meet to keep its organization dynamic and growing. Swanson is still striving for that delicate balance between freedom and discipline. "Now I'm cracking down on the design group a little. The trick is that if I get them too organized, I'll destroy some of the free spirit, the creativity." Swanson is a very hands-on CEO. He is the driving force for growth, the source of the energy that propels the company forward. He is also still searching for a means to create engines of growth at the next level, so the company can continue to expand rapidly, without everything relying on him. "There is an organizational challenge awaiting me here in the future.

That is, how to create an organization where there is a focus of energy on each key area of the business. It can't all come from me any more."

Swanson has succeeded in implementing corporate values, such as coordination, integration, and freedom at a high level, that are critical for the continuous growth of an organization. But he has not yet been able to institutionalize that implementation to the extent that it becomes a self-generating and self-perpetuating source of energy for nonstop growth. The challenges he faces are the challenges that confront every company that wants to create a living organization.

CREATING A LIVING ORGANIZATION

An organization becomes creative when its capacities are fully utilized and it functions at peak levels. Otherwise, it degenerates, its component parts operating in isolation from each other, and ceases to be an organization. It becomes a bureaucracy.

The secret to keeping an organization alive and youthful is to keep it operating at its maximum capacity and to keep increasing that capacity by constantly upgrading the quality of its subunits and the coordination and integration between them. Then the organization flowers into a living organism with its own energy and dynamism for growth.

Organization is most alive when its every act is fresh and vibrant. Usually in a company each fresh, energizing experience is counter-balanced by thousands of routine acts which dull our sensibilities and drain our energies. Yet it need not be so. It is possible for companies to structure and carry out work in such a way that every activity, every job, every individual act becomes a refreshing and energizing experience for the individual, and a stimulus for further growth of the company. Chapter Fourteen presents practical strategies to energize individual acts and thereby energize the corporation as a whole.

STRATEGIES TO ENERGIZE YOUR ORGANIZATION

1. Establish clear job descriptions for every position and create a system whereby the responsibilities and authority of each position are clear to other people in the company.
2. Analyze the jobs of executives, managers and supervisors to identify tasks that can be delegated to lower levels and the conditions necessary to make that delegation effective.
3. Conduct an analysis of major activities in the company such as selling, advertising, order taking, invoicing, product development, project management, purchasing, maintenance, customer service, dispatch, and so on

to identify ways to increase the speed, reduce the cost, eliminate unnecessary steps, and improve the quality of these activities. Then extend the analysis to minor activities as well.

4. Assess the effectiveness of important systems in the company in terms of their speed, personnel requirements, quality of work, and cost of operation. Identify steps to improve their performance on these variables.

5. One way to ensure that your organization remains youthful, vigorous, and perpetually fresh is to implement values to a high level. Every value has a direct or indirect impact on the organization, but the most powerful are the organizational values such as coordination, integration, discipline, freedom, standardization, teamwork, and communication.

APPLYING THE TOOLS OF ORGANIZATION

A. *Analyze Your Job*
Here are ten steps to energize your personal organization.

1. Make a list of the actual tasks that you perform in the course of a month.
2. Categorize the tasks by frequency and importance into major, minor, infrequent, and nonrecurring.
3. Break down each task into its actual steps.
4. Estimate the time required to perform each step. Calculate the time required for each task per month. Total up the time to see that you have accounted for all your working hours during an average month.
5. Identify those steps that could be carried out effectively by someone who reports to you.
6. Now assess lost opportunities that occur because you have no time to do other important things. List all the tasks you are not performing or not performing as fully as you should be in order to carry out the responsibilities of your position.
7. Calculate the benefit in terms of time, money, and opportunities from transferring those steps or tasks.
8. Identify the appropriate position to which these tasks should be transferred.
9. Identify the conditions necessary to effect the transfer successfully.
10. Reorganize your job.

B. *Analyze Key Systems*
1. Conduct an analysis of five key systems in your company.
2. Evaluate each system in terms of four criteria: speed of operation, personnel requirement, quality and reliability, and cost effectiveness. Rate the system on each of the four criteria on a scale from 0 (low) to 25 (high). The maximum score for each system is 100 points.
3. Identify specific actions you can take to improve the performance of these systems on these criteria.
4. Repeat the analysis for other major and minor systems.

C. *Analyze Key Activities*
1. Conduct an analysis of five key activities in your company.
2. Evaluate each activity in terms of the following questions:
   a. Do the people responsible for the activity have all the information and skills they require for the job?
   b. Do they have all the authority required?
   c. Are the proper systems in place to carry out and monitor the activity?
   d. Can these systems be improved?
   e. Can the activity be done with fewer people?
   f. Can quality and reliability be improved?
   g. Can speed be increased?
   h. Can coordination between this and other related activities be increased?
   i. Can cost be reduced?
3. Identify specific actions you can take to improve the performance of the activity.
4. Repeat the analysis for other major and minor activities.

PROFIT PLANNING

1. Review your answers to the questions on organization at the end of Chapter Two.
2. Identify the practical steps you will take to raise the performance of your company/division/department on this component.
3. Develop a detailed action plan for carrying out these steps.

4. Estimate the growth in your company's revenues and profits that can be achieved by applying the ideas presented in this chapter to energize organization and convert it into an engine for growth.

SUMMARY

- Organization is the most powerful and creative, but least understood and appreciated, of the five engines.

- The analysis of an organization in terms of its three fundamental subunits—positions, activities, and systems—is a powerful tool for releasing the energies of this engine.

- Implementation of organizational values such as coordination, integration, and freedom makes an organization alive and creative.

Chapter Eleven

MAKING THE MARKET COME TO YOU

To grow means that you must expand your market. In that sense this entire book is about ways to energize the component market for the growth of your company. In Chapter Six, we looked at the market in its widest sense as co-terminous with society. Every change in society creates new needs and new markets for companies that are quick to perceive their significance and to seize the opportunity. New technologies, new life styles, new laws and political configurations, and new types of organization are social developments with major impact on market opportunities. Companies like Liz Claiborne, Reebok, AMRE, Expeditors International, Gartner Group, P.A.M. and Mesa perceived such changes and converted them into opportunities for rapid growth.

In other chapters we have looked at companies that have developed their markets by implementing values like customer service, quality, and on-time delivery. SAS and Linear Technology are dramatic examples of the power of value implementation to attract customers. These two approaches to the market, one focused on external changes and the other on internal developments, are important elements of a comprehensive approach to the market.

Our goal is to convert each of the five components of your business into an engine for rapid growth. Many people and companies consider market the most important of the five, yet the one that is least under our control. There is an almost superstitious reverence for the munificent market, which is the provider of all bounty, and an equally superstitious fear of the fickle or despotic market, which takes away as quickly as it gives. "After all," they argue, "businesses are created to meet the demands of the market and to thrive on it. When the market falls, there is not much you can do but hang on and pray for a speedy recovery." On the other hand, today there are many large successful companies that seem to dominate the market and actually command it to do their bidding. They boast, "We create the market. We decide what the customer will have. We provide it and the customer buys."

Both views of the market express a partial truth. The market creates businesses and business creates markets. The market is at once something vast and external to a company and at the same time something with which every company is in close and intimate contact. It can be cold and aloof. It can also be warm and embracing. But the relationship is not as one-sided as it may seem. The market is not just an enchanting temptress that leads us along and shares its charms and riches for a while, before looking elsewhere for its pleasure. It can also be an enchanted lover, true to the core, which seeks after us passionately and clings with everlasting devotion. In this chapter we explore strategies to convert the market into an eternal partner and an engine for endless expansion.

WHAT IS YOUR MARKET?

The market exists at three different levels. Companies relate to the market in three different ways. At the first level, the market consists of a finite number of recognized needs, and companies compete to meet those needs. There is a strong demand for computers, so we make them. There is a widespread demand for fast and convenient food service, so we provide it. This is the basis of niche marketing. Study the existing market and find a segment or subsegment where your company can effectively compete. Niche marketing is effective, because it enables a company to focus on what it does best. But the niche approach is also limited. It starts and ends with the existing market and tries to maximize gains within the present field. If your company approaches the market from this point of view, its growth is confined to the already established needs of the market.

At the second level, the market consists of needs which exist, but are unrecognized by society and companies, and therefore are unmet. Companies grow by recognizing those unfulfilled needs, creating a general awareness of them and then meeting them. This is what Fred Smith did when he founded Federal Express. He recognized the latent demand for overnight parcel delivery, generated public awareness of the importance of that need, and established a company to meet it.

Vipont Pharmaceuticals has done something similar. It recognized an unmet need in an increasingly health-conscious population and created a product to meet that need. Toothpaste is a $1.2 billion a year commodity business, in which dozens of giant suppliers compete with one another for valuable shelf space in supermarkets and drugstores. What chance would a tiny start-up toothpaste company have against Goliaths like Procter & Gamble and Colgate? Vipont realized it was fighting against heavy odds in 1981 when it introduced a new toothpaste containing sanguinaria, a natural medicinal compound from the bloodroot plant, which has been proven effective in preventing the formation of oral plaque, a major cause of gum disease that afflicts some 40 million Americans.

When Vipont started, there was very little awareness of the dangers of plaque and no manifest demand for an antiplaque toothpaste and mouthwash, especially at twice the price of regular brands. Vipont did not enter an existing market at all. It created a new one. Instead of trying to compete on national television against the majors, Vipont chose another strategy. It went directly to dentists and oral hygienists—the ones who knew all about plaque and its dangers—to educate them about the virtues of a sanguinaria-based toothpaste and mouthwash. The strategy worked. The professionals recognized the value of the product and began recommending it to their patients. The awareness they created gave birth to a new market for antiplaque toothpaste and mouthwash. Vipont has risen on the crest of that emerging market from sales of $12,000 in 1981 to $33.5 million in 1988 and is still growing at 30% a year.

You do not have to be an original thinker or visionary to identify unmet needs. You need an open, curious mind and careful observation. What are the unrecognized needs in your industry? What new dimension or incremental improvement can you add to an existing product or service that will meet a latent need of society or your customers and create a new market that does not now exist?

Not every company can create a new product or a new market. But the third level of market is open to all. *There is in every industry a gap between what the market actually needs or wants and what companies perceive it wants. That gap represents fertile untapped ground for any company that can become more conscious of the market's real wants.* Even as great a marketing company as Coca-Cola failed to perceive correctly the wants of its customers when it introduced the "new Coke" in the mid-1980s. And the American automobile industry is notorious for its blatant inability or unwillingness to understand what the market wants and to provide it. The gap created by that failure served as an open invitation for invasion by European carmakers in the 1960s and the Japanese in the 1980s.

How do you become conscious of something of which you are unconscious? One method is to ask! That is what Ford Motors did about five years ago when it finally realized that the old way of doing business in a comfortable shared monopoly industry was dead. When Ford launched its project to develop the Taurus, it identified and adapted some of the best features found on competitors' cars. Then it did the unthinkable. For the first time, Ford asked customers detailed questions about what they wanted. The company compiled a list of 1,401 customer wants, including apparently insignificant details such as lettering under the hood to help the nonmechanically minded distinguish the radiator from the battery and to know where to put in the oil! More than 700 of these ideas were incorporated in the Taurus and Sable models. Behold the response. Ford sold about half a million of the new models in the very first year.

The Taurus went on to become one of the best selling cars in the United States for three years in succession. *Car and Driver* called it "the most agile and capable sedan Detroit has ever produced."[1]

Closing the gap between what the market wants and what we think it wants is an exercise in objectivity and humility. For many companies, this one strategy is enough to double sales. Small improvements can make a big difference. When is the last time you really and systematically asked your customers about their preferences? If it was not today or yesterday, perhaps you should ask again.

Asking for the customer's preferences opens up new avenues for growth, but by itself it is a partial approach. Many companies have come to understand a general truth of human nature. The individual is not fully conscious of what he or she wants or likes or why. The same is true of the market. *The market is conscious only at the minimum level of its needs.* If a company offers a new product or an improved service, the market knows whether it likes it or not. It can even make suggestions for minor improvements, but rarely more than that. This is what Federal Express has learned asking customers about their needs. Carole Presley, senior vice president of marketing, says, "People don't have a clue of what to ask for beyond what they currently are getting. They want what they are currently getting to work precisely 100% of the time." That does not mean that preferences do not exist, it only means they are not conscious.

If the customers cannot tell you their preferences, then how do you find out? That requires a new attitude and an effort to identify with the customer. C. E. Woolman, founder of Delta Airlines, described the attitude as "putting yourself on the other side of the counter and looking at things from the customer's point of view." The effort required is one of careful observation, perception, and thoughtfulness.

The level at which your company relates to the market determines the scope for its expansion. Relating to unfulfilled needs and unmet preferences opens up endless opportunities for growth in any industry.

WHO IS YOUR CUSTOMER?

As companies relate to the market at three different levels, they also view the customer from four different perspectives. The wider and deeper the view, the greater is the market that opens. First and most commonly, companies relate to the customer from the point of view of the product. "I have a product to sell. Anyone who buys it is my customer." Companies with this view have a very limited idea of who their customers are, what their needs are or how to attract more of them. They rely on the product to do that.

The second view is more expansive. Look at the customer as a member of society. Identify the social characteristics of the customer and think of ways to meet the needs of specific social groups. Julius Rosenwald followed this approach when he introduced

Sear's famed money-back guarantee at the turn of the century. Sears was selling to rural farmers, who were highly suspicious of urban merchants, especially mail-order merchants! Understanding the need of that social group, Rosenwald introduced the money-back offer to assure them of quality and complete satisfaction. Henry Ford did the same thing when he built a low-priced car for the working-class buyer. He understood the urge of the working class to live the American dream of owning a car. So he designed and built the Model T at less than half the price of existing models and revolutionized the automotive industry. When Liz Claiborne introduced a line of garments specially designed for working women, the company was looking at the customer as a member of a social group with distinct characteristics. When Gideon Gartner packaged information on the computer industry specifically for decision-making computer users, he was looking at a social subset, too.

Looking at the customer as a member of society with distinct characteristics and specific needs has enabled these companies to expand vastly the market for their products and services, in some cases to a size greater than the entire original industry it started in.

The third view of the customer opens even greater vistas. Look at the customer simply as an individual. Recognize the needs and preferences that any individual would have and cater to them. Apple Computer thought from the individual's point of view when they created the user-friendly Macintosh computer.

It did not take a genius to realize that companies that pay high prices to get valuable documents delivered overnight would like to have access to up-to-the-minute information regarding the location and status of their parcels—but it did take a company with an open mind, thinking about what other people think. Federal Express realized that getting the parcel there quickly was really only half of what the customer wanted. In many cases the customer also wanted to know that the parcel had arrived, and if not, when it would. In practice, the company discovered that immediate information about the parcel was even more important to many customers than on-time delivery itself.

The fourth and most powerful view is to relate to the customer, not merely as an individual who shares much in common with everyone else, but as a unique individual who has unique needs, preferences, and identity. Hotel customers do appreciate the chocolate on the pillow—everyone likes chocolate—or the newspaper under the door even when they know that the same treatment is given to every other customer as well. But nothing evokes such a powerful response as when the customer realizes that the company relates to him or her as a unique individual. The effort a company makes to custom-tailor a product or service to meet a specific need, to solve problems to the customer's total satisfaction, or just to recognize the customer by name makes a lasting impression.

Who are your customers? How well do you know them? How deeply do you cater to the specific needs and characteristics which distinguish them from others? What more can you do to differentiate your products or services, so that they more closely meet your customers' social or individual characteristics?

MAKING THE MARKET RESPOND

When a company appeals very deeply and powerfully to the conscious or unconscious need of the market, the market rushes toward it and literally drives its growth. It is possible for any company to make the market respond with that intensity by what the company does within itself, without going out to seek the market at all.

The market is attracted to a company by the intensity and quality of the work it does. Virtually every strategy described in this book to release and utilize corporate energies more effectively, to raise the quality of work by implementing values, and to energize and balance the five components can directly or indirectly attract the market.

The following nine strategies can be used to energize the market for your company and bring it to your door.

Hard Work

How do you feel when you enter a store where the employees are too preoccupied by talking among themselves to attend to your needs or when the luggage carrier at a luxury hotel sees you walking in with a heavy bag and lazily gets up from his chair and strolls over to greet you? Contrast this with your feeling when you enter a company where people are alert, active, brisk, and busily engaged in work. Even if you are kept waiting, the energy and activity itself is attractive. Hard work attracts the market.

Organized Work Can Energize the Market

When work is well organized, streamlined, and smooth running, it attracts the market even more. Customers who come in contact feel a sense of competence and confidence that brings them back. Any improvement in the functioning of your organization can have a direct or indirect impact on the market. Organization influences quality, friendliness, speed of response, accuracy, reliability, orderliness—literally everything your company does.

Organization even helps you to know your customers better. Knowing exactly who your customers are enables your company to utilize the most effective means for reaching them. AMRE has a sophisticated customer tracking system that enables it to track every response to its TV advertisements and direct mail to determine precisely which state or zip code generates the highest rates of response and the highest closing ratios. All advertisement responses come in through postage-paid return cards or over WATS lines to a centralized point where the customer is qualified by well-trained phone operators and appointments are made for salespeople in offices around the country. This eliminates the necessity for salespeople to identify their own leads and enables them to concentrate on making sales. AMRE's sales force averages a closing rate of nearly 20% on average sales of over $6,000.

Perfect Work

Perfect work means work that is done by happy employees in a harmonious and flawless manner by implementing corporate values to a high degree. Companies that achieve this level of performance are irresistibly attractive to customers. People enjoy making contact with the company and seek every opportunity to come back.

Raising performance on any value can energize the market. SAS did it with speed and customer service. Ford did it with quality. Merck has done it with credibility. Northwestern Mutual has done it through a commitment to teamwork and customer service. AMRE did it with systematic functioning and development of its people. Any value can evoke an intensely positive response from the customer. P.A.M. has discovered what McDonald's has known for decades. Even a simple value like cleanliness can have a tremendous impact. P.A.M. prides itself on maintaining its trucks in mint condition. Frequently, existing and would-be customers comment on how impressed they are by the sparkling cleanliness of the equipment. Cleanliness attracts too. If you do not believe that, watch your own reaction the next time you go into a restaurant that is not clean.

People Can Energize the Market

Knowledgeable, well-trained, cheerful people with pleasant, positive attitudes toward the customer can make a world of difference. You cannot order people to be cheerful. If you want your people to please your customers, make sure your people are happy. Carole Presley of Federal Express explains: "Every time our customers make a phone call to us, they notice exactly what the agent's tone of voice is and whether that agent went to the full extent to answer the question or resolve the issue." In fact, Federal Express has found that the attitude and behavior of their front-line employees is rated by customers as the real reason why they prefer the company over its competitors—not the fact that it has a higher on-time delivery rate. "Every time we ask the customer to evaluate the company, they always rate our couriers number one, our telephone agents number two, and our customer service agents in the field as number three. These are the top-rated attributes. They are rated much higher than on-time delivery."

Capital Can Energize the Market

Managing finances properly can enable a company to expand its market or create new markets. By maintaining itself as the low-cost airline on commuter runs, Mesa has been able not only to compete effectively, but actually to create new markets in some cases. Federal Express also found that by improving operational efficiencies, it was able to reduce costs and prices by 30% over the last ten years. Lower prices dramatically expanded the market.

Technology Can Energize the Market

Many technologies can be adapted to improve the product or the quality of service to customers and evoke a response from the market. When Federal Express installed DADS computer terminals in trucks and a few years later gave a SuperTracker hand-held terminal to every courier, it really energized people. The couriers were suddenly at the leading edge of technology. Their sense of pride and motivation increased dramatically. Customers also evinced great curiosity about the new technology. So the couriers were trained to make a brief presentation to interested customers about the SuperTracker and were given small brochures they could leave with the customer. What technology from other industries could your company adopt to give it a leading edge in service to your customers or in product quality?

Extend the Application of Your Product or Service to One New Area

As Vipont extended the use of toothpaste for treating plaque, the use of every product and service can be extended to serve new purposes. Perrier converted mineral water into a popular social drink. The use of aspirin has been extended from treating headaches to heart ailments. How can you extend the use of your existing products and services to serve new purposes or meet new needs?

Improve the Quality and Accuracy of Information to the Customer

Merck has done it through its commitment to the value of credibility with the customer. Listen Up did it through a computerized tracking system for orders in the service department. Whatever the means, providing customers with information they can rely on confidently is a real energizer.

Relate to the Customer as a Unique Individual

All that we have said about the power of giving attention to people within the company applies in equal measure to the customer. Nothing makes people respond more than genuine interest and personal attention. Take sincere interest in your customers for their own sake—and not merely because they are customers—and they will seek excuses to relate to your company for the sheer joy of the attention they receive.

ATTENTION TO THE CUSTOMER

Children respond to attention, but many children are deprived of it. The same is true of husbands, wives, friends, employees and shareholders. It is also true of customers. Nothing attracts customers like personal attention in the form of pleasant, courteous, high-quality service. The phone answered on the first ring with a warm, cheerful voice is a pure delight to the customer. The thank-you note, the phone call "just to see how you are doing," the sympathetic listening to a problem, the order promptly and properly dispatched, the literature thoughtfully conceived to answer the customer's real questions—rather than raising new ones!—the letter telling the customer the products have been back-ordered and specifying the date when the order is expected—these are just a few of the small ways in which companies can give attention to their customers.

Two things are essential to give that attention. First, management and every employee must understand fully and believe that it is good to do so and feel enthusiastic about pleasing the customer. If it is done out of a genuine desire to help and make happy, it is most powerful. All negative attitudes—for example, the customer is unreasonable, the customer is foolish, the customer is ripping us off—must be tempered by a genuine desire to please.

Second, the company and all its people must have sufficient energy to give that attention. As the child's inexhaustible demands for attention can exhaust the most energetic parent, the needs of the customer are endless. Therefore, the effort requires an enormous energy, which the company must be able to release from its people and harness effectively without waste. People must be enthused and continuously learning new skills, so that their energies are constantly overflowing. Systems must be fine-tuned and smooth running, so that all available energy is properly utilized for service. Attention is given through prompt service, which requires an alert, highly efficient organization. It is conveyed through pleasant service, which is possible when people within the company are naturally happy in their work and not under stress. Attention is given through personalized service to the customer. Personalized service can be given to all customers only when impersonal systems are employed to manage routine work down to the last detail. The systems must be developed enough to smoothly handle even heavy bursts of activity and yet flexible enough to adapt to unusual, individual customer demands.

When we refer to the customer, we think of individuals. When we refer to the market, we usually think of an impersonal capacity to buy. But by market, we mean the sum of all actual and potential individual customers in the society. Giving attention to the market means to be genuinely interested in the needs, requirements, ways of life, tastes and levels of appreciation of people in the society. This effort has several dimensions.

There should be a full knowledge of the needs of present customers and the way your products or services are used by them. This knowledge comes from being in constant and close touch with buyers, dealers, and actual users. There has to be an awareness of how the ultimate customers actually live or work and how they actually use the products or services as part of that living and working. The company must be constantly thinking about the customer's convenience and finding new ways to serve it. There should also be a full knowledge of the future needs of the customer, new ways in which the products can be used to meet new needs or to raise the level of comfort, convenience, productivity, and so on. This requires an analytical study of the customer to discover what might bring greater satisfaction.

In other words, for a company to energize the market it must be continuously striving to know, understand, serve, please, and anticipate the needs of its customers, while at the same time constantly fostering the growth and fulfillment of its own employees to release their enthusiastic energies and perfecting the systems needed for delivering attention to the customer.

YOU ARE BEING WATCHED

Make no mistake about it. Every company is being watched all the time. Just as we remember exactly how we were treated or mistreated when we went into that restaurant four years ago, just as we can recall exactly how we felt when our new car had to go back for servicing the day after we bought it, just as we can fondly recollect the patience and sympathy unexpectedly shown by a customer service representative after our warranty had expired, in just the same way every customer remembers or does not remember your company.

Every company is being talked about, too. Both the good experiences and the bad are eagerly shared with family, friends, and coworkers. Word-of-mouth is as powerful an advertisement today, as it was in the centuries before TV and radio.

Customers perceive differences. Those differences do not have to be very great to make a great deal of difference in our market—just great enough to distinguish us one way or the other from our competitors. Every time we make a purchase or choose a company, we select on the basis of conscious or unconscious preferences that are often minutely small. Therefore, even a small effort, a small improvement in the product, the service or any other facet of our operations can have a disproportionately positive impact on our business. The same is also true of a small error or failing.

That is why focusing on corporate values is so powerful. Values raise the quality of our performance by significant increments, which become directly visible or indirectly perceptible to the market, even when they are implemented in the depths of the company away from the public eye.

PROFIT PLANNING

1. Review your answers to the questions on market at the end of Chapter Two.
2. Identify the practical steps you will take to raise the performance of your company/division/department on this component.
3. Develop a detailed action plan for carrying out these steps.
4. Estimate the growth in your company's revenues and profits that can be achieved by applying the ideas presented in this chapter to energize market and convert it into an engine for growth.

SUMMARY

- It is possible for a company to energize its market so that the market is attracted and moves toward the company.

- The market can be viewed from three different perspectives: existing needs, unrecognized needs, and the gap between what the market needs and what the company perceives that it wants.

- The customer can be viewed from four different perspectives: in terms of the product or service, as a member of a social group, as an individual, and as a unique person.

- The market moves toward a company in response to hard work, organization, and commitment to values.

- People, technology, and capital can also energize the market.

Chapter Twelve

TUNING IN TECHNOLOGY

No one needs to be convinced that technology can be an engine of growth. We see all around us examples of companies that have exploded upon the scene and rocketed into prominence on the basis of a new technology or a new product. But that is to view this component in a narrow sense as the technology of a product or an industrial process. Whereas the component technology is equally applicable to a trucking company or an airfreight forwarder.

In its essence, technology is the know-how that enables a company to produce and distribute a product or provide a service to the market. It includes the equipment companies employ for sales, design, production, storage, delivery, accounting, training, measurement, and so on. It includes the knowledge, know-how, and skills they employ for all these activities as well.

Each of the five components can be energized in several different ways. In this chapter, we explore two basic strategies for energizing technology: implementing values and integrating technology more closely with the other four components.

The values most directly related to technology are innovation and creativity, quality, safety, and maintenance of equipment.

INNOVATION AND CREATIVITY

There are three levels of technology—productive, innovative and creative. Productive technology is any technology which has a practical utility. By innovative technology, we mean technology which has been improved to add greater value, function, economy, or quality. Creative technology contains an original element. It is not just improved, it is something new. Technological creativity can be achieved by combining or relating technology to the other four components in new ways. Following are some basic principles for identifying potential areas of technological innovation and creativity.

Add One New Dimension to the Value of the Product

In 1960 there were more than 30 manufacturers of radios, TVs, and hi-fi equipment in Denmark. Today there is only Bang & Olufsen. The others have been swept away by the rise of the giant electronics corporations in Japan and in Europe, which produce in such huge volumes that smaller manufacturers cannot compete. Bang & Olufsen not only survived, it has grown nearly 50-fold in 26 years by adding a totally new dimension to home electronics products—beauty—by combining acoustical quality with elegant design. The company has succeeded so well that its products are displayed in the Museum of Modern Art in New York City.

A change in any aspect of the product or service can add a new dimension to its value or convenience. Minit International introduced shoe repairing to prestige department stores and train stations throughout Europe to make the service more accessible. California wine is now being sold to Europe in milk containers to reduce the costs of transportation. What new dimension can you add to the products or services you offer, to the way they are packaged or the places they are available?

Integrate New and Old Technology

There are so many possible technological innovations of which we are unconscious that even without the advent of any new technologies, it is possible to improve virtually any product. Detroit is putting new technology in its cars—the on-board computer—and under them—stainless steel mufflers and coatings to prevent rust. Chrysler has added luxury and convenience with an old technology by installing a small motor to close the trunk in some models. It has become fashionable to put digital clocks on almost everything. What new or old technology can you add to enhance the value of your product or service?

Look at Technology from the Market's Point of View

Make a conscious effort to identify ways in which your products or services could be made to better serve the needs of the market. Ford and Bang & Olufsen have done this. Merck adopted this approach in the 1950s, when it encouraged its research scientists to talk directly to marketing people at a very early stage in the research process, so that the direction of scientific inquiry could be more closely tuned to the needs of patients. This approach enabled Merck to develop drugs to meet previously untreated conditions and drugs suitable for treating patients who could not benefit from existing medicines. It also was a principle reason for the rise of Merck from fifth to first in the U.S. drug industry.

Create or Innovate Technology to Meet Psychological Needs

Apple's user-friendly Macintosh is a computer which people really enjoy working on—some would even say "love" working on. Studies have shown that the average Mac user spends much more time on the computer than users of other brands. It is a technology that has psychological appeal—fun. Providing enjoyment or security or educational value to a technology enhances its value.

Look for Innovations That Reduce Cost

Federal Express searches high and low for every possible means to bring down the cost of transporting parcels. It even looked at the way its planes were built and decided it could improve that too. The planes the company uses were originally designed for carrying passengers, not containers of packages. The length of a Boeing 727 plane's body is sufficient to hold 11 standard containers of freight with some room left over. Federal Express found that by modifying the internal frame it could fit an extra container on each flight. This resulted in additional capacity equivalent to the purchase of 13 new aircraft for a nominal cost, saving the company millions of dollars on equipment.

QUALITY

Quality applies to everything—product, service, production technology, showroom displays, packaging, accounting, and so on. Regardless of where this value is applied, quality has the power to improve morale, reduce costs, and minimize the necessity of redoing work. Effective implementation of quality involves the five stages outlined earlier in this book—a firm commitment, setting clear and quantifiable standards, assigning responsibility, putting in the right systems to achieve and monitor performance, and training for the right skills.

America's basic manufacturing industries have been under enormous pressure over the past decade to improve quality in everything they do. The *commitment* to quality is no longer a matter of choice. It is a pressing necessity. Larger customers are insisting on better quality from all their suppliers. In many industries customers are not waiting for vendors to raise their quality *standards*. The customers are imposing their own. The companies most committed to quality have two sets of standards, the one imposed by the customer and the one they impose on themselves, which is significantly higher.

In the past, quality control departments and inspectors were responsible for quality and empowered to stop production lines and reject products below standard. Today the structure for quality has changed. Everyone has a responsibility for quality. Machine operators are being given the responsibility to monitor their work and the authority to send back substandard parts that come to them. Systems such as statistical process control are being used to provide immediate feedback on quality deviations as they come off the machine. Training is being given to managers, supervisors, operators and workers to improve awareness and skills for quality. Wherever such a comprehensive approach to quality improvement is introduced, the results are impressive.

The experience of Sectional Tool and Die of Ohio is typical. John Babbitt, the founder, launched a major quality program last year. He hired a quality manager who reported directly to the CEO, developed a detailed quality manual, introduced statistical process control systems, and did extensive training. Instead of giving all authority to the quality control inspectors, machine operators were made responsible for monitoring the quality of parts they produced and they were given the systems needed to do so. This really got people involved in finding ways to improve quality. The effort had a dramatic impact on his people and his profitability. Energy, motivation and productivity went way up. The scrap rate fell from 5% to 1%, which added $250,000 to the company's bottom line on sales of $6 million.

Quality has no end and no limit. Think about quality in your company. What more can you do to improve it?

PUTTING TECHNOLOGY IN PROPER PERSPECTIVE

Technology is so powerful that those who are deeply involved with it sometimes forget that in business it cannot function by itself. The full productive and creative power of technology becomes available only when it is kept in proper balance with the other four components.

Vipont Pharmaceuticals was established back in 1968 as a research company to develop products based on sanguinaria. During its first 13 years in business, it never sold a product. By the time Larry Frederick became CEO in 1981, the company had spent the $4 million invested in it over the years and had a negative net worth of $500,000. About the only thing the company had left was a very good product and a great technological potential. The product was the toothpaste. The potential was a technology for using sanguinaria to treat gum disease, which the company felt could help Vipont become a $500 million company.

To bring the toothpaste to market and create the financial and organizational basis for developing the new technology, Frederick and his team had to build up the other four components of the company. They resorted to some creative financial techniques to raise additional capital. They recruited talented and experienced people to head up marketing, sales, and research positions. They put in sophisticated systems for planning, budgeting, financial control, and tracking customers. The company which had been treading water for 13 years suddenly starting growing rapidly. Its ability to generate increasing sales and profits over the last few years has also enabled it to invest the funds needed to accelerate development of its technology for gum disease.

Vipont's growth illustrates how dependent technology is on the other components for its full development and flowering. Larry Holt, vice president of finance, agrees: "All five components were important." Until the other four components were suitably developed, the potentials of its technology could not be exploited. The full creative potentials of technology can be tapped by exploring the linkages between this component and the other four.

MATCHING TECHNOLOGY WITH THE MARKET

One of the reasons Mesa Airlines has been able to survive the heavy competition from other commuter and regional airlines has been its knack for properly matching its equipment with the needs of the market. Some new airlines rushed to buy big, fancy Boeing aircraft and then lost heavily by flying the highly competitive, larger commercial market routes just to fill all the seats on the bigger planes. Mesa followed a different strategy. It decided to fly only the lower volume commuter routes, where it could maintain a cost advantage and bought smaller 19- and 13-seat aircraft to suit its strategy. CEO Larry Risley explains: "The thing that has propelled our growth has been the ability to recognize the potential markets and fit the right size equipment to those markets. We size the equipment to the market demand, even if it means going to smaller equipment. I am not concerned about how many people I can carry, as much as I am about how many people I can carry profitably."

Robert Ross may not have understood or appreciated government regulations too well, but he certainly understood and appreciated what his customers wanted. Their biggest concern was with the safe disposal of solid hazardous waste that could not be easily burned. Incineration of liquid wastes was relatively easy, but disposal of solids was so difficult that many commercial incinerators would not touch them. Years ago Ross and his son Gary began experimenting with better ways to handle the incineration of solids. After years of experimentation, they came up with a technology that enabled Ross Incineration Services to incinerate solids profitably and made it a technological leader in this important segment of the industry.

LINKING TECHNOLOGY AND ORGANIZATION

Just as the market can energize the development of technology, organization can too. When the demand and price for incineration of solid wastes skyrocketed in the early 1980s, Ross Incineration found giant Fortune 500 companies literally standing in line to avail themselves of its services. Its only problem was that the technology it employed for handling solids required frequent shutdowns for cleaning and maintenance. As a result the incinerator was operating less than three weeks in the month.

To meet the demands of its customers, it became essential for the company to keep the incinerator operating at the highest levels of efficiency with the minimum of unscheduled shutdowns. Maureen Cromling and Gary Ross realized that they did not have the organizational structure in place to achieve and maintain such high levels of performance on their incinerator. So they hired a new vice president of operations and a more qualified plant manager to build up a structure that could achieve higher levels of operational efficiency. New systems were installed to monitor and analyze performance of the equipment. Detailed schedules and preventive maintenance procedures were established to reduce downtime to an absolute minimum. Coordination between sales, transportation, the loading dock, and the testing laboratory were improved to ensure nonstop flow of materials. Virtually every activity and system related to the incinerator were reviewed and upgraded to improve performance. The new organization enabled Ross to increase the annual throughput of the incinerator by nearly 100%.

Organization can have an energizing impact on R&D as well as on production. The structure of R&D should be tailored to the unique needs of that department, with an academic as distinct from a purely commercial atmosphere. We have already described the type of organization Linear Technology uses to bring out the creativity of its chip designers—close coordination with production and the market and freedom to choose the products they work on.

The research division at Gartner Group is structured to provide maximum freedom to the individual researchers within well-defined guidelines. The division is divided into more than a dozen service groups focusing on different aspects of the computer industry. The research method has been systematized to ensure consistency and uniformity. There are also quality control functions to ensure accuracy and objectivity. In addition there are weekly all-hands meetings at which researchers present their findings to their peers, who may challenge and openly criticize them.

Gartner's research division is plagued by one inherent organizational weakness. The job of a program director, as presently defined, is so complex and demanding that the company has difficulty recruiting people to fill these positions. "My biggest fear," says vice president Craig Symons, "is how are we going to meet our personnel requirements in the future. We expect the program directors to be the world's best presenters, prolific writers, good on the phone with customers, gurus on their special field." This illustrates to what extent the structure of an organization can influence the development of technology.

PEOPLE AND TECHNOLOGY

The development of technology is directly linked to the way a company recruits, trains, and motivates people. Gartner has a very rigorous recruitment screening process to ensure that it selects only the very best candidates. All applicants have to prepare reports and make their presentations to demonstrate their verbal and written skills. Gideon Gartner himself conducts training programs for the researchers to ensure that they fully understand the company's approach to information research. Earlier we described the unique salary incentive system Gartner employs to ensure that researchers remain highly sensitive to the needs of the customer and do not get carried away by their interest in the subject for its own sake.

ENERGIZING TECHNOLOGY IN YOUR COMPANY

Think about the know-how of your business. Apply these 12 strategies to energize technology in your company.

1. Improve the technology of your product or service by adding one new dimension to it.
2. Combine a new or old technology with your product or service to enhance its value.
3. Look at the products or services your company provides from the market's point of view. What can you do to better meet the needs of your customers?
4. Can you attune your product or service to meet a psychological need, so that it provides greater enjoyment, security or educational value to the customer?
5. Examine every technology your company employs and identify ways to reduce cost.
6. Implement the value quality in every possible area through all five stages of value implementation.
7. Improve and systematize preventive maintenance programs for all equipment and machinery.
8. Match your technology as closely as possible with the needs of the market.

9. What improvements can you make in your organization that will improve the development and operation of technology?
10. What new or improved technologies can you introduce that will improve the functioning of your organization?
11. What can you do to improve the development and operation of technology by better recruitment, training and motivation of your people?
12. How can you utilize technology to make work easier, more interesting and more rewarding for people?

PROFIT PLANNING

1. Review your answers to the questions on technology at the end of Chapter Two.
2. Identify the practical steps you will take to raise the performance of your company/division/department on this component.
3. Develop a detailed action plan for carrying out these steps.
4. Estimate the growth in your company's revenues and profits that can be achieved by applying the ideas presented in this chapter to energize technology and convert it into an engine for growth.

SUMMARY

• The engine technology is the know-how that enables a company to produce and distribute a product or provide a service to the market.

• Technology is most powerfully energized by integrating it more fully with the needs of the market.

• Technology is energized by implementing values such as innovation, quality, safety, and maintenance.

• Technology is also energized by linking it with the components organization, people, and capital.

Chapter Thirteen

GROWING CAPITAL

Ask entrepreneurs and executives about what holds back the growth of their business. Chances are the first word in reply will be "money"—capital. Capital is a reincarnation of the fickle, Greek goddess of fortune. Everything seems to depend on her generosity and benevolence. At least that is how we perceive it.

But no enlightened twentieth-century businessperson need be subjected to the whims and fancies of an ancient goddess. Capital is a power that can be attracted, mastered and harnessed for productive purposes by any company. In the Chapter Eleven, we looked at ways to make the market respond to your company and generate higher sales. As the market is attracted to companies which create the right internal conditions, so is capital. In this chapter we examine ways to make money move toward your company and generate higher profits.

Capital differs from the other four components. It is at once a productive resource and a result of productive work. It is an essential requirement for the activities of a company and an essential end result of those activities, too. Capital and profit are two different forms of the same thing.

Capital is a symbol of productive power. It contains all the other components within itself in potential. It can be converted into many different forms and used to stimulate the growth of any of the other components—to purchase or develop technology, hire people, build organization and develop a market. The linkage and interrelationship between capital and the other components is a key to energizing capital and converting it into an engine of growth.

HOW DO YOU MAKE MONEY COME TO YOU?

Larry Frederick must have known the answer to this question in 1981, otherwise he never would have consented to leave a secure executive position at International Teledyne Waterpik to become CEO of a company with a long history of research—and little else. Imagine trying to convince investors to put more money into a public company on the verge of bankruptcy, which has spent $4 million over 13 years trying to make toothpaste and never sold a single tubeful. But that is exactly what Frederick did when he joined Vipont Pharmaceuticals and walked into what he later described as "a total disaster." Frederick spent the first 18 months restructuring the company to make it financially viable and talking to financial institutions, shareholders, and the investment community to raise more money. The analysts were in unanimous agreement: "It's impossible!"

Finally Frederick and his team came up with an imaginative solution. They created a new R&D partnership that would raise money and conduct research, then sell the research results to the parent company. The research would generate a good tax write-off for investors and enable Vipont to spend more on research without showing further losses on its balance sheet. The idea worked. Vipont was able to raise $1.25 million to carry on its research and bring the toothpaste to market. In fact, it worked so well that within two years Vipont bought back the partnership and paid the investors three times their original capital in return. By then Vipont was able to go to Wall Street and raise further capital through a fresh $4 million stock offering.

Vipont's success is a dramatic example of making capital respond to the needs of a business. Two things made it possible. First, the experienced management understood the close linkage between capital and the other components. They knew that having a good technology and even a good market for its products were not enough. They understood what had to be done to build up all five components of the business to make the company profitable and attractive to investors. They drew up a comprehensive strategic plan for developing all five components, so that investors could see that the company had a viable basis and tremendous scope for growth. In other words, they created the five components in essence before seeking finance to create them in fact.

Second, they believed in the hidden potentials of the component capital and knew how to tap them to convert capital into an engine for growth. According to vice president of finance, Larry Holt, who has been with the company since 1973, "We have always been able to finance ourselves. We are creative enough to do unusual things. Capital has never been a constraint on our growth. We have always raised the capital we needed without resorting to a leverage type of financing. We've always stayed away from debt and had equity." Michelle Morgan added, "I almost think we are better at raising capital than we are at selling products, and I think we are excellent at selling products. We have built up a good track record that has made the capital funding easier."

CREATIVE FINANCING

When Robert Swanson and four other people left National Semiconductor to start up Linear Technology, they had a wealth of managerial experience, technological expertise, organizational know-how, and market knowledge. What they needed was money. Their plan was so solid that venture capitalists offered $15 million to fund the new company in return for a 60% share in the business. The entrepreneurs almost accepted the proposal, but then decided to think creatively. Instead they persuaded a real estate builder to borrow $3.5 million from his own bankers and put up a building for Linear to lease from him. They also found a leasing company that was willing to lease $9 million in equipment for their production facility based on 20% collateral security. So they went back to the venture capitals and said they wanted only $4.5 million and offered a 40% share of the business in return. The surprised investors reluctantly agreed. By investing only $500,000 of their own money, the entrepreneurs got 60% of a $15 million start-up company. That is creativity!

In an enterprising business environment like ours, society is constantly creating new ways to raise capital for business. Companies that need funds for growth should concentrate on developing all five components of their business and maintaining a balance between them. They should be constantly thinking and looking for innovative ways to attract capital for nonstop expansion.

SOME SIMPLE, BUT POWERFUL PRINCIPLES

In an earlier chapter we discussed the many different ways to motivate and energize people for greater productivity, profitability, growth and enjoyment. There are many ways to energize capital too.

Give It the Attention It Deserves

As do people, capital responds to attention. Companies give attention to capital through the way they account for money and other assets. It may sound surprising, but many companies do not know what they earn or what they lose—especially companies that are in financial trouble. The crisis that hit Waltz Brothers came as a surprise because the owners had always taken profits for granted and never insisted on accurate or timely accounts. One entrepreneur was driving down the Hollywood freeway when he received a call from his accountant telling him he was bankrupt. The businessman responded in disbelief, "But how could that be? My sales are up by 25% over last year." To which the accountant replied, "That's true, but your expenses are up by 35%!"

It took Iacocca quite some time to really understand the depth of Chrysler's troubles, because it took that long to sort out the real meaning of numbers on the income statement and the balance sheet. Some companies strive so hard to conceal the bad news from Wall Street through favorable accounting adjustments that they successfully conceal it from themselves as well, until it is too late.

One of the major offending areas is inventory. From very small companies to very large, keeping an accurate count and valuation of inventory is a task many find daunting, because accurate inventory accounting requires flawless systems at virtually every point connected to the product from inspection of incoming shipments and correct data entry to writing of sales receipts and control of inventory transfers. Fred Lokoff's Bryn Mawr Stereo in Pennsylvania has one of the best inventory control systems we have encountered in a retail business. Lokoff's system enables him to manage inventory levels carefully to obtain more than 6 turns a year on his inventory, compared with an industry average of less than 3.5 turns for audiovideo electronics stores. This means that with the same amount of capital, he can finance 70% more business than the average store in his industry. Lokoff's financial systems have paid off: "In twenty years in business, I have never had a year where I have done less business or made less profit than the year before. The only thing that has happened in bad years is that the increase was smaller."

Accounts Should Be Up to Date

Sounds easy? Then, why in the world is it so uncommon? Look at any company that is losing money. Chances are very good that its accounts are far behind schedule. Typically such companies complete their accounts just in time to go to their bankers for further finance. You can hear an infinite variety of explanations for slow accounting, yet the fact remains that getting and keeping accounts up to date has a great power— and it is not easy. Vance Pflanz, founder of Pflanz Electronics in Sioux City, Iowa, developed and installed in his store an online system that tells him the company's daily profit at the end of every working day.

How long does it take your company to close the books at the end of each month and find out how much it made or lost? Every day's delay is a real deenergizer to the growth of your business. Close the gap and watch the results.

Conventional wisdom says that companies should pay their bills as slowly as possible and collect receivables from others as quickly as they can. But there is a deeper, more profound wisdom, whose validity the most successful companies have discovered, that says *pay your bills as quickly as you can and collect receivables as quickly as you can too.* There is a logic behind this wisdom. How enthusiastic would your employees be if they were never quite sure if and when they would be getting their paychecks? Paying others quickly goes a long way in energizing them in their relationship with your company. The energy and commitment of a supplier who is positively disposed and appreciative can be as powerful a driving force for growth as the positive attitude of your most important customers. Winning over your vendors is worth ten times more than the deals a company can make or the interest it can save by slowing down payments to suppliers.

Use the Accounts as an Active Instrument

The word *accounting* is commonly used to refer to two related but distinct activities. Most companies use accounting primarily as a passive tool for recording and monitoring income and expenditure. But accounting can also be employed as an active instrument and powerful tool for monitoring and improving the performance of any business.

Gartner Group produces an income statement within seven days after closing its books at the end of every month. The statement details the performance of every department and service which the company offers and shows which ones are making and losing money. Management closely monitors financial performance to eliminate unprofitable services. "The key to success is to stop an idea in time when it is not working," says vice president of finance Bernard Denoyer.

AMRE completes 175 home remodeling jobs around the country every day. Within two days, corporate controller Dennie Brown knows exactly how much the company earned on each individual job. When the company opens a new office in a new area, this system enables it to adjust its pricing immediately to a profitable level, without waiting till the end-of-month financials are ready to know whether it lost or earned money. "If something is changing, the managers know immediately," says Brown. "They don't even care about month-end financials, because they already know their results."

It also enables AMRE to identify the precise characteristics of profit-making jobs, so that the marketing department knows what they should and should not be selling. "We have parameters set up to tell us what works in terms of prices, commissions, labor costs, material costs, etc.," Brown says.

Both of these companies utilize accounting as an active tool for making up-to-the-minute management decisions that directly impact on the bottom line. That requires up-to-the-minute accounting.

Use Cost Accounting as an Index of Performance

When Mike Zazanis of Audio Associates in Fairfax, Virginia, bought out a struggling retail business, he scrutinized the business's financial statements with a magnifying glass to find out why it was losing money. Then he took meticulous efforts to eliminate all wasteful and unnecessary expenditures. But no matter what he did, one thing kept bothering him: the cost of electricity. All his experience told him it should not exceed 1% of gross sales, yet even after putting in electricity-saving lighting, it still exceeded 3%. He began to suspect the air conditioner was at fault, so he called in an expert to check it. It checked out fine. He continued his efforts without success, but could not trace the reason for the high electricity bill. Finally he asked a friend to check the air conditioner again. The friend came back with this report: "The air conditioner works just fine. But every time you turn it on, the heater goes on too!" Zazanis was able to eliminate the waste of electricity and even get a refund from the owner of the building for the excess charges he had paid in previous months. This one change added 1.5% to his bottom line and helped to turn the company from losses to profits. That is the power of using the numbers constructively.

Saving Money versus Cutting Costs

The most profitable companies are not the ones that constantly cut costs across the board. They are the ones that know how to save money. The cost cutters achieve marginal short-term profit gains at the expense of midterm growth and long-term profitability. Cutting costs means to look at expenses, say they are too high, and order someone to reduce them—without the knowledge or understanding of how that reduction will really impact on the future of your business. The cost cutter says: do not hire more people, regardless of the need; postpone putting in that system, in spite of what it will do to improve quality or efficiency; live with the cramped quarters, even if they impact on morale and productivity.

Cost cutting is a negative activity—it achieves its results through contraction—whereas saving money is a positive and expansive activity that achieves its results by raising the quality and quantity of performance. Saving money means to analyze every job, system, and activity carefully and then ask: How can we do it better or for less money? Saving money requires clear goals, an intimate knowledge of the business, and a genuine commitment to building up the company to higher levels of performance.

Federal Express is firmly committed to saving every cent it can, provided that saving takes them a step closer to realizing Smith's vision of the future and provided it does not contradict the company's commitment to its core values—people, service, safety, and so on. Since 1975 Federal Express has brought down the cost of transporting a package from $9.15 to $2.70. This achievement is not the result of scrupulous cost cutting. It is the result of a constant effort to improve the overall efficiency of the system at every conceivable point.

Federal Express looks at every operation from the viewpoint of how it can help reduce the overall cost of handling a package, so that costs and prices can be further decreased and volumes can be further increased. This is how the company stumbled on the ideas of lengthening the body frame of its planes to add an extra container, introducing interactive video to reduce the number of training days for pilots, using peelable labels to save courier time, and introducing countless other cost innovations. All these improvements are generated by a positive, expansive attitude of wanting to do things better, not one of wanting to cut jobs or travel expenses.

The company constantly monitors critical success factors, such as the cost of transport per available ton mile (ATM). So it looks at every activity to see how it can be improved to help achieve that goal. Every department in the air-operations division is asked to scrutinize its activities to see what can be done to reduce flying time, reduce maintenance costs, increase productivity, and so on. Each manager is asked to determine the performance parameters on which his or her department should be evaluated. Jim Riedmeyer, former senior vice president of the division, says: "Don't force measurements down on people. They must buy into them. They must perceive them as reasonable. If there is a productivity improvement, it is not likely to come from the finance department. It is going to come from the ground level." The guiding light for saving money is adherence to the company's values. Riedmeyer constantly told his managers: "Don't worry about finance raining death and destruction down on you. Don't change or compromise our values, whatever you do."

The key to saving money at Federal Express is not overzealous cost cutting. It is an insistence on a proper balance between all the essentials of the business. "I don't believe in the least cost approach. I want to demonstrate improved production efficiency," Riedmeyer says. "You earn your future in the airline business by displaying a balance of technical, operational, and economic excellence."

Capital Can Energize People

The right financial indicators can be powerful people motivators. Gartner Group employs an index called net contract value increase (NCVI), which Gideon Gartner adapted from his experiences when working at IBM. Gartner sells its services on an annual contract basis, and it measures everything in terms of impact on the total value of contracts. NCVI measures the net increase in the value of total contracts on hand from one period to the next. Salespeople are paid commission only on the net increase in contracts they have on the books from one period to the next. This implies that Gartner debits commissions for any contract that is not renewed. The company uses NCVI to set budgets for its growth on each service it offers and for evaluating the performance of salespeople, service managers and researchers. Gartner has a 15-year plan to reach revenues of $750 million by the year 2000. Everything has been reduced to NCVI goals. According to Gideon Gartner, the NCVI measure motivates salespeople to sell, on an average, twice as much business as its competitors do. It even motivates the service managers and researchers to concentrate on growth. Because of NCVI, "the people providing the product really are focused on growing the business. That promotes entrepreneurism even among the people who are just writing research. And ironically, focus on growth has a positive effect on quality."

Henry Triesler of Precision Grinding, Inc., in Phoenix developed a simple indicator that has had tremendous impact on the motivation of his people and the profitability of his grinding business. Highly paid skilled workers in this industry are paid on an hourly basis. Work for customers is also quoted on an estimate of total work-hours required to complete it. Triesler developed a system to measure the amount of revenue the company earns from the work completed by each worker in terms of revenue dollars per hour. Performance of each worker on each job, each day and each week is tracked and reported to the shop manager and the individual workers. When the new measure was first introduced, the average shop rate was $37 per hour. Within 18 months, the average had risen to $52 per hour—with no direct linkage between performance on the index and compensation—and the company went from 10.6% losses to 11.6% profits. A simple index increased productivity by 40% and turned a losing business into a very profitable one.

Be sure your measures really reflect the result you want to achieve. A company measuring the net earnings of each of its branch offices ran out of cash, because the system encouraged each branch to accumulate high inventories to ensure they had materials to sell. The system did not take into account the cost of the inventories they carried or the number of turns each office achieved. It did not measure or reward good inventory management, so branch managers ignored that aspect of their jobs.

For financial measures to motivate people, they should be simple and easy to understand. Buzz Jensen introduced a complex commission system for his salespeople to encourage and reward them for selling the right products at the right prices to maximize the company's profits. In practice the salespeople found the system so difficult to understand that it did not serve as a guide for their sales strategies at all. When he simplified the system and made it easy to understand, the sales force immediately took up the cues and improved the company's margins.

Financial measures should not only be easy to understand. They should be easy to calculate and track too. One company became so obsessed with using numbers to motivate that it negotiated different commission arrangements with each of its branch managers and his or her key staff. The system was so difficult to manage that the central accounting department needed sixty accountants to handle the work that would normally be done by thirty people in a company of this size.

Attitude Is Critical

The moment you talk about money, people get uptight, especially those who are responsible for paying it out or collecting it. Everyone who handles money exercises a great power. It can be used to intimidate or threaten people, either overtly or subtly—just a day's or a week's unexplained delay in payment is enough to do it. To make capital a positive energizing power, it should only be used in a positive way by people with a positive attitude. Taking a positive and expansive attitude toward spending and collecting money is not easy, but it can be very energizing.

Dennie Brown of AMRE tells his accounting staff: "On payday you are in the attitude business. If a salesman doesn't dot an 'i' or cross a 't,' pay him anyway. If you try to teach him a lesson, he is going to have a bad attitude and he is not going to go out and sell a job that night. And if the salespeople don't sell, we don't need payroll accountants!"

ENERGIZING CAPITAL

Think about the way capital is managed in your company and answer these basic questions:

1. Is your company exploring and taking advantage of every conceivable source of finance to make your business grow?
2. What can be done to improve the accuracy and timeliness of accounting, so that information on performance is available as soon as possible after the day, the week, the month, or the job is over?
3. How can your company utilize financial information as a positive instrument for tracking and monitoring performance on key activities?
4. What type of indicators can you develop as positive motivating tools to help managers and employees evaluate their own performance?
5. What are the key areas in which the company can save money by improving performance? What can be done to raise performance in those areas?
6. What can you do to generate a more positive attitude in your company regarding the way money is used to motivate employees and vendors?

PROFIT PLANNING

1. Review your answers to the questions on capital at the end of Chapter Two.
2. Identify the practical steps you will take to raise the performance of your company/division/department on this component.
3. Develop a detailed action plan for carrying out these steps.
4. Estimate the growth in your company's revenues and profits that can be achieved by applying the ideas presented in this chapter to energize capital and convert it into an engine for growth.

SUMMARY

• As society continuously evolves new opportunities in the market, it is also constantly developing new ways to generate capital for the growth and expansion of businesses.

• No resourceful enterprise need be held back in its growth for want of sufficient capital, provided it practices the principles for attracting money.

• Companies can make capital come to them by fully developing the potentials of this component and integrating it with the other four.

• Capital is energized when we take the right attitude toward it and used it as an index for performance rather than merely as an end in itself.

• Accounting can be an active instrument for energizing capital when payables and receivables are completed in time and records are accurate and up to date.

Chapter Fourteen

DOUBLING STRATEGIES

We began this book with an emphatic assertion: there is a process that can be utilized by any company to grow rapidly and profitably, provided that it really wants rapid growth. We defined rapid growth as doubling revenues or profits in 12 to 24 months, but added that for some companies a much higher rate of growth is possible. To us, doubling refers to the maximum rate of growth in revenues and profits that a company wants and believes it can achieve.

In the first 13 chapters of this book, we have described different aspects of the process for doubling. We began by challenging some of the basic myths and superstitions about growth that limit our awareness, tie up our energies and prevent us from achieving what is actually well within our reach. In the second chapter we looked at the five engines, each of which contains vast, untapped potentials for the growth of any company. Chapter Three explained how the maximum power of these five engines is released when they are developed in a balanced and harmonious manner. Next we described the process by which companies release, direct, channel, and convert energy to achieve high performance, high profitability, and rapid growth. The fifth chapter explained how energy that is normally dispersed and wasted can be conserved and harnessed for maximum results. In Chapter Six we explored ways to increase awareness of emerging opportunities in the external environment as a means to release and mobilize more energy for growth. The next two chapters focused on the power of values to raise the process of energy generation and conversion to the highest level in your company. Chapters Nine to Thirteen presented practical strategies to energize each of the five components of your business—people, organization, market, technology and capital—and convert them into engines for rapid growth.

In this chapter, we attempt to tie all these ideas together and apply them to your company through practical strategies for accelerated growth. These strategies are divided into three major categories—partial and comprehensive strategies to energize the company from above downward and isolated strategies that work to energize each individual from below upwards.

AN ACCOUNTANT'S TREASON

In 1982 an accountant named Eduardo Malone was appointed president of the $275 million industrial division of the $2 billion French conglomerate Chargeurs S.A. Chargeurs is an amalgamation of century-old companies whose operations include U.T.A. airlines, textiles, a truck manufacturing division, and a shipping line. The company is owned by one of the wealthiest men in France, Jerome Seydoux of the Schlumberger family. The appointment of Malone as president of this conservative, traditional company was an extraordinary event. Chargeurs was a company that respected age and family heritage. Malone had neither. He was only 36 years old, and he was an Argentinian who had previously been controller in one of Chargeurs's Argentine subsidiaries. The appointment was so unusual that when Malone first broke the news to his wife, she exclaimed, "Why, that's treason!"

When Malone moved to Paris and took up his new position, he found a company with notable strengths and weaknesses. Its greatest strength was in the component technology, where it excelled in engineering and production know-how. There was a predominance of family members in top management who possessed intelligence and education but lacked professional management skills. The company maintained a paternalistic relationship with its people, providing good compensation and benefits and jobs for many of their children. There was a dynamic, entrepreneurial culture in the overseas operations. In the foreign subsidiaries authority was decentralized, and managers were given a great deal of freedom. In contrast, the organization in France was highly centralized, bureaucratic, and authoritarian.

Malone's assignment was to improve the financial performance of the industrial division, which had earned less than 1% profit the previous year, as soon and as much as possible. Everyone was watching and expecting Malone to fail. Apart from an MBA degree and his experience in Argentina, Malone brought to his new job a deep personal belief in people and a sense of responsibility to the welfare of those who worked for him. At the head office he found people working in an atmosphere of fear and insecurity, where ideas were stifled and individual initiative was discouraged. He decided that the greatest urgency and greatest potential lay in the company's people. Despite the company's poor performance and the pressure he was under for quick results, he announced that no one in the company would be fired. With the help of his management team, he identified all those managers in the company who were not performing adequately and he approached each one of them individually with the following question: "How can I help you do your job better?" He encouraged people to communicate their ideas and suggestions and pushed authority to lower levels to empower people to act on their own initiative.

The results of these changes were startling. People who had felt frightened and constricted became expansive and excited. Not only those who had feared for their jobs, but all those who felt demotivated and discouraged began to express fresh energy in their work. The result, as Malone described it, was "Profits exploded!" In one year the net income of the industrial division rose eightfold, from 0.75% to over 6% of revenues. That was the power Malone released by giving positive attention to his people.

PARTIAL STRATEGIES

The dramatic growth in profits at Chargeurs is an example of a partial strategy for releasing the energies of a company for higher profits or revenues. We call a strategy partial when it focuses on tapping the potentials of one aspect of the business, either 1 of the 5 components or 1 of the 30 values listed earlier.

In the preceding chapters, we have cited many examples to illustrate that harnessing the energy from even one of these areas is sufficient to substantially increase revenues or profits or both. Bang & Olufsen of America grew by 35% in a year by energizing the component market through its commitment to the value of customer service. Precision Grinding, Inc., converted a 11% loss into 12% profit within a year, primarily by focusing on improving its financial systems and performance on quality and on-time delivery.

BEN & JERRY'S

Ben & Jerry's is not a company that anyone would take seriously, if it were not for the company's impressive record of growth from $614,000 to $45 million in seven years. A partial strategy has been the driving force for that growth—commitment to two powerful corporate values: quality and service to society.

The company insists on very high-quality standards, which include less than half the amount of air used in most other brands of ice cream. Every year tons of ice cream are thrown away, just because they do not meet the company's stringent requirements for perfect texture and blending. Ben & Jerry's has actually pioneered in the development of improved machinery to permit blending of larger and heavier add-in ingredients.

Ben & Jerry's social mission has been the subject of much debate both within and outside the company, but its role in the company's growth is undeniable. It has had an energizing impact on people, the market and the community. When the company went public in 1984, it offered the shares for sale only to residents of its native Vermont. The company supports local industry by purchasing only Vermont milk products at a premium price. Both these actions have won loyalty and support from the local population. To promote a more egalitarian, family feeling, it maintains a maximum 5 to 1 ratio between the pay of executives and hourly workers. The company also does what it calls "socially conscious marketing," which means it spends most of its advertising dollars sponsoring public radio and folk concerts. Recently the company introduced a new product, called Peace Pops, of which 1% of the sales proceeds is being donated to the cause of world peace. The company's commitment to quality and serving society have made its market respond.

MATCHING STRATEGIES WITH GOALS

Most of the companies referred to in this book have achieved very high rates of growth and high levels of profitability by focusing on one or two components or one or two key corporate values. Mesa Airlines' real strength has been in careful financial control and proper matching of its equipment to meet the needs of the market. Gartner has excelled in systematizing its research process and energizing its people through an innovative compensation package and a lot of freedom. Vipont's greatest strengths have been in creative financing and innovative research.

The companies referred to in this book are not held up as models of perfection. We cannot even state with confidence that all of them will continue to perform as well in the future as they have in the past. In fact, if the subject of this book had been how the lack of balanced development retards and limits growth, we could cite some of the same companies as examples, since most of them have significant weaknesses offsetting their impressive strengths. But our purpose has been to show how even the development of one or two components or one or two values to a high degree can energize a company and raise it to a far higher level in its industry. All of these companies have tapped the potentials of at least one area and grown dramatically as a result. Not that we advocate or recommend such a one-sided approach. But if your company's goal is only to double or triple in size, a partial strategy, which focuses on one component or one value that is relatively weak, is more than sufficient in most cases to accomplish that limited purpose.

However, if your company's goal is something more than a mere doubling, a partial strategy may not be for you. If, for instance, your goal is to become the leader in your area or your industry, locally, nationally, or internationally, you need a comprehensive strategy for accelerating the growth of your company through the process described in this book.

COMPREHENSIVE STRATEGIES

We have described two aspects of the process of growth. The five components are the resources and engines. Each is an inexhaustible source of energy. The bringing together of these five to form a business is the creative act that releases the energy of the components and turns them into engines for growth. The interaction between the components is a creative process which continuously generates new opportunities. Since each component by itself is limitless and the possible combinations and interactions are countless, the creative potentials of their interrelationships are infinite.

The five components are like the structure of an atom or molecule—a finite number of atomic or subatomic particles combining and interacting in countless different ways to form an infinite variety of forms and physical forces. Science has uncovered the physical and chemical processes by which atomic and molecular energies are released from the atom and molecule and recombined to produce more complex substances and more powerful, more intelligent forms of life. The physics and chemistry by which the five components release their energies and recombine to produce more powerful and productive types of companies is the process of energy conversion described in Chapter Four.

Any company that fully understands the structure of the five components and their interactions and the process of energy conversion can launch itself on a never-ending cycle of growth that generates higher revenues and higher profits year after year and decade after decade. This is not just an abstract possibility. There are many companies that have done it more or less consciously and continuously. Because they have done so for an extended period of time, they are very large corporations today—companies such as AT&T, Delta Airlines, DuPont, IBM, Merck, and Northwestern Mutual Life.

But the moment companies of this awesome size are mentioned, the management of the average $1 million, $10 million, or $100 million company thinks, "What has that got to do with me?" The answer is, "Everything." IBM was once a $12 million company too. The very fact that there is a process by which one company has grown 5,000-fold from $12 million to $60 billion should be a source of inspiration to every company that has a more modest goal, because one company's achievement proves that it is possible.

Regardless of whether your company is a $600,000 company reaching for $6 million like Ben & Jerry's was in 1981, or a $7 million company striving for $70 million like Linear Technology was in 1984, or a $22 million company aiming for $200 million like AMRE was in 1985, or a $258 million company shooting for over $4 billion like Federal Express in 1979, the process is the same.

Because these companies did many different things to propel their growth and because that growth has taken place over a number of years, it is difficult for us to see clearly the relationship between their actions and the results. Therefore, the most dramatic and revealing examples of the process are those that involve a sudden change in direction or policy that results in a sudden change in performance. We have already described dramatic changes of this type at SAS, London Life, C & J Industries, Bang & Olufsen, and Waltz Brothers.

ENERGIZING A LIFE SAVER

The same process occurred more recently when Howard Cooper took over as CEO of Trimedyne in early 1988. At the time, Trimedyne was a company with one marked strength, technology. The company developed and was marketing a high-tech medical device called a laserscope, which can be inserted into a patient's arteries and used to destroy arterial plaque. Plaque is the cause of the arterial blockages that, until recently, could only be treated by surgery.

When Trimedyne received approval from the Federal Drug Administration to market the laserscope in February 1987, the company was caught unprepared. It had 65 people and sales of $5.7 million. There were no real marketing function, no marketing strategy, no sales organization or no sales systems. The company did not even maintain a record of customers for its earlier products, so that they could be contacted to buy the laserscope. Its small production facility was unable to meet demand. The limited manufacturing capacity worried Wall Street analysts, who felt that Trimedyne could not deliver on its orders. There was no qualified financial manager, no financial controls, no forecasting, no budgets, no business plan, not even a credit or collection department. There was no personnel function either, no standard wage and salary scales. The company also lacked experienced managers and management information systems.

In other words, Trimedyne had one developed component and little else. Driven by the engine technology, the company's sales doubled in 1986 to just over $12 million. But in the absence of the other four components, the company could not go very much farther. Cooper was brought in by the board of directors, because he was a very experienced executive who had earlier purchased a struggling medical equipment manufacturing company for $60 million, built it up and resold it for $140 million. After joining Trimedyne, he quickly set about assessing the company's strengths and weaknesses and taking steps to build up the weaker components.

Cooper's first major step was to set a clear direction for the growth of the company. Together with other executives, he developed a mission statement and drew up a strategic plan, which gave a new direction to both marketing and research. The company stopped development and marketing of other medical devices which it had been making to focus on the area of cardiovascular disease. At the same time, it widened the field of research beyond the laserscope to cover other high-technology methods to remove plaque. Through the plan, Cooper also established clear goals for each department to work toward. "Previously, the company was task-oriented as opposed to goal-oriented," Cooper explained. "Now we have tasks as an orientation, but all within the framework of goals."

In the component market, Cooper recruited and trained a team of clinical specialists to educate the public about the advantages of laserscope therapy over other forms of treatment. He doubled the sales force and built up a regional sales management structure. By carefully analyzing the country's demographics, he discovered that 70% of the company's market fell within 17 states, so he decided to concentrate the sales effort on that target territory.

As a businessman and not a technologist, Cooper understood the power of attuning technology to the needs of the market.

> Any company that has some technology can find a small market and grow to $500,000 or $2 million a year. But to grow beyond that there must be a vital difference. . . . Companies run by engineers or technicians without reference to the market typically fail. Usually companies develop technology before they understand the market. *I believe technology must take a lead from the market.*

To improve coordination between these two components, salespeople were asked to report back their experiences directly to the research staff, and research engineers were sent out into the field to meet physicians and sense the needs of the market. This coordination led to significant improvements in the product line. The company also accelerated its clinical research program to enable the sales staff to document the advantages of its technology.

Cooper strengthened the component people by recruiting qualified individuals with managerial experience for key positions in engineering, finance, sales, marketing, quality control, and personnel. "We can't reach the next plateau of revenues, unless we bring on enough of the right people and incur the expense early enough," he explained. To ensure that people and technology stayed in balance, he cataloged the company's research projects to assess future personnel requirements and drew up a plan to meet them. He also brought in a consultant to develop competitive wage and salary scales to ensure the company could attract all the people it needed. A generous bonus and incentive program was also introduced. At the end of 1988 the company paid bonuses to every employee equal to 13% of corporate net income.

The company also made a major effort to build up the systems it needs to function smoothly and efficiently as it grows. New systems were introduced for monitoring sales performance, managing R&D expenditure, controlling manufacturing costs, and providing marketing information. Cooper found that no distinction was being made between orders booked and orders shipped, so that monitoring the order backlog was impossible. Therefore, he introduced a computerized system to track bookings and shipments by product line.

Cooper modified the company's manufacturing plans to bring them into balance with marketing forecasts. To augment production quickly to meet rising demand, the company went to outside manufacturers to supplement its own capacity.

The component finance was so poorly developed that Cooper chose to replace the entire department with more qualified people. Then he introduced detailed financial planning and budgeting.

Cooper understood that for Trimedyne to keep growing and become a dominant force in its field, it had to develop in a balanced manner. "There are several areas that we have to excel in, not only in technology and the quality of that technology. We have to also excel in marketing skills, in expense control, in asset utilization. . . . It is important to build a strong management team which can make decisions to encompass finance, marketing, technology, and manufacturing. I really believe in the theory of the ubiquitous manager."

The result of these efforts to build up each of the five components and to energize them by closely integrating each with the other four had a sensational effect. In one year the company's revenues increased 250% from $12 million in 1987 to $31 million in 1988. Net income during the same period rose more than 1000% from $494,000 to $5.3 million or 17% of revenues.

THREE ASPECTS OF THE PROCESS

There is nothing that Cooper did that cannot be done by any company. Trimedyne's growth is impressive, both because it is so rapid and because it is based on a comprehensive and balanced effort to release the potentials of all five components.

The process that took place at Trimedyne in a period of one year is the process by which every company grows, regardless of whether that growth is swift and continuous or slow and halting. The process has three fundamental aspects:

1. Development of the inherent capacities of each of the five components.
2. Linkage and coordination of the components with one another to attune them to a common purpose and form an integral whole.
3. This development and coordination is achieved by releasing energy, directing it to achieve corporate values and goals, channeling it through appropriate organizational structures, and expressing it with the right skills.

Although the process always has these common dimensions, it can vary considerably in terms of its speed, intensity and comprehensiveness. It can also vary in one other important respect: the type or level of energy released and harnessed.

THREE LEVELS OF ENERGY CONVERSION

In an earlier chapter, we described three graded levels of energy that can be released and channeled for growth:

1. *Physical.* The first level is the physical energy we express through hard work. Physical energy is released when people are disciplined, hard working and interested in the work. This energy is reflected in a company by alert, brisk movements and a clean work environment.
2. *Organizational.* The next higher level is the social or organizational energy we express when people work together in an organized manner to achieve common goals. This energy is released when there are smooth running systems, good communication and cooperation between people and departments.
3. *Individual.* The highest level is the mental or psychological energy of the individual, which is released by commitment to inspiring values. This energy expresses itself through intense individual involvement, personal growth, continuous creativity, and a constant sense of freshness and fulfillment.

The process of energy conversion can take place at any of these levels with any one or mixture of these three types of energy. The process that occurred at Trimedyne was predominantly physical. This was necessarily so, because the company lacked even the basic physical structures needed for the development of the five components. The process involved recruiting people, adding new positions, installing systems, expanding the sales force and production capabilities, and so on.

The effort that Lee Iacocca made to save Chrysler in the early 1980s was also predominantly physical. Here, of course, the basic constituents of the five components were already in place, but the energies of the company were stifled and scattered in all directions. Iacocca had to release and redirect those energies more effectively and efficiently to improve the performance of the company. Under the impending threat of corporate bankruptcy and the even more imminent fear to the workers of losing their jobs, he had to restore discipline among an assertive and intractable unionized work force. In actuality, 34 vice presidents, countless white-collar workers, and tens of thousands of blue-collar workers did lose their jobs. He had to impose coordination between isolated and narrow-minded departments. He literally had to force design engineers, production engineers and marketing people to talk with one another and produce a car which was well designed and well built. He even had to threaten Congress with the political consequences of letting the company sink. The magnitude of Iacocca's effort and achievement were heroic. He transformed a bankrupt, comatose giant, which every financial analyst in the country had already pronounced dead, into a dynamic, responsive, very much alive and rapidly growing company, which not only became highly profitable, but actually doubled in size over the next five years.

REENERGIZING AN ORGANIZATION

Chrysler amazed America in the early 1980s by surviving its crisis and re-emerging healthy, vigorous, and highly competitive. Equally extraordinary has been the radical transformation of Ford Motors in the mid-1980s and its reemergence as the leader of the U.S. automotive industry after 60 years as a successful, but second-class, citizen. The process by which Ford transformed itself into a trend-setting, pace-setting sprinter and the most profitable car maker in the world is an example of energy conversion at the organizational level.

At its colossal inception some 80 years ago, Ford Motors shook the whole world and changed it forever. It emerged out of nowhere to become the largest, most sophisticated mass-manufacturing company of its day. It put the price of an automobile within the reach of almost everyone and revolutionized life in America. As if exhausted by this remarkable effort, 15 years later Ford was overtaken by General Motors and settled down to a life of success and mediocrity, which lasted more than half a century. In the early 1980s Ford reawoke and once again startled the business world with a feat of a different character, but almost equal in magnitude to its initial achievement.

In 1980 Ford shared much in common with Chrysler. Its products had developed a reputation for poor design and shoddy quality. Its entire focus seemed to be on producing quantity, not quality. Its organization had become militaristic, highly bureaucratic and divided into independent fiefdoms. People seemed to be more interested in office politics and fostering their careers than in making good cars. The management style was highly autocratic. Production methods were outmoded and inefficient. The company was overstaffed and underproductive. And, like Chrysler, the company was losing market share and losing money too. In 1980 it recorded a loss of $3.26 billion, and over the next few years its domestic car sales declined by 25%. "Running scared," is how one leading industry analyst described the company. "Ford in 1980 and '81 was really looking at the end of the earth."[1]

Then suddenly the colossus awoke and in a period of three years turned itself into one of the most dynamic and profitable companies in the country. The turnaround was orchestrated by Philip Caldwell, who succeeded Henry Ford II as chairman in 1980, and Donald Petersen, who became president under Caldwell and then chairman in 1985. Together they instituted sweeping changes in all five components and liberated fresh torrents of energy from all parts and levels of the company.

One of their most significant achievements was to realign the component technology to attune it to the needs of the market. We have already described Ford's effort to find out from customers exactly what improvements they would like in an automobile, carrying back 1,401 suggestions to its engineers. It invested $3 billion to design rounder, aerodynamically styled cars, culminating in the development of the world's best-selling car, the Escort, and then the Taurus.

Ford also energized technology by implementing the value quality through the five stages—commitment, standards, structure, systems and skills. The company brought in quality guru Edward Deming and instituted his 14-point program for improving quality and productivity. An employee involvement program was instituted to get workers involved in quality improvement and give them the authority to make it happen. Plants and workers were given quality goals in place of production quotas. In one plant the percentage of engines accepted by inspectors the first time they reached the end of the line rose from 60% to 96%, while productivity increased by 27%. By 1987 Ford's quality had improved by 60%, as measured by consumer surveys and repair costs under warranty plans. Elimination of reworking due to improved quality and increasing factory automation have enabled the company to raise productivity by 36% since 1981.

In the component capital, the company introduced stringent cost-cutting measures. To reduce production capacity to bring it in line with declining market demand, management closed 15 manufacturing facilities, including 3 U.S. assembly plants. It also cut total employment by nearly one-third. It realized a savings of $3 billion by switching to just-in-time inventory management. Now Ford achieves 9 turns a year on its inventory, compared with the former 6 turns.

Ford energized the components people and organization by replacing the old, authoritarian management style with one based on open communication, participation, and teamwork. To overcome the habits of the past, company executives underwent week-long training programs at Ford's Executive Development Center on participatory management and on how to listen to subordinates. Petersen told executives, "Everyone with legitimate input to your decision should have the chance to be heard."[2] Executive bonuses and incentives were linked directly with quality and with people skills. There was an unprecedented drive to push responsibility down to lower levels of the organization. The company minutely analyzed each aspect of its operations to understand how the different parts affected each other and to find ways to improve coordination between them. The emphasis on improving communication and understanding between people had an electrifying effect on the organization and its people. Even Wall Street took note of the change. One analyst remarked: "Ford has opened channels of communication. You've got people sharing data and under-standing each other's problems. Decisions are being made with more and better information, which leads to better decisions."[3]

The result of all these efforts is current history. In 1985 Ford earned $2.5 billion on sales of $52 billion. In 1986 its earnings rose 30% to $3.3 billion on revenues of $63 billion, surpassing General Motors in profitability for the first time since 1924. By 1987 the company had slashed its costs by $5 billion and lowered its break-even point by an astonishing 40%. It had also accumulated a cash surplus of $9 billion. *Fortune* cited the example of Ford and six other major U.S. corporations as "compelling testimony that restructuring can indeed lower break-even points substantially and *lead to a doubling or even tripling of earnings*."[4]

And when just about everyone believed that Ford had accomplished the utmost that could be achieved, Ford's automotive division proceeded over the next two years to rack up an additional 30% rise in revenues and 39% increase in profits, closing 1988 with profits of $4.6 billion on sales of $82 billion. In three years this megacompany had increased revenues by 58% and profits by 84%.

Newsweek's comment on Ford's dramatic turnaround is revealing. "There is nothing startling or even original in Ford's better ideas: the remarkable thing is that they are so obvious and Ford once ignored them and now it embraces them."[5]

The steps that Ford took to achieve these results are an expression of the process of corporate energy conversion. The company took systematic efforts to build up the five components, to improve coordination among them, and to establish a greater balance. It released fresh energies from the components by a combination of strategies. The focus on reducing costs and the consequent cutting of the work force had an effect similar to the one at Chrysler. It released enormous physical energy from those who had previously felt secure and complacent. The effort at restructuring, streamlining activities and systems, and opening up communication released organizational energies. The commitment to quality, teamwork, and the greater involvement of individuals at all levels in decision-making released higher-level psychological energies as well. The outcome was a result of the process of energization, partially carried out at these three different levels, but predominantly at the middle level of organizational energy.

Chrysler and Ford illustrate the truth in the adage that great difficulties can be converted into great opportunities. Very often opportunities come to us in the form of difficulties. When we do not recognize or respond to a new opportunity when it presents itself positively, it sometimes comes back in the form of a physical pressure which we call a difficulty. If a company responds positively to that physical pressure, it releases powerful, latent energies that are pent up below the surface and explode into growth. Therefore, the physical pressure generated by a difficulty is often the most opportune occasion for doubling.

THE HIGHEST LEVEL OF THE PROCESS

We selected Federal Express as one of the companies to be cited in this book for two reasons. First, it is a company that has grown very fast over a very short period of time to emerge from the ranks of the small and midsized growth companies and enter the ranks of today's giant corporations. In this respect, it has completed the transition which AMRE, Expeditors International, Vipont and many other midsized growth companies aspire to achieve. It reveals the next stage of the growth process and dramatically illustrates how quickly this phase can be accomplished. Second, Federal Express is a company that has achieved its phenomenal success through a well-balanced and harmonious development of all five components, and it has energized itself for this growth by a serious commitment to a range of high corporate values including reliability, customer service, systematic functioning, safety, open communication and development of people.

Federal Express is not a perfect company. It has made its share of mistakes and had its share of problems, such as the $350 million net loss on its Zap-Mail facsimile program. But it has gone about as far as any company we know to energize each of the five components at the third and highest level of energy conversion process—by releasing the psychological energies of the individual.

The process of energy conversion is a living organic process. It is the process of growth. So in its highest expression it transforms an organization into a living organism with a life and vitality of its own. The energy and intensity generated at Chrysler and Ford are very impressive, but the dynamism, vitality, and élan we felt at Federal Express is of a higher order than these forces. The company is propelled, not by the fear of bankruptcy, not by the spectra of huge losses or job insecurity. It is powered and actuated by a lofty vision of a distant possibility and an aspiration to realize that vision. Not that Federal Express is lost in the clouds. There is nothing ethereal or ephemeral about this company. It is supremely practical and down to earth. But it is also fresh, vibrant, and alive. People in the company, like Roger Podwoski, managing director of service systems administration, feel it too:

> There is something more alive about this company. The difference is two-fold: there is this unbelievable commitment to the customer, and employees see we are constantly improving what we do. This company talks a lot. This company is alive, and as long as it's alive you feel part of it. We are constantly looking at different ways to improve. The attitude of improvement is not just at the top. *It goes all the way down.*

The most noble and inspiring characteristic of being human is this aspiration for growth, the striving to go higher and be better than before, what Ted Weise called "a fanatical urge to do better." That is the esprit de corps at Federal Express.

Think about the process of growth in your company. Is your company growing as fast and as far as you want it to? If companies the size of Federal Express and Ford can grow so quickly, why should you be satisfied with anything less? What can you do to accelerate the process? What type of energy is your company releasing and expressing for its growth? Is your company tapping physical, organizational, or individual energies? What can you do to elevate the process to a higher level of intensity?

Patience is a great virtue and sign of wisdom, but it can also become a rationale for accomplishing much less than you are capable of achieving. The process we are describing does not require a lot of time. As soon as the right conditions are provided, the energy is released and acts instantaneously. If you are thinking that growth has to take a long time, think again. Life is filled with examples of individuals and companies rising with lightning speed to the top. The real determinant of time is only the intensity of the aspiration that inspires you to grow.

ENERGIZING FROM ABOVE AND FROM BELOW

The partial growth strategies are very potent. The comprehensive strategies are extremely powerful. Yet there is one more strategy that can be at once easier to initiate and even more effective than either of these.

The partial and comprehensive strategies start at the top of the company and work their way down. In most companies the process works something like this: the CEO has an intense aspiration or inspiring vision which releases his energy. He communicates this idea to his management team and tries to inspire them with his vision and win their enthusiastic support. The management team conceives of a plan to implement the idea and develops a consensus at the top as to what can be achieved and how. Then senior management translates the plan into practical programs for action and presents them to middle management. Middle management formulates detailed operational plans for execution by first-line managers. At each step in the process both the idea and the energy to achieve it have to be passed on from one person to the next, from one level to the next, so that the plan will carry the necessary power for realization. If the CEO succeeds in fully inspiring senior managers with his vision, and if they in turn succeed in fully enthusing middle management with their plan, then the process gains momentum and releases fresh energies at successive stages as it travels down through the organization.

When the movement is fully successful and the entire company is energized by the vision to achieve the goals of the plan, then even small, routine individual acts express something of the energy and inspiration of the overall vision. The telephone operator answers the phone with an eager, cheerful friendliness that is genuine and irresistible. The production operator works with a briskness, pride, and meticulous care worthy of the finest skilled craftsman. The whole company radiates and overflows with happy, buoyant, confident, exuberant energy. This is the end result of the process of energy conversion when it releases the highest level of psychological energies and when it is taken all the way down to the level of the individual act.

Instead of starting at the top with a comprehensive strategy to energize the whole company and working down to energize successive layers of acts, it is also possible to start at the bottom, at the level of individual acts, and by energizing many of them release fresh energies that spread by contagion from one act to the next, from one level to the next, until ultimately they energize the whole company to the top and to its core. The essential elements of the process are the same in either case, only the direction is different.

The process that moves from the top down starts with the CEO and with a central plan and is propelled by the authority of those at the top. The process that rises upward from below can be initiated by any manager, any individual, and spreads spontaneously in an atmosphere of freedom.

The principle underlying the comprehensive and partial strategies is that each component of the company can be managed in such a way as to release fresh, productive energy in that component and through their interrelationships in other components as well. The principle underlying the process that begins from below is that every act in a company can be carried out in such a way that it releases fresh productive energy during the act and in the people who are involved in it and by contagion in related acts and people too.

When the dispatcher at P.A.M. listens attentively and sympathetically to the personal problem of a driver who is 2,000 miles away from his family, that act can evoke a response of appreciation in the driver and satisfaction in the dispatcher which spills over into other acts they perform and spreads to other people they interact with. The grateful driver may smile infectiously as he meets the next customer or go out of his way to solve the customer's problem. The dispatcher becomes more alert, because he now finds his job less monotonous and more challenging, and that alertness enables him to identify a better routing for the trucks that saves time for the customer and money for the company. One thoughtful act can energize service to the customer, human relations within the company and productive efficiency as well.

FIFTEEN WAYS TO ENERGIZE AN ACT

Every act in a company can be energized, no matter how small and how routine it is. Here are some basic ways to energize an act.

Act from the Other Person's Point of View

This one principle is enough to transform any company into a living mountain of vibrant energy. Mayflower Moving Company has discovered how to convert the mundane act of knocking at a door into an act as sacred and refined as a Japanese tea ceremony. Mayflower understands how a wife can feel when her husband has gone off to work and left her alone, the door bell rings, and suddenly she finds herself standing face to face with a big, burly hulk of a man, whom she has never seen before in her life. The first natural conscious or subconscious reaction is fear. So Mayflower trains its moving people with the customer uppermost in mind. The movers are dressed in immaculate uniforms. When they approach a home for the first time, they carry a clipboard with the company name emblazoned in large letters on the back. They position the clipboard across the chest, so the name is highly visible. Then they ring the bell. To whomever answers, be it man, woman, or child, the mover smiles broadly and makes eye contact, then slowly lowers his eyes down to his feet, so that the customer's eyes naturally follow and see the clean uniform and name on the clipboard. Simultaneously the mover takes a slow step backward to signify his non-aggressive intentions. The momentary fright is avoided and replaced by a warm, positive initial meeting that carries over as a sense of confidence, security, and relaxation in the customer's mind, and influences her entire experience and impression of the company.

Taking the other person's point of view applies to everyone—even to our subordinates! In the midst of the Great Depression, Tom Watson went down to the factory floor and asked machinery operators how their jobs could be made easier and more productive. Taking his employees' point of view really energized his people and resulted in significant productivity gains as well.

Federal Express permits its customer service telephone agents to knit a sweater or read a novel between phone calls, because they understand how boring it can be just sitting around waiting for the phone to ring. The operators are a lot more alert and cheerful as a result.

All outgoing, expansive movements energize, such as wanting your employees or your customers to earn more. Vipont has consciously adopted the concept of "mutual benefit" as corporate policy. "Our goal is to provide a benefit to everybody," says CEO Larry Frederick. "Our products provide a benefit to the consumer, to the dentist and hygienists, to the retailer." Employees benefit as shareholders. Dentists and hygienists, whose clients have fewer cavities to treat than in the past, are able to offer additional services to them for treating plaque. Retailers earn higher margins on Vipont products.

Be Thoughtful

This is a corollary of the first principle. Give to another person a little bit more than they have reason to expect, and both you and the other person will be energized. It happened to us when we called Delta Airlines for a flight from Washington National to Newark, New Jersey, six years ago, and we still remember that tiny, totally insignificant little act.

The Delta agent explained over the phone that the airline does not fly that route. Before we could say "thank you" and put down the phone, the agent told us the names of three airlines that did. This time we managed to get in a "thank you" before the agent asked us what time we wished to fly and proceeded to read off the departure times of six flights that might be suitable. Then after a second "thank you" and a second attempt to hang up, the agent asked to our amazement, "Would you like the phone numbers of the other airlines?" What customer would not remember a company that remembers the customer this way?

Strive for Perfection

To do better than another is competition. It can energize you as long as you are in second place. When you achieve the goal, it leads to satisfaction. To do better than yesterday is to strive for perfection, competing against yourself. Striving for perfection continuously releases greater energy in the individual and in the act. When a company can generate this attitude in small routine acts, it leads to continuous innovation and improvements, like the 3 seconds saved by a peelable label at Federal Express. Every act becomes a subject for observation and possible modification. Every unconscious habit comes under conscious scrutiny. Every act gets energized.

Relate to the Uniqueness in Every Act

The surest way to take all the energy out of an act is to respond from habit to the sameness in the act. Every act is unique in some way, even if we have performed it a thousand times in the presence of the same people, because neither we nor they are ever the same again. If you relate to the uniqueness in any act and respond out of freshness, it gets energized. A door-to-door saleswoman goes from house to house all day presenting the same sales pitch at each stop. But the person who answers the door is never the same. Each has different thoughts, different needs, different feelings, a different face. If the saleswoman takes interest in observing those things and relating to them, her job becomes fascinating, her presentations become energized.

In the same manner, every customer, every employee and every situation is unique and responds differently when we treat it that way.

Create a Sense of Ownership by Giving Authority

Giving a person authority and responsibility over any act is energizing, even when the authority is over something very small. At C & J Industries each worker is given authority over a few square feet of work area around his or her machine. In that small territory the worker is a sovereign ruler with complete authority to enforce safety and cleanliness. Terry Crabbe of Sound Hounds gave authority over one of the store's product lines to each of his salespeople. Each was made responsible for maintaining the product displays, stocking and monitoring inventory levels, reordering merchandise and conducting training classes for other salespeople on his or her product line. This policy created a very active sense of ownership, motivated the sales force, and helped the company to triple its profits in 1987, then to raise them 60% in 1988 and another 30% in 1989.

The Federal Express hub in Memphis receives thousands of visitors every year. The people who act as tour guides behave like well-trained and seasoned professionals, full of useful and fascinating information, and bubbling with enthusiasm. Yet these tour guides are actually regular hub employees who take up the special assignment on a rotating basis. Being asked to tell the public about their company is an enjoyable and satisfying experience for employees and makes their presentations enjoyable and satisfying to visitors too.

Federal Express customer service operators also rotate teaching classes on customer service to new batches of employees. Since every executive must take the customer service classes, too, occasionally an operator finds herself giving instruction to her boss's boss's boss. That is energizing!

Put in a System Wherever It Is Missing

Establishing order, ease and harmony in place of chaos and confusion relieves stress and frustration and can be very energizing. The order desk at Bang & Olufsen of America is run by four dedicated women who handle hundreds of calls a day from customers wanting anything from a $12,000 stereo system to a 12-cent replacement screw. The real challenge comes when a service technician in a repair shop, who cannot find his service manual, calls in without a part number and asks for "one of those tiny black plastic things that go in the left-hand corner at the back of the case." The operators just about go crazy trying to find out what part the customer needs. Two years ago one of the operators got it into her head to rectify the situation. She went out to a hardware store with her husband and bought materials to build a catalog stand for each operator and then compiled four complete sets of service manuals to stand by the operators' desks. This simple system relieved frustration in the order department and pleased many service technicians, who were no longer treated so negatively for calling in without a part number.

Relate an Act to Another Act

This is a scaled-down version of the principle of coordination. Every act is related to other acts. It either depends on them or influences them. Taking the effort to relate two or more acts which are normally carried out independently of one another relieves irritation, improves efficiency and releases energy.

Impart or Upgrade a Skill

We related earlier how Dave Gray of Nedlloyd's London office was put in charge of the new computer system and asked to learn the whole thing from scratch. Dave is the most energized person in the company, and his positive attitude is positively infectious.

Implement Any Value in the Act

When the guard at the parking lot gate of a DuPont factory reminds departing drivers to buckle their safety belts, he communicates in a nutshell the company's fanatical commitment to safety and its intense concern for the welfare of its employees. Bringing down any value to the level of the individual act can have that same energizing impact. The smaller the act, the greater the power. Every company gives excellent and prompt service to its largest, most important customers. If you give the same royal service to your smallest, least significant customer, you win that customer for life and the market rushes toward your company. If you treat even job applicants like customers, people will flock to the company.

Recognize the Power of Attitude

A positive attitude has the power to energize any situation. When Eduardo Malone went to failing managers and asked how he could help them, his positive attitude sent waves of energy through the company. Taking a positive attitude toward poorly performing people, troublesome problems and frustrating circumstances can evoke unexpected and energizing responses from other people. With the right attitude, every poor performer can be helped to improve and even tough problems get resolved.

Create Challenges and Opportunities for People to Be Successful

This principle is a way of life at Federal Express. Karl Birkholz remarked: "You can make any job challenging, if you want to. It is a manager's job to find out what turns people on . . . what they like." Challenges of any description are energizing. Jim Barksdale says: "The most motivating thing for any member of a team is the feeling that they belong to a winning team. It transcends pay. It transcends personal ambition. It transcends almost anything." Recognize achievement and create opportunities for people to be successful. Success is a self-gratifying experience.

Give Personal Attention

This principle has been fully discussed in Chapter Nine. Give personal attention and recognition to anyone or everyone. Nothing energizes more.

Introduce Tools of Measurement

Psychologists have found that immediate feedback on performance dramatically increases the speed of learning. Measures that reflect individual performance improve the quality and speed of performance. Henry Triesler's measure for the productivity of his machinists, the TV monitor at Federal Express that flashes the day's volume of parcels the list in the customer service department that reports the average speed of response to incoming calls, and Jerry's Audio list of sales by salespeople on the bathroom wall are examples of energizing measures. If the measures are directly linked to compensation, they can be even more powerful. Any work becomes more lively when objective measures are introduced for evaluating it.

Take an Active Interest in the Promotion and Progress of Your Subordinates

It is self-explanatory, but not very common.

Focus on Work, Not the Person or the Position

In any group work situation, we are conscious that someone is the boss and others are subordinates, someone is the "expert" or "authority" and others are not. Eliminating that distinction from thought, speech, and action has a very energizing impact on the group. That is why participatory management is so effective.

SPLITTING SECONDS

John Banks, CEO of Audio Centre in Montreal, understands the power of the individual act. When a new phone operator was recruited, John spent one full day sitting with her and listening to how she answered the phone. After each call, he told her how her words and tone of voice made him feel. His theme to the operator was, "I spend a fortune on advertising and what do the customers get? They get you! Energize every word you speak with a smile in your voice." When a new accountant joined the firm, Banks asked him to spend two weeks out on the sales floor, so he would become sensitive to the needs and feelings of the customers.

Banks is equally concerned about the smallest word and gesture of his sales force. When the store is busy and all the salespeople are engaged with customers, he still expects one of them to rush over to greet each new customer who walks in the door and promise them attention at the earliest possible moment. In his training sessions, John focuses on understanding exactly how the customer feels, the doubt, distrust and anxiety that are inherent in the relationship of customer to salesperson and the importance of tiny gestures, such as failing to make eye contact for a few seconds when the customer is speaking. "I have tried through 547 morning meetings to stimulate our salespeople's compassion for the typically confused or intimidated customer. This constant effort has energized our client relationships and has been responsible for a great part of our growth," he says.

John adds: "There are no miracles in this business. It all comes down to simple acts. Never having a dirty ashtray. Never walking past a piece of fluff on the carpet. My biggest challenge is to energize my managers, so they will energize their people. *Every single small act has a significance to the overall result.*"

Just exactly how small an act does John refer to? "I tell my staff that if two salespeople are talking when a customer walks in the door, they should end the conversation right in the middle of the sentence and directly attend to the customer. I tell them, 'Don't even wait to finish the joke.' The customer is so sensitive. Split seconds make the difference. We have been able to split seconds here." It is no wonder that Banks's business has grown fivefold over the last five years, from $2.0 million in 1984 to $10.5 million in 1988.

INSTITUTIONALIZING THE ACT

Every act performed in a company can be energized by any individual through 1 or more of the 15 methods just described. Each energized act infuses fresh energy into the organization and makes work more alive and enjoyable. People begin to think, feel, and respond differently. Employees come to work with a different attitude. Customers approach the company with new expectations. The contagion of freshness spreads to other people and other acts, until it becomes a culture or way of life within the company.

Such a spontaneous process can flower and spread by itself up to a point. But often it will stop at the boundaries of one department or one level of the company. The process can be facilitated, accelerated, and extended throughout the company by institutionalizing it at four different levels. The higher-level methods release greater energy and freshness, but they depend to a great extent on the personal understanding and attitude of each individual who employs them. The lower-level methods are less powerful and effective, but they are much easier to extend to many people and many acts. Any company striving to energize itself from below will find that all the methods are useful.

Awareness

The highest and most powerful way to energize an act is by being aware at a higher or wider level. John Banks is aware of how his customers feel; therefore, he knows precisely how to behave so as to make them feel most comfortable. Nedlloyd's Rick de Rooy is aware of how energizing it can be to learn a new skill; therefore, he could transform Dave Gray from a troublesome employee into an energized one. Fred Smith is conscious of the enormous untapped potentials for his company, so he speaks with conviction when he challenges his people to be the very best. Lee Southard of Vipont really believes it when he says: "You can be whatever you resolve to be. Everything is possible!" This awareness itself is ultimately energizing.

Attitude

It is not always possible to make every employee, especially in larger companies, fully share the awareness of how an act can be energized. Therefore, the same act can be energized by teaching people an expansive attitude. Banks teaches his salespeople to empathize with the customer. C. E. Woolman taught Delta employees the attitude of thinking from the customer's point of view. AMRE's Dennie Brown teaches his accounting staff the importance of a positive attitude when handling money.

Rules

Attitudes are psychological. Not every person can take the right attitude all the time. But it is always possible to follow a rule and train people to follow it. That is why P.A.M. has specific rules about how dispatchers should conduct themselves over the phone with drivers and what they should do if the driver has a problem. We often think of rules as something cold and impersonal, but that is only because they are usually framed that way. Federal Express has framed rules that state exactly what the rights of employees are in situations where they feel they are being treated unfairly, including the right of personal appeal to the CEO. Such rules have a powerful energizing influence on the way both managers and employees conduct themselves.

Instructions

At the lowest level, it is possible to add an energizing element to a small act, even when the person carrying out the act is not aware of the purpose and lacks a higher attitude, by giving precise instructions as to how the act is to be performed. This is how Mayflower energizes the act of knocking at the door. Perhaps the company cannot teach psychology to every mover it employs, but it can give specific instructions that will go a long way to improving customer satisfaction.

UNFORGETTABLE MOMENTS

C. E. Woolman was a simple man of great personal warmth, who won an endearing loyalty from his people, yet was forever urging them on to higher performance. Woolman was a man of many values, but two—which in many companies oppose one another—stood out most prominently: his respect for people and his thriftiness. He had the open friendliness of a farmer and the frugality produced by the Great Depression. There are many stories recounted at Delta about this legendary man. One in particular illustrates just how powerfully a single, small act can energize a whole company.

A young man was posted on the night shift at Delta's airport repair hangar, where planes are serviced for the next day's flights. He was responsible for managing the spare parts room and providing parts to the technicians working on the planes. Usually most of his work occurred early in the night, when the maintenance process was beginning. So he sometimes found there were long hours with nothing to do. On one such occasion, the young man fell asleep at his desk—for how long he did not know. Then suddenly he was aroused by a most uncomfortable feeling and immediately realized that there was someone standing in front of him in the room. As he raised his head and glanced up at that man's face, his worst fears were confirmed. It was C. E. Woolman. Woolman looked down at the man with an expressionless face, paused for a few moments, and then said: "Young man, if you are going to sleep on the job, the very least you can do is turn out the lights!"

This unforgettable story, told by the young man with humor and affection to everyone he met and retold by them countless times to thousands of other employees, friends and customers, is the epitome of an energized act. In a split second Woolman had reinforced two of his most precious and apparently contradictory values—cost consciousness and his commitment to his people. This story and many others like it loom large in the minds of Delta employees when they speak to customers on the phone, when flight attendants share their own sandwiches with hungry customers on late-night flights, and when managers discover the errors made by their subordinates.

And each time they recall or recount these stories, they release more energy and add a little more freshness to their work.

ENERGIZING EVERY ACT

There are rare, wonderful moments in life, when you feel totally alive and fresh and joyous, when you really believe that anything and everything is possible. At such moments you are fully alert, fully confident, overflowing with energy. And very often at such times, the thought occurs: "If only this could last. If only I could feel this way always. Life would be unbelievable."

The highest and greatest goal a company can strive to achieve is not to double or triple its profits or revenues. It is not to become the largest or best of its kind in the country or even in the world. The very highest aspiration a company can have is to fill its every working day with unforgettable moments like these, so that every employee and every act is overflowing with energy and constantly growing as far and as high as they can. Such a company need not even think about doubling, because it will double every year.

SUMMARY

- Any company can employ three different strategies to double revenues and/or profits in 24 months.

- Partial strategies tap the potentials of one or two components or values for dramatic short-term results.

- Comprehensive strategies develop all the components and create a dynamic equilibrium between them by energizing all stages of the energy conversion process through value implementation. This strategy acts from above downward to achieve long-term growth and high profitability.

- Energizing every act is a strategy that begins at the bottom at isolated points and spreads outward and upward until it transforms the entire company into a vibrant living organization that can expand without limit.

Chapter Fifteen

PLANNING FOR PROFIT

We move now from idea and example to application to your company. But perhaps there is one last lingering doubt to be answered. In spite of our explanations and illustrations, some readers may still be wondering what all our talk about energy has to do with doubling the profits of your company. This raises a very fundamental question that is rarely ever asked: Where does profit come from?

Let us dispense with metaphysics and talk practically. What exactly is the difference between a company that makes money and a company that loses money? What, for instance, was the difference between the Chrysler Corporation that lost $3.3 billion between 1978 and 1981 and the Chrysler Corporation that earned $3.3 billion between 1982 and 1984? Think about it.

There is no single answer to these questions. There are many sources of profit, many factors that generate it, many differences between the profitable and unprofitable business. But all the answers follow a pattern and conform to the central process described in this book.

HIGH ENERGY

Without energy there is no work, no profit. The higher the energy, the greater the profit. Eduardo Malone stirred up the energies at Chargeurs and profits multiplied eightfold in two years. Ben Thompson-McCausland dramatically increased the energy level at London Life, and new premium income grew 87.5% the first year.

HIGH VALUES

Without values, work is substandard. The higher the values that are actually achieved in physical work, the greater the financial results. Jan Carlzon significantly improved customer service and punctuality at SAS, and profits soared by $80 million in one year.

CLEAR OBJECTIVES

Work becomes efficient only when the objectives are clear to everyone. Harold Corner set clear objectives to cut delivery time on his molds in half and cut costs so C & J Industries could compete with the Japanese. Those objectives mobilized his whole company to a united effort that reduced the operating costs of C & J by more than $500,000.

RIGHT STRUCTURE

Profits are generated by good organization. Good organization is based on the right structure. Putting in the right structure enabled Marty Wiegel to raise the profits of Wiegel Tool Works 40% in one year.

RIGHT SYSTEMS

Systems are the foundation of efficient operations, and they can always be made better. The addition of a 13-digit code to P.A.M.'s computerized dispatch system improves the utilization of equipment, drivers' time, and service to customers and will save the company hundreds of thousands of dollars. The measurement system Triesler developed at Precision Grinding for monitoring the productivity of his machine operators helped to raise the shop rate (measured in revenues per employee per hour) by 40% and convert operating income from a 11% loss into a 12% profit.

GOOD COORDINATION

Unless activities and systems within the company are well coordinated, profit just falls through the gaps. Improving coordination enabled Bang & Olufsen's machine shops to increase productivity by 25% and East Asiatic Company's timber division to raise profits by 30% a year for three successive years.

GOOD COMMUNICATION

Communication between people, departments, and levels of the company and between the company and its vendors and customers is a large part of what being in business is all about. Communication is the very essence of teamwork. Every breakdown in communication affects the bottom line as directly as a breakdown on the assembly line. Improved communication was a driving force for the 25% increase in revenues and profits in one year at Elizabeth Carbide, the 5.5-fold growth of J & M Incorporated over the last three years, and the amazing profit performance of Ford Motors over the last half decade.

HIGHER EDUCATION

Education has made this nation the most prosperous in the world. It has made IBM the most profitable company in the world, too. Education improves the quality of every idea a company generates, every decision it makes, and every action it takes. Better ideas, better decisions, and better actions mean better profits.

BETTER SKILLS

Virtually every time an employee handles a product, processes a piece of paper, and interacts with a customer, that person has an impact on the profits of your business. A minute difference in skills can make the difference between a perfect $25,000 die and a useless hunk of steel, between a lifelong customer and a lifelong enemy. Motorola calculated it achieved a 3,000% return on its investment in training. Better physical, technical, organizational, interpersonal, managerial, and psychological skills generate more profits on every corporate activity.

Figure 5 depicts the process of energy conversion and illustrates how each of these factors act to increase the generation, transmission, and conversion of energy into results. Each factor acts as one of the three lenses to energize the corporation by improving the concentration and magnification of energy as it flows through the system. The end result of this process is higher productivity, higher revenues, and higher profits.

CHOOSING YOUR GOAL

In the preceding chapters we have presented elaborate explanations and many examples of the process of corporate growth and how it can be consciously utilized by

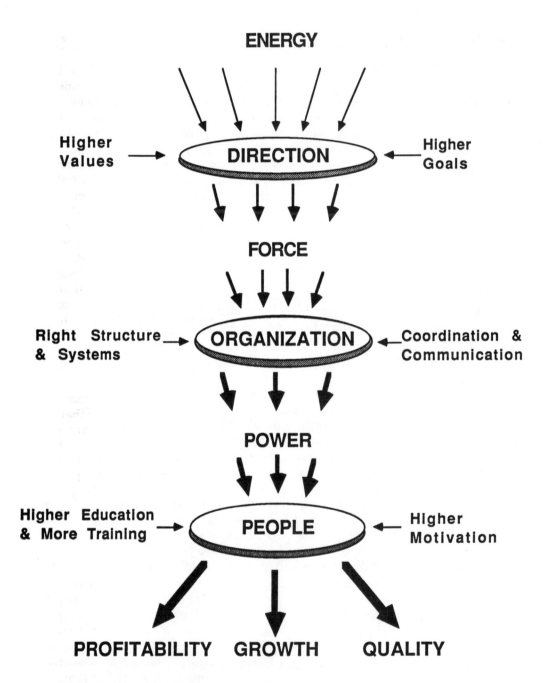

Figure 5. Corporate Energy Conversion.

your company for rapidly increasing revenues and profits. Explanations can be interesting, but they rarely inspire us to action. Examples can fill us with admiration for those that have accomplished great things, but they seldom prompt us to follow in the footsteps of those we admire.

What then can inspire us to take the practical steps needed for high achievement? For that, we need an inspiring practical goal and a practical plan of action.

Choose a goal for the growth in revenues and profits of your company over the next two years, or if you have already done so, review that goal now. Choosing the right goal is of utmost importance. A practical goal is one that you can and will achieve. It must be sufficiently challenging to release your energies for action, and yet not so high as to seem unachievable. If you choose a goal that you fully know you can achieve, it does not inspire, it does not release and mobilize your energies for action. After some time, interest wanes. The goal and the effort are forgotten. If, on the other hand, in a moment of boldness or enthusiasm you fix a goal a little beyond your maximum capacities to achieve, after a while doubt and skepticism creep into the mind. In the light of common day, the goal looks impossible. It ceases to inspire and energize you to action. Or if you choose a goal that mentally you know is achievable, but that demands an effort you are unwilling to make to attain it, after a few halting efforts the goal will be forgotten and the effort abandoned.

Therefore choosing wisely in the first place is of the greatest importance. The best way to choose a goal that will work for you is to review all the characteristics of your company and compare them with the characteristics of high-performance companies which you have read about, heard about, and know from firsthand experience. Weigh the relative strengths and weaknesses of your company in comparison with these other companies. Consider how far your company has come and the capacities needed to accomplish what they have accomplished. Now think of a goal for your company about which you can feel enthusiastic. It should be a goal that you feel a physical urge to accomplish. That is the best goal for your company—not a dollar more or less.

CALCULATING PROFIT AND REVENUE GOALS

During the course of this book, we have suggested several exercises to help you objectively assess the relative strengths and weaknesses of each of the five components of your company and the company's ability to generate, direct, and convert energy effectively into results. We have also identified a large number of strategies that your company, your division, or your department can employ to convert the five components into engines of growth and to intensify and accelerate the process of converting energy into results. These exercises can assist you in formulating a goal that is at once challenging and realistic.

If you have completed these exercises, pause at this time to review your responses to them and assess their cumulative significance. The following exercise asks you to review the original goals you set at the end of Chapter One and the subsequent plans you have developed in response to the questions we have raised to see whether your original goals still seem challenging and realistic. Since several of your action plans may contain duplication and since it may not be possible to carry out all the plans simultaneously, a provision is made to adjust your goals taking into account these factors.

Use the Profit Plan form in Appendix B to record your answers to the following questions:

1. Review the original revenue and profit goals which you entered in the Profit Plan line 1. Are they sufficiently challenging? Are they realistic? If not, modify them and enter the revised goals on line 2.

2. If you have not already done so, enter baseline data for the current year's revenues and profits on line 3 of the Profit Plan.

3. Review your assessment of the five components in the questionnaire at the end of Chapter Two and the Action Plan for the five components referred to at the end of Chapter Three. What impact will these actions have on the revenues and profits of your business? Calculate the estimated net increase in revenues and profits that will result from completing these actions and enter these figures on line 4.

4. Review your answers to the energy questionnaire at the end of Chapter Four and the Action Plans for improving the energy flow referred to at the end of Chapter Five. Calculate the estimated net increase in revenues and profits that will result from completing these actions and enter these figures on line 5.

5. Review the opportunities you identified and the decisions you recorded in the Action Plan for opportunities referred to at the end of Chapter Six. Calculate the estimated net increase in revenues and profits that will result from completing these actions and enter these figures on line 6.

6. Review the Action Plan on value implementation referred to at the end of Chapter Eight. Calculate the estimated net increase in revenues and profits which will result from completing these actions and enter these figures on line 7.

7. Review the Action Plans you developed for energizing each of the five components of your business in response to the questions at the end of Chapters Nine to Thirteen. Calculate the estimated net increase in revenues

and profits which will result from completing these actions and enter these figures on lines 8 to 12.

8. The different Action Plans you have made and the estimates of their impact on revenues and profits may contain duplication. Go back and try to estimate the amount of duplication and enter those figures as negative numbers (to be subtracted from the earlier entries) on line 13.

9. Even though each of your Action Plans may be realistic and achievable in itself, it may not be possible for you to carry out all of them during the same period. Review the plans, realistically assess the company's ability to carry them out, and adjust the schedules for completing each plan accordingly. Revise your revenue and profit figures and enter any reduction in estimated additional revenue and profits during the plan years as negative numbers on line 14.

10. Add up the figures in lines 3 to 12 for each year and enter the total anticipated revenues and profits on line 15.

11. Add up the total deductions in line 13 and 14 and enter the total in line 16.

12. Now calculate the total estimated revenues and profits during the three years by subtracting the figure in line 16 from the figure in line 15. Enter the grand total on line 17.

13. Now review once again the goals you set and recorded in line 1 and 2. Do they still seem challenging enough? Do they still seem realistic? Enter your final revenue and profit goals on line 18.

ENVISIONING THE FUTURE

Once you have established clear goals, you must develop a detailed strategic plan for achieving them. Your aim is to accelerate the natural, unconscious process by which companies grow by consciously initiating actions that will accelerate that process. That requires imagination, forethought and careful planning.

Many companies prepare strategic plans to develop new opportunities in the marketplace, financial plans for investment of capital, production or sales plans. But that type of planning is inadequate for this purpose. Plans which focus only on one or two of the five components often fail, because the other components are not developed enough to support the growth. When Trimedyne's sales exploded in 1987, its production capacity was inadequate to meet the demand, it was severely understaffed and undermanaged, and it lacked the organizational structure and systems necessary to handle the expansion. That is why AMRE plans far ahead for its human resources and systems requirements as well as for its sales strategy and financial needs.

A very powerful method to clarify your understanding of the steps needed to achieve your goals is to envision what the company will look like when these goals have been achieved. Federal Express conducts exercises like this to help it anticipate its future needs and develop sound plans for meeting them. Recently the company undertook an exercise called Butterfly 2000 to help it envision what the company will be like when it achieves its corporate goal of increasing the number of packages it handles every day from the current 1 million to 6 million. Through this exercise management identified the resources it will require in each of the five components and the strategies it will employ to develop them.

Smith explains the concept: "Planning for the future is very difficult when an organization is this complex and this capital intensive, and the size and scope is really very large. What I have done periodically is to create a snap-shot vision of some point in the future, a vision of the future. The important point is that we thought about what the company was going to look like at some point in the future and then we worked backward to the present. We did not extrapolate forward from the present to the future."

This exercise enabled Federal Express to project how many parcels or tons of freight it will be transporting, how many people, planes and trucks they will need to carry that freight, how many hubs and sorting facilities will be required and where they should be located, what type of service facilities will be needed to handle all those planes and trucks, and so on. But the exercise goes beyond this. It also enabled management to identify the type of organization the company will need to manage this size business; how many phone calls it will have to handle every day; how many invoices; how much information; what type of systems it will need to handle these large volumes efficiently; how many seasoned managers, pilots, engineers, drivers, couriers, and customer service agents it will need for its worldwide operations; how it will attract them; and how it will train them in the Federal Express way of doing business.

Jim Barksdale talked about planning at Federal Express:

> We do a lot of planning in this company. We have to plan. That keeps us from making enormously expensive mistakes. It also enables us not to get overwhelmed by the stress of growth, because we know what is coming.

THINK DOUBLE

Imagine your company/your division/your department twice as large and twice as profitable as it is today. Or if the goals you have chosen will more than double revenues and profits, think of how the company will be when it achieves these goals.

Ask yourself, what does doubling really mean? What does it involve? How will things be different than they are now?

Think about the impact of doubling on each of the five components of the business. There are several different ways or levels at which it can be done. First start by visualizing the physical results of such an expansion. How many customers will you have when you achieve the goals? How many products or services will the company be producing and delivering? How large a facility will be required? How many stores, offices, plants? What new or additional equipment will be required? How much additional investment will be needed in plant and machinery, in raw materials and finished inventory? How many people will be necessary to produce and market these products and services?

Now take a second look from a slightly different angle. What knowledge and skills are necessary to accomplish your goal? Will greater sales and marketing expertise be required? Will greater design capabilities or production know-how be required? Will your employees need better technical, organizational, or operational skills? Do your managers have all the skills they will need to make decisions, solve problems, plan and direct new activities, and motivate and communicate with their employees and customers?

Third, try to imagine how all these people will function together within the organization? Who will train the new people and upgrade the skills of existing employees? What new departments will have to be added? What new positions will be needed at the level of operators, supervisors and managers in sales, marketing, finance, production, administration, and so on? Do you have the systems needed to handle the larger volume and complexity of work—systems for recruitment, training, production, quality control, customer service, financial control, reporting, decision making, and so on? How will the company ensure good communication and proper coordination of activities as the organization expands?

Fourth, look at the ideas that direct the activities of the company. Does the company have a clear mission statement to guide its future growth? What type of company does it want to become? What are its values? Does it have clear quantitative goals or objectives? What type of plan is needed to build up each of the five components to achieve those goals?

Fifth, look at the force that will be needed to accomplish the goal you have set. Who will provide the energy for all this work of planning, directing, and monitoring progress? Of building up each of the five components to the required level? Of attracting new customers, creating new products, raising capital, building up the organization and developing the people? How much energy and effort will it require? Where will it come from?

Finally, look into yourself. What skills and capacities will you need to accomplish the goals? How much personal effort and dedication will it require? How do you feel about pursuing the goals you have set and the plans you have drawn up? Are you inspired, enthused, excited, and overflowing with energy? Pause here and reaffirm your decision and commitment to the goals. The surest sign of your future success is if you can feel at this point a calm, happy solid aspiration to take up the challenge and expand yourself and your company as far and as high as possible.

Take the time to develop a vision of your company in the future at the six levels just described. Set down your vision on paper in as much detail as possible. Discuss it with your associates. Work out the alternatives in your mind until your vision becomes so real that it seems like you can almost see into the future.

FROM PLAN TO IMPLEMENTATION

Once you have established the goals for your company/division/department and developed a clear vision of what it should become, follow these steps to translate your vision into reality:

1. Create a full awareness within the company, at least at the higher levels and preferably at all levels, of the opportunities that exist for doubling both externally and within each of the five components.
2. Strive to communicate your knowledge and conviction to create a consensus among your people for achieving the goals you have established.
3. Get people actively involved in identifying opportunities and contributing their ideas of how the company can achieve these goals.
4. In collaboration with your management team, draw up a detailed plan of action for the next two years to achieve the goals.
5. Ask each executive in the company in collaboration with his or her managers to work out detailed plans for the development of each of the five components of the company to meet the requirements of the plan.
6. Ask each manager to study the major activities under his or her responsibility and identify the precise requirements in terms of personnel, systems, space, equipment, finance, knowledge, skills, and so on to implement fully the plan.
7. Impart an understanding of the plan to all your people and win their enthusiastic support for implementing it.

8. Implement the plan. Even if you carry out only 50% of what you propose, your results will surely double.

9. Along with these other efforts, try to energize as many acts in the company as possible. This will generate a very positive and supportive climate for achieving your goals.

THE THREE CONCLUSIONS

We ended the first chapter by presenting three fundamental conclusions about rapid growth.

Our first conclusion stated that rapid, sustained and profitable growth is possible for any company that really wants it and is willing to make the effort. Through the explanations and examples in this book, we have shown why and how we believe this statement to be true. We have particularly emphasized the central importance of the human aspiration in the process of corporate growth. To achieve the maximum possible in the life of your company and in your own life, you must feel something like Trimedyne's Howard Cooper. "I am impatient for success," he says. "It is my burning expectation to get there, my aspiration. . . . It is a very strong dream I have. I have to tell you that I dream this stuff."

Our second conclusion states that rapid growth in revenues and profits is the result of a process, a process that can be learned. Many entrepreneurs may be born with innate talents for enterprise, but the knowledge and skills needed to make a company grow and keep growing can be acquired by anyone. We have attempted to describe this process as clearly and fully as possible in a book intended for the general business reader and for companies ranging in size from $100,000 to $100 billion. This process is not a theory or construction. It is a description of the dynamics we have observed in hundreds of companies of all sizes and in a wide variety of businesses. The process is naturally occurring in every company all the time. Our aim is to make that natural process more conscious and, therefore, more precise, swift, powerful, and effective. We have cited many examples to show that a conscious utilization of the process can dramatically accelerate the pace of growth and multiply its results.

Our third conclusion states that the process of growth is fundamentally the same for the individual, the company, and the nation. In fact the three are inextricably intertwined, that is, personal growth, corporate growth and national growth go together. At many points in the book, we have attempted to show the direct and intimate relationship between the growth of individuals within a company and the growth of the company itself. The parallel goes even deeper, because personal growth of any type within or outside the company involves the same process of releasing, directing, and harnessing energy to achieve results.

DOUBLE AMERICA

We have said very little about the relationship between the growth of companies and the growth of the nation as a whole, but here too the connection is direct and very close. Nations grow through the growth of individuals and organizations. All the achievements of the U.S. economy thus far are the cumulative result of countless individual and corporate contributions. Yet at the same time, these individual and corporate achievements are made possible by the general atmosphere and supporting commercial climate in the country as a whole.

Today the American national climate *permits* companies to grow and to double. It does not actively *support* them. Companies that choose as their goals to double or triple revenues and profits are pioneers and trendsetters serving the nation as a whole. Their example can be a source of inspiration for thousands of other companies to follow, just as today's great corporations have inspired countless others to emulate them.

But imagine what could be achieved if the nation as a whole adopted the objective of doubling as its inspiring goal and offered social recognition and support to any and every company that consents to serve that goal by doubling their own business. Suppose that instead of looking with indifference or concern on the growth of other companies, we viewed their success as our own achievement at the national level. We could create a national environment that actively fosters the unlimited growth of its members and its own endless expansion.

Today our country is preoccupied by national economic problems—the trade deficit, the national debt, inflation, and unemployment. But if the productivity and profitability of American industry doubled, all those problems would disappear. If a company like Chrysler Corporation could convert horrendous losses into tremendous profits and eradicate its enormous pile of debts seven years before they were due for repayment, why cannot our country do it too? The scale is different, but the the process is exactly the same.

The process is the one described in this book. At the national level it requires the releasing of some of the enormous, pent-up, latent potentials of this young and vibrant nation and a restoration of the balance between the essential components of national development. This is a country that abounds in energy and resourcefulness. We have seen what this nation could accomplish when faced with the challenge of saving freedom and democracy in the last world war. If even a portion of these capacities were released and channeled for national prosperity, this country could feed and cloth all its members and have enough left over to feed and clothe the entire rest of the world.

To double revenues and profits is a fitting short-term goal for a company. To double the prosperity of our nation, to *double America*, is a fitting collective goal for a people with the energy and potential we possess.

SUMMARY

Profit is the direct result of high energy, commitment to values, clear objectives, the right structure and systems, good communication and coordination, higher education, and better skills.

- Choosing the right goal, which is at once challenging and realistic, is critically important for doubling.

- Envisioning how the company will be when it achieves the goal generates knowledge of all that needs to be done to achieve it at six different levels.

- The goal takes on life when it is converted into a practical profit plan, which identifies the steps to be taken to energize the five components and the anticipated results of that effort.

Appendix A

===

ACTION PLAN

Use the Action Plan form beginning on page 242 for recording the specific actions you have decided to take to improve the performance of your company. Breakdown the actions into as many steps as possible and identify the person who will be responsible for carrying out every step and the date by which it should be completed.

Date:————————— Page:——————————— Updated:——————————

Purpose:————————————————————————————————————

Steps To Be Taken	By Whom?	By When?	Completed

Estimate the impact of this Action Plan on the revenues and sales of your company during the next 12, 24, and 36 months:

Year I Additional		Year II Additional		Year III Additional	
Revenue	*Profit*	*Revenue*	*Profit*	*Revenue*	*Profit*

Appendix B

PROFIT PLAN

Action Plan	Year I Additional		Year II Additional		Year III Additional	
	Revenue	Profit	Revenue	Profit	Revenue	Profit
Proposed goals						
Revised goals						
Baseline						
Five components						
Energy flow						
Opportunities						
Values						
People						
Organization						
Market						
Technology						
Capital						
Duplication (—)						
Adjustment for timing (—)						
Total lines 3 to 12						
Total lines 13 + 14						
Estimated performance from implementing plans (Total lines 15 + 16)						
Final goals						

NOTES

The quotations in the text that appear without note numbers were obtained in the course of personal interviews. The sources for quotations are indicated in these notes.

Chapter Two

1. Survey of 770 U.S. corporations conducted by Garry Jacobs and Frederick Harmon in collaboration with American Management Association.
2. From an article in *The New York Times*, January 8, 1989.

Chapter Four

1. *The Vital Difference: Unleashing the Powers of Sustained Corporate Success*, coauthored by Garry Jacobs and Frederick G. Harmon, AMACOM Books, 1985, p. 27.
2. *Moments of Truth*, by Jan Carlzon, Harper & Row, 1987, p. 27.
3. *Ibid.*, p. 38.

Chapter Five

1. All quotations on London Life are from an interview with Thompson-McClausland except those cited and footnoted from his book, *Change, Business Performance and Values: The Experience of London Life*, Ben Thompson-McCausland with Derek Biddle, Gresham College, England, 1985, p. 11.
2. *Ibid.*, p. 17
3. *Iacocca: An Autobiography*, Lee Iacocca with William Novak, Bantam Books, 1984, p. 141.
4. *Moments of Truth*, by Jan Carlzon, Harper & Row, 1987, p. 121.
5. *Ibid.*, p. 121-126.

Chapter Six

1. "America's Fastest Growing Companies," *Fortune*, May 23, 1988, pp. 29-30.
2. *Ibid.*, p. 30.

Chapter Seven

1. "The Entrepreneur of the Decade," *INC.*, April 1989, p. 120.
2. "Companies That Serve You Best," *Fortune*, December 7, 1987, p. 81.
3. "How Managers Can Succeed Through Speed," *Fortune*, February 13, 1989, p. 30.

Chapter Eight

1. "Companies That Serve You Best," *Fortune*, December 7, 1987.
2. "Sky the Limit? Federal Express Corp. Is a Triumph of Free Enterprise," *Barron's*, February 8, 1988.

Chapter Nine

1. "Companies That Serve You Best," *Fortune*, December 7, 1987.
2. *Fortune*, June 8, 1987, p. 87.
3. *Pygmalion*, George Bernard Shaw, Act V.

Chapter Ten

1. *Moments of Truth*, by Jan Carlzon, Harper & Row, 1987, p. 32.
2. *Ibid.*, p. 38.
3. "How Managers Can Succeed Through Speed," *Fortune*, February 13, 1989, p. 32.

Chapter Eleven

1. "Donald Eugene Petersen," in *Current Biography*, March 1988, p. 45.
2. "Can Ford Stay on Top?" *Business Week*, September 28, 1987, p. 81.
3. "Ford's Idea Machine," *Newsweek*, November 24, 1986, p. 65.
4. "Old-Line Industry Shapes Up," *Fortune*, April 27, 1987, p. 23.
5. *Ibid.*, "Ford's Idea Machine," p. 66.

Index

Questionnaires, managers rating of
    company, 39–40

R

Recruiting, 102
  for education, 139–40
Redfern, Tom, 174
Reebok, 75
Reregulation, effects of, 77–78
Restructuring, example of, 31–33
Richardson, Ward, 168
Riedmeyer, Jim, 145, 205
Risley, Larry, 35, 195
Rosenwald, Julius, 183
Ross, Gary, 98, 140, 195, 196
Ross Incineration Services, 97–98, 140,
    195
Ross, Robert, 97–98, 195
Rules of conduct, 230
Ryan, Hillsdon, 20

S

Safety, as energizer, 131–32
Sahlen & Associates, 5
Scandinavian Airlines, 49–52, 67–68,
    105, 160
Sear's, 183
Sectional Tool and Die, 194
Skills
  as institutionalized value, 106–7,
    111–12
  institutionalizing for delegation,
    160–61
  types required, 106, 127

Smith, Fred, 5, 39, 71, 75, 107, 108,
    137, 163, 164, 169, 170, 180, 230
Smith, Rick, 122
Social awareness, Ben & Jerry's, 211–
    12
Social change, growth opportunities,
    75–76
Social recognition, importance to
    employees, 132–34
Sound Advice, 140
Sound Hounds, 7, 225
Southard, Lee, 7–8, 80, 230
Standards
  as institutionalized value, 103–4,
    108–9
  quality and, 193–94
Sterling chemicals, 7
Stinson, Walt, 74, 102, 131, 133, 140
Stock-option plans, 123
Stoneback, John, 135–36
Strategic Planning Institute of
    Cambridge, 87
Strategies
  comprehensive strategies, 212–16
  direction of implementation, 222–23
  matching with goals, 212
  strategic planning, 69
Structure, as institutionalized value,
    104–5, 109
Swanson, Robert, 16, 100, 123, 173,
    175, 201
Symons, Craig, 196
Systems, as institutionalized value,
    105–6, 109–11
Systems of organization, 155
  analysis of, 166–69
  ease of use, 168
  improvements and power, 168–69